Cosmology and Social Life

Cosmology AND Social Life

Ritual Exchange among the Mambai of East Timor

ELIZABETH G. TRAUBE

The University of Chicago Press · Chicago and London

Elizabeth G. Traube is associate professor of anthropology at
Wesleyan University.

Title page illustration: An old man keeps watch over the
sacred rock of Raimaus

The University of Chicago Press, Chicago 60637
The University of Chicago Press, Ltd., London
© 1986 by The University of Chicago
All rights reserved. Published 1986
Printed in the United States of America
95 94 93 92 91 90 89 88 87 86   54321

Library of Congress Cataloging-in-Publication Data

Traube, Elizabeth G.
  Cosmology and social life.

  Bibliography: p.
  Includes index.
    1. Mambai (Indonesian people)—Rites and
ceremonies. I. Title.
DS632.M28T73 1986   306'.0899922   86-16166
ISBN 0-226-81149-2
ISBN 0-226-81150-6 (pbk.)

Contents

Contents

Illustrations

Figures

Plates (following page 124)

Preface

In eastern Indonesia, extending in a line that runs east from Java and toward New Guinea, there is a chain of islands known as the Lesser Sundas. Timor is the largest and easternmost island in the chain. Formerly, the island was divided into an eastern and a western part, controlled by the Dutch and the Portuguese respectively. Western Timor was incorporated into the Republic of Indonesia in 1950, whereas eastern Timor remained an overseas province of Portugal until 1975. From October 1972 through November 1974, I conducted field research on what was then Portuguese Timor. The primary subjects of my research were a people known as the Mambai.

This study represents a stage in my thought about the Mambai. It remains closely tied in many respects to my experience in the field. My focus is on ritual practices which Mambai themselves regard as central to their way of life. In this the study reflects my activities in the field, where I attended a variety of collective ritual performances. Mambai carry on an intricate, richly textured, energetic ritual life. Many performances are drawn out over weeks or months, and I spent the better part of my second year with the Mambai traveling on an almost continuous ritual circuit.

I had not exactly told people that this was how I intended to pass my time among them. It seemed to happen naturally, as a matter of course, and it is only in looking back that I can discern what might be described as choices made on their part and on mine. My fieldwork was shaped by an interplay between instructions that I received from my Mambai acquaintances and certain intellectual and personal dispositions of my own, including a tendency that I have to follow, or try to follow, instructions. I was told by Mambai to visit certain places, and I visited them; I was invited to one ritual after another, and I endeavored to attend them all, often trekking back and forth between different performances; I was urged to look for what Mambai call the "trunk" of their ritual practices, and I came to feel not only that this allegedly concealed base was obtainable, but that it indeed represented the true goal of my research.

From an intellectual perspective, both my original research project and my wider interests were consistent with the directions that I received from Mambai. I went to Timor with an interest in dual classification, and I had incorporated into my research proposal a claim advanced by my teacher and supervisor, James J. Fox. Fox has argued that the key to dual classification in eastern Indonesia lies in what he calls "dyadic ritual languages," based on a principle of semantic parallelism. Mambai use this principle of composition in all formal speech events, and the ritual performances to which Mambai directed me provided ample opportunity to study oral poetry. In nonritual contexts, moreover, significant knowledge of the past is expressed in the same ritual language, so that when various individuals began bit by bit to narrate for me the sacred histories of their villages, and to speak cautiously about the origins of the cosmos, they cast their utterances in dual terms.

My interests, however, were not confined to the linguistic form of these utterances. My original training as an undergraduate was in the study of folklore and mythology, and throughout my graduate career I retained a strong interest in oral narrative. It soon became apparent to me that Mambai saw themselves as the possessors of a rich narrative tradition handed down from the past (although we shall see that the sense in which they actually possess such a tradition is problematic). The puzzling snippets of myths that I heard were enough to captivate my attention and to make the "collection" of myths into a primary research interest.

Mambai themselves insisted that there was really only one narrative, a single, unified story that begins with the creation of the world and continues until the present. They spoke of the original, cosmogonic events as the "trunk" of present reality, and I learned soon enough that these events presupposed an opposition between a male sky and a female earth. Theirs was, in other words, a "dual cosmology" such as I had expected to find, and it appeared to be a powerful one, a cosmology suffused with agonistic themes of suffering, sacrifice, separation, and loss. A compelling cosmology, one might say, but the source of my own compulsion to master it was as much external as internal to the "text" I pursued. For while the content of Mambai cosmological knowledge intrigued me, it was the way that Mambai invoked it, the peculiar place that such knowledge seemed to occupy in their affairs, which determined my course of study and transformed an intellectual interest in mythology into a fascination bordering on obsession.

There is also another, more personal dimension to my readiness to conceive of my study as a quest after valued knowledge of the past. To explain, I must turn briefly to a period that I would just as soon forget, the first months of my stay on Timor.

I only came to the Mambai after five increasingly unhappy months of residence in a town called Laleia, and of intermittent drifting across Timor in search of a new place to settle. Laleia on the northeast coast is occupied by Galoli speakers, and prior to my fieldwork I had more or less arbitrarily selected the Galoli as the group I intended to study. But Laleia and its inhabitants disappointed me. The town itself had a dusty, mundane appearance, and the Galoli, most of whom spoke fluent Portuguese and professed to be Catholics, struck me as "acculturated" natives. Traditional practices had been discarded, I was told, though no doubt there were a few old people who could describe them to me. And possibly, people suggested, I might find more "traditional" Galoli in scattered outlying settlements south of Laleia. But no one seemed to think it feasible for me to live in those settlements, and I took them at their word.

So I stayed in Laleia, fretting in the oppressive heat of the town, half-heartedly studying the Galoli language, and wondering if the remote settlements would someday disclose to me a more exciting cultural tradition. I was befriended during this period of discontent by a young woman named Joanna, and I eventually moved into the house that she shared with her husband and children. Joanna had the kind of gaiety and high spirits that I too possess in better times, and I responded to her warmth and openness by becoming deeply dependent on her.

It was during my residence in Joanna's household that I first began to consider the Mambai as possible research subjects. I had taken a week off from Laleia to visit the Mambai district of Same, and this area seemed to me to offer everything that Laleia lacked. Talking with reserved and dignified Mambai elders, peering into stately sacred houses almost palpably laden with meaning, visiting quiet shrines centered around great rocks and trees, I sensed the plenitude of a rich, traditional culture. Mambai life, from what little I glimpsed of it on this rapid tour, seemed exotic, mysterious, other, and above all, full and intact. Yet I returned uncertainly to Laleia and to Joanna, and crept back into the shelter of our friendship, glumly asking myself if I would trade the one true friend I had made for "a handful of rituals."

It was not only my attachment to Joanna that held me. For much as the Mambai attracted me, they frightened me at the same time. On Timor the Mambai have a reputation as a remote and impenetrable people who possess special ritual knowledge. They are also spoken of as "backward" (*atrasado*), and they are regarded by the coastal peoples as being ignorant of modern ways and suspicious of outsiders. They were represented to me as an ideal choice, if I wished to learn about ancient traditions, but various individuals also expressed certain misgivings. Educated Timorese in the capital town of Dili wondered openly if I would be able to communicate with the Mambai. "They know many things," said one man, himself of Mambai origins, but reared in Dili, "but they will not even tell them to us."

Eventually I decided to take the risk. I left Laleia and moved to the administrative district of Aileu, which is the first district directly south of Dili. Aileu is inhabited by Mambai, and the colonial administrator, a man named Alfredo Pires, had expressed his enthusiastic support of my plans. Pires helped me to settle in a Mambai household called Era Bisa, located within walking distance of the *vila*, or administrative center, of Aileu. The head of the household, Silvestre, was the chief of a local territory known as a *suku*, by name, suku Seloi. His wife, Dona Silvina, was a highly respected and well-liked woman in Aileu. Pires chose this particular household for its proximity to the vila, and also for the companionship that he judged it would provide. Era Bisa included a number of young women who spoke Portuguese as well as Mambai; I have always suspected that Pires took one of them aside and told her that Menina Elizabeth was lonely and in need of companionship.

At all events, Maria Fatima, who at nineteen was the oldest of the daughters in the household, became my companion and instructor in the Mambai language. My first months at Era Bisa were spent largely in her company. She proved to be a patient and skillful language teacher, and before long we had abandoned Portuguese entirely and were conducting halting conversations in Mambai. We spent our days lazing around Era Bisa, working in the family gardens or visiting various of Fatima's female relatives. I had an idea that I should find and put myself under the tutelage of some wise older woman, and I was scouting around for such a person when our living situation changed. Fatima went off to Dili to enroll in a schoolteacher's training course, and at about the same time her mother left Era Bisa to supervise the harvest of the rice in Seloi. And I went along.

Silvina, or Adão Inan (Mother of Adão) as she is known in the tekonym system, had waited until I had a primitive control of Mambai. She herself spoke no Portuguese, only Mambai and Tetum, but she took over my education after Fatima's departure. I called her *in-kai*, "my mother," and she called me (as she did most younger people) *au ana*, "my child," or else *Menina*, which is the Portuguese term for "Miss." The Mambai avoid using personal names, and I was known throughout my stay as "Menina," an appellation that I came to respond to as to my own name.

In Seloi, Adão Inan allowed me, with some amusement, to "tag-tag along behind her" on her daily rounds. I watched the rice harvest and observed, without understanding them, the simple harvest rites. I went visiting with Adão Inan, who began to explain the Mambai system of marriage, introducing me to her various affines and explicating the twisting paths of marital alliance relations. She was, as I soon discovered, masterful at elucidating important Mambai concepts, such as the "house" or the "cult."

Adão Inan was a Catholic, and she told me that she had never attended an indigenous Mambai ritual. So it was a first for both of us in the rice fields of Seloi, where we watched the priests perform the harvest rites. Together we attended our first death ritual, a postburial rite held late at night, which I might sleepily have avoided, had she not roused me and said: "Let us go, Menina. We shall see many things." I do not think it is simply a projection of my own wishes to say that those experiences were imbued with a sense of mutual excitement and shared discovery.

Months later, after I had become involved in grander ritual events, my relationship with Adão Inan changed in subtle ways. In a sense, I became her informant. Whenever I returned to Era Bisa, she and I would dine together, and she would ask me to recount the things that I had witnessed, things which she herself had heard of but had never seen. Yet it was she who was indirectly responsible for this new stage in my research, which began when I left both Era Bisa and Seloi and proceeded southward to the mountain homes of "rock and tree."

Hohul and Raimaus are centers of Mambai ritual activity. I first heard the names of these villages in Seloi. There they are, often hopelessly mistranscribed, in my notes on the rice ritual or on interviews with Seloi elders. And many were the times when Fatima and I had listened to village headmen, and even her father, the suku chief, narrate tales about the strange ritual goings-on in Hohul. Pires himself had told me that I would have to visit Hohul, which he called "the Rome of Timor."

But Hohul, unlike Rome, has a designated "door," and that door is Raimaus. I do not think that Adão Inan was aware of this order, but she helped me to follow it. Several men who regard Raimaus as their origin place also maintain residences in Seloi. When the suku members convened for the yearly census, Adão Inan consulted with one of these men, the headman of a Seloi village. Later on she would explain to me that she had judged it time for me to acquire new, more qualified teachers. "I am too ignorant of the things that Menina seeks," she said. But the people of Raimaus were reputed to "know many words," and, on her instructions, some of them met with me during the Seloi census.

The headman was known as Mau Balen Chief. He was a big, blustering man, given to orating ritual chants after downing a glass or two of palm liquor. It was he who relayed Adão Inan's instructions to his kinsmen. Among these was Mau Saka, a leading priest of Raimaus. Mau Saka was a young man, and he described himself as a "little child." He was the most modest and unassuming of all the priests whom I met. Throughout our long acquaintance, he told me repeatedly that his father had died when he, Mau Saka, was still little, and hence his words remained "incomplete."

Our first meeting was brief. Mau Saka "fled" (or so my friends would laughingly describe his abrupt disappearance) after one evening of nervous conversation, in which he repeatedly invited me to come to Raimaus, where he said we might talk at length. When I did so a month later, Mau Saka drew me aside. "My words are tied together with those of Kai Seu Aman," he said. "They are not different."

Kai Seu Aman, or Mau Balen, the man of whom Mau Saka spoke, had lingered in Seloi after Mau Saka's disappearance and had met with me each day and night for a week. I understood very little of what Mau Balen said to me during that period. This was due in part to my linguistic shortcomings, which were intensified by my lack of familiarity with the poetic language that Mau Balen used and in part to the sheer unfamiliarity of the story that he was unfolding. Assisted by several other men from Raimaus and silently monitored by his mother, the taciturn and proud Tat Lo, Mau Balen narrated bits and pieces of the sacred histories of Hohul and Raimaus. It was many months before I understood the narrative structure underlying the scrawled texts that had filled two notebooks by the end of that week. At the time, I learned the names of the sacred rocks and trees in Hohul and in Raimaus, I began to acquire some idea of the relationship between Father Heaven and Mother Earth, and I learned that certain questions provoke tense silences, followed by abrupt shifts of subject.

But Mau Balen, unlike Mau Saka, clearly loved to talk. He was in his early thirties, and he had an expressive voice that would sink to a whisper when he wished to explain some particularly important point. Indeed, my strongest impression of him during that first week, an impression that set and intensified over time, was that Mau Balen urgently wanted to make me understand him. He was a skillful and captivating raconteur who, when he resolved to clarify some element of cosmology, would let his words tumble out in a turbulent stream.

Mau Balen is not a priest, as he took great pains to inform me at our first meeting. He distrusts priests in general, and he would often question the capability of particular practitioners. However, he omitted to tell me for several months that he is the "master" of Nunu Fun, the eldest house in Raimaus. He inherited this role from his father, who had surrendered all public, priestly responsibilities to Mau Saka's father after a quarrel. Now it is Mau Saka who performs the priest's role, but it is Mau Balen who must sit in the place of the "house master" during ritual meals in Nunu Fun.

Mau Balen's residence is in Seloi, where he lives with his unmarried younger brother, his two wives, and his children. Before we met he had been employed irregularly as a carpenter by several Europeans and Chinese in Aileu. He returns unfailingly to Raimaus for ritual occasions, and he was one of the central organizers of the elaborate ritual held for the rebuilding of his house. Yet he would often tell me that his extended dealings with foreigners had drawn him away from the world of rock and tree, and had taken a toll on his knowledge. Nevertheless, he was widely reputed to "have words," and it was he whom Adão Inan had specifically intended for me to meet. "He is young," she told me, "but people say that he is one who knows."

I doubt if Adão Inan had guessed that my relationship with Mau Balen would extend over the duration of my stay on Timor. What I do know is that both she and her husband acquiesced readily when I proposed to begin accompanying Mau Balen to ritual performances. "It is on your back now," Adão Inan told Mau Balen when she formally surrendered to him responsibility for my well-being. Her husband, Adão Aman, approved of the plan enthusiastically and confided to Mau Balen and me that he himself had an interest in the "words" that we two would seek. "For I also seek those words," he said to us, and he promised that he would dedicate a water buffalo to celebrate the success of our mission.

No water buffalo was sacrificed, but Adão Inan and Adão Aman never wavered in their support of my new course of action. Looking back, what strikes me is that over the course of my fieldwork, I bridged the two major positions in the Mambai political system. I began as the "child" of an executive figure and then gradually penetrated into the realm of ritual authority, which is embodied in the sacred rock and tree of cult life.

In my second year with the Mambai, I came to work more and more exclusively with persons associated with ritual authority, although I continued to meet, from time to time, with political executives. I must concede that what I present here is in many ways a one-sided view of Mambai society, and that more intensive research with those who exercise political power would have brought competing views into focus. Nevertheless, there is among the Mambai a deep-seated, collectively held conviction that significant knowledge belongs to those entrusted with ritual authority. And it was the rulers of Seloi who not only endorsed my connection with centers of ritual activity, but who actively assisted me in establishing it.

As time passed, I became intimately associated with Hohul and Raimaus. Mau Balen became my research assistant and received approximately forty dollars a month in return for escorting me to a variety of ritual performances. Many of these took place in either Hohul or Raimaus, and it was at a Hohul ritual that I met the man who became my other assistant, Mau Tersa Aman or Mau Bere.

Like Mau Balen, he came well recommended. Mau Bere, then in his late twenties, was the eldest son of a minor Hohul priest, and he was widely regarded as one who "had words." More important, he had the reputation of one who "speaks straight," and whose words do not "wind about," as often happens in the discourse of priests. When I visited Hohul, Mau Bere's name came up repeatedly. One night he came to witness an interview that Mau Balen had arranged with a Hohul priest named Mau Lear, and Mau Balen accorded to Mau Bere the honor of pouring liquor for the priest. Mau Lear left fairly drunk, and a storm of denunciations of his discourse broke out among the various onlookers. Mau Bere's voice rose loudest of all, until all the others fell silent and listened to him. Clearly, he was a man of stature.

I approached him later, without a conduit, and invited him to come and talk with me. He came that same night, and together he and Mau Balen took up the thread of a story that Mau Balen had in fact begun in Seloi, the dark story of Mother Earth's death (see chapter 2). Much later, Mau Bere told me that he had come "with sadness," resolved to entrust his words to me in that one night and then to withdraw. His speech, which I recorded on tape, shows the strains of such an endeavor and alternates between elliptical allusions and barrages of details.

Whatever Mau Bere's original resolve may have been, it was clear when we parted on that first night that the story was not complete. He returned the next night, and the night after that, and so a new triangular partnership took shape. Toward the end of the ritual event, I asked Mau Bere if he would accept a position similar to Mau Balen's. He seemed to me to agree eagerly. Had he lost his "sadness"? Had he seen the economic and social advantages of the position? Did he consider it improper for Mau Balen of Raimaus to be my sole guide? All of these elements may well have been present in his decision. What I know is that once he had accepted my offer, Mau Bere placed himself under a solemn obligation: to speak his words "from trunk to tip," to speak "until it reaches the names." As with Mau Balen, and for reasons that will always remain in part obscure to me, it became important to Mau Bere to "pass on" his words to me. In the end, perhaps we three never really understood one another. Nevertheless, a trust grew up between us, and I hope that I have not violated it.

In the eight months that intervened between that Hohul ritual and my departure, we three were almost constantly together, observing four major ritual performances and visiting a number of different origin villages. Our relationship was not without its strains. I am not sure if "jealousy" is an accurate description of the tension that I began to detect between Mau Balen and Mau Bere, but I found as time went on that we formed two dyads as often as one triad. When we ventured off to distant places, then we clustered together as in the first weeks. But when we took up residence in Raimaus during the lengthy house-building rites, each of the two men took to conferring with me privately. In the last weeks of my stay, when I used our imminent parting to pressure them for "missing words," the rift became pronounced. Mau Bere said flatly that he would speak his last words to me alone, without Mau Balen present.

We used various metaphors for our relationship. On the one hand, I was always "Menina," their employer, and they were my assistants, my *asudante*, as they called themselves (from Portuguese *ajudar*, "to help"). At times we described our tie as one of sister and brothers, and other people regularly referred to us in these terms. We also spoke of ourselves as "little children," tagging behind after the elders. And we were friends. We lived together, ate together, laughed together, fought together, and above all, we worked together.

It was agreed from the beginning that their service would be of "two kinds." As each man claimed to "have words," they were to convey to me their own knowledge regarding the past, especially as it bore on the rites that we witnessed. One or both of them usually accompanied me during ritual performances and offered on-the-spot exegeses. Afterward, usually on the same day, we would meet to discuss the overall significance of the rite. If I had taped any segments of a performance, they would assist me with transcriptions by slowly repeating and commenting on the often slurred speech of the priest.

The second kind of service involved arranging and participating in my meetings with other people, priests and notable elders whom we encountered during our travels. This was a task that they both seemed to relish, and they performed it with considerable skill. Their assistance was invaluable. To an outsider, Mambai narratives often seem uneventful, repetitive, and confusing. Mau Balen and Mau Bere shared a gift for prompting speakers to elaborate upon important themes. When the topic of conversation was a ritual performance, they directed the discussion to small but essential features and thereby gave me access to materials that, unprompted, the priests would not have introduced.

This method of inquiry also had its drawbacks. Add the prestige of their villages to Mau Balen's and Mau Bere's forceful personalities, and one may rightly suspect that informants could be intimidated. Gradually, I began to sense that certain people felt that Mau Balen and Mau Bere were there to evaluate their discourse. To make matters worse, although we three had devised a formal etiquette to regulate interviews, the two of them did not always abide by our rules. Usually, they were patient and polite and would feign interest, even if they privately judged the speaker's words to be trivial. But both of them could become arrogant and domineering. Several times I had to rebuke them for openly displaying their incredulity, or for badgering and bullying recalcitrant speakers.

Eventually, I took to conducting private interviews with persons whom I felt had suffered from my assistants' zeal. I do not, however, assume that the absence of my two mediators made for more "natural" communicative situations. If anything, it had the reverse effect, and this needs explanation.

Although I spent two years with the Mambai, becoming fluent in their language, familiar with their traditions and their way of life, I was always "Menina," a white European from across the "water and sea." I was distinguished from other foreigners only by my stubborn interest in the affairs "of rock and tree." Yet I came bearing with me the "book and pen," symbols of European identity, which are repeatedly contrasted in Mambai poetry to the sacred rock and tree. My project, as Mambai represented it, was to record with book and pen "the walk of rock and tree." The participation of Mau Balen and Mau Bere worked to incorporate this unusual project into a larger, familiar cultural concern with the acquisition of sacred knowledge.

Moreover, as I learned gradually, my association with Hohul and Raimaus was not accidental in Mambai evaluation. I mentioned previously that Raimaus is represented as the "door" to Hohul. Hohul is located due south of Raimaus and, in this spatial symbolism, Raimaus is also defined as the threshold that mediates between the southern interior and the northern sea. A stranger from overseas did well to enter Mambai lands through the "door of the sea." In effect, with the assistance of my friends, I had stumbled upon a proper path.

But the question that still remains is why did they open that door to me at all. No doubt there are many answers, but there is one that I have found both intellectually and emotionally satisfying. I believe that Mambai saw in me a wanderer who had returned to the homeland in search of her own origins, a seeker after a treasure that they had long held in keeping. That perception provoked among them a measure of alarm, for Mambai are chary of their knowledge, and they take great pride in their status as unique custodians of a past that others have forgotten. Yet one cannot be long among them without detecting an anxious apprehension that they themselves are included in what has been forgotten. Hence there was also, I believe, a measure of relief at obtaining, in a would-be receiver of knowledge, a chance to tell their story. My persistent questions, shaped as much by their enigmatic replies as by any prior interests of my own, allowed them to recreate and renew their sense of themselves through sharing it with an outsider.

I, however, must tell their story in my own way. I cannot present it (as I sometimes perceived it in the field) as received, sacred truth. The Mambai conceptions of the past that I am concerned with here may be provisionally defined as narrative fictions for living, which shape and are shaped by the conditions of Mambai social existence. This process, of which the Mambai themselves are not conscious, involves the use of narrative discourse and discourse about narrative to create a meaningful social world.

The present study is not intended in any sense as a "full story" of the Mambai, for I have done my best to put aside the nostalgic faith in plenitude that first led me to them. What I encountered was not, of course, an untouched culture, and its apparent wholeness was in many ways a transient product of discourse, something made and remade by speakers who insisted on the necessary character of their practices. There is, nevertheless, a certain "timeless" character to this study, inasmuch as it focuses on the internal dynamics of Mambai social life and neglects Mambai interactions with a larger world, except as that world was embodied by me. My entry into Mambai life was not a sign of a mythic past (as many Mambai seemed to think), but rather a particular moment in a long history of involvement with outsiders. Our conversations were situated in a historical context which, however, is not treated directly in this volume. My concern here is limited to describing social and cultural processes of integration, and I leave for treatment in another place the historical forces that also influence these processes. In part, this ethnographic strategy represents the process of my own thought, as I moved from an almost aesthetic appreciation for the coherence of Mambai culture to a sense of the effort required to produce that coherence, and then to an understanding of a larger context in which Mambai efforts are called forth.

Regretfully, I must conclude this preface by commenting briefly on an aborted process of decolonization and its grim aftermath. It is my hope that this book will provide a new perspective on a little-known tragedy that has taken place on Timor since my fieldwork.

Serious talk of decolonization began on Portuguese Timor after the fall of the Caetano regime in April 1974. New political parties were formed in the province. One of these, Fretilin, organized itself around a call for national independence and had gained considerable support throughout the province by the time of my departure. In August 1975 a civil war broke out between Fretilin and a rival political party. Fretilin emerged the victor after three weeks of fighting, during which the Portuguese colonial administration had withdrawn from the island. The victors called upon the Portuguese to return and resume a peaceful process of decolonization, but these calls went unheeded. The leaders of Fretilin set up a caretaker government to administer the province. At length, however, under the pressure of Indonesian incursions at the border with West Timor, they declared the independence of the Republic of East Timor. Two weeks later, on December 7, 1975, the Indonesian government launched a full-scale military invasion of East Timor.

Information about East Timor since the invasion and occupation of the territory is neither abundant nor easy to assess. But there have been persistent reports of an ongoing, Fretilin-led resistance to Indonesian rule. There are also reports that somewhere between 60,000 and 300,000 East Timorese (that is, between one-tenth and one-half of the total population) have died since the invasion began, from war, starvation, and disease. Today the political status of East Timor remains subject to dispute. Indonesia officially annexed the territory in 1976, in what was represented by the Indonesian government as an act of self-determination. Neither the United Nations nor the Portuguese government has recognized the legitimacy of the annexation. Yearly resolutions passed by the General Assembly of the United Nations have consistently reaffirmed the right of the East Timorese people to determine their own political future.

At the time of this writing, the chances that the East Timorese will be allowed to exercise that right appear slim. My scholarly activities will not obtain for them that chance. But I hope that, at the least, my work will testify to the capacities of one particular Timorese people to think imaginatively and profoundly about the meaning of collective life.

Acknowledgments

I have already acknowledged those Mambai to whom I feel most deeply indebted: the members of the household of Era Bisa and my teachers and friends from Hohul and Raimaus. I want also to mention the people of Er Hetu and Kai Kas, who "ruined" so many of their pigs and chickens in entertaining me; the people of Ol Fan, who invited me to a ritual which other obligations kept me from seeing to its conclusion; and the heads of the ruling house of Bar Tai, who assisted me in many ways and who showed to me personally the greatest courtesy and respect. I also thank Shepard and Leona Forman, Peter and Susan Parrington, Alfredo Pires, and Michael Oliver for their friendship and support.

The research on which this study is based was supported by a grant from the National Science Foundation and a grant from the National Institute of Mental Health. I thank the Anthropology Department of the Research School of Pacific Studies at the Australian National University, and Derek Freeman in particular, for the hospitality they offered me during my field-break.

My greatest debt is to my teacher and supervisor at Harvard, James J. Fox, who directed me to Timor. Many other individuals have contributed to this manuscript in various ways. They are Marie Jeanne Adams, Marylin Arthur, Shelley Errington, Johannes Fabian, Shepard Forman, Hildred Geertz, Josué Harari, Richard Huntington, Rhys Isaac, James Kavanagh, John Kirkpatrick, David Konstan, Joel Kuipers, David Maybury-Lewis, Peter Metcalf, Rodney Needham, Richard Price, Michelle Rosaldo, Marshall Sahlins, David Sapir, David Schneider, Michael Silverstein, S. J. Tambiah, Khachig Tölölyan, Valerio Valeri, and Elisabeth Young-Bruehl. My deepest gratitude goes to my parents, Mildred and Shepard Traube, and my sister, Victoria Traube, for their love and support.

Introduction

This book is a study of the social and ritual life of an eastern Indonesian people, the Mambai of East Timor. It is also intended as a contribution to a topic that has long been important in anthropology, the relations between symbolic classification and social life. The term "classification" is intended to call up Durkheim and Mauss's essay on classificatory systems (1963; orig. 1903), and the wider intellectual tradition associated with these two theorists. I regard this work as a product of that tradition, and I intend these opening remarks as an acknowledgment of origins, not of ultimate origins, but of certain privileged precursor texts.

A tradition, as Ricoeur remarks, "is not a sealed package we pass from hand to hand, without ever opening, but rather a treasure from which we draw by the handful and which by this very act is replenished" (1974, 27). The French sociological tradition, or the Année Sociologique tradition, as it is also known, has indeed been an accessible treasure. Not all the projects envisioned by Durkheim and his collaborators have proved productive, and some of their major ideas have been challenged and superseded. Yet the tradition has been carried on in diverse places, both within anthropology and in other fields, and in the sense intended by Ricoeur, it remains very much alive.

One place where French sociological thought was taken up was in Leiden, by the Dutch structuralists who studied under J. P. B. de Josselin de Jong during the 1930s. Of the studies carried out by de Jong's students, that of F. A. E. van Wouden is of particular relevance for the ethnography of eastern Indonesia. Van Wouden's doctoral dissertation, a comparative analysis of a number of eastern Indonesian societies, was completed in 1935 and appeared in translation in 1968 as *Types of Social Structure in Eastern Indonesia*. The influence of Durkheim and Mauss is evident in van Wouden's conception of his research as a study of embracing systems of classification that orga-

1

nize both cosmos and society.[1] In retrospect, however, van Wouden's causal explanation of classificatory systems appears as a major weakness in his comparative model. That model was in fact premised on an aspect of Durkheim's thought that more recent studies have called into question.

Durkheim advanced in the 1903 essay with Mauss an argument that he later developed and elaborated in *The Elementary Forms of the Religious Life* (1965; orig. 1912). In essence, he argued for the logical, and indeed the temporal, priority of the social order over symbolic representations. Various commentators and critics have called attention to a number of ambiguities in Durkheim's thought regarding this relationship (Needham 1963, xxiv–xxix; Lukes 1972, 462–477; Augé 1982, 25–32). Yet the overwhelming impression left by *The Elementary Forms* is that society is not only perpetuated by means of symbolic representations, but also precedes, generates, and is the object of those representations.[2] The argument, as one critic points out, presupposes that a "represented social reality may be defined independently of its 'representations'" (Augé 1982, 31).

Contemporary structuralist thought in anthropology has broken with the radical social determinism of Durkheim's approach to symbolic forms and has rejected the "social origins of symbols" in favor of the "symbolic origins of society." In structural analyses symbolic forms are not treated as products of prior social realities but are held to be in some way constitutive of those realities. Hence for Lévi-Strauss, whose chiasmus I have borrowed, the anthropological object is always of a "symbolic nature" (1976, 11); and anthropology itself becomes a study of multiple forms of "communication," the circulation of goods and services (economics), of women (kinship and marriage), and messages (myths, rituals, and other forms of classification). Lévi-Strauss has implemented this concept of social life as communication in his major studies of marriage systems, "totemic" classifications, and mythology.[3] In launching what may be described as an effort to integrate French sociological theory with Saussurean linguistics, Lévi-Strauss drew less on Durkheim, and more on Mauss. The particular inspiration, many times acknowledged by Lévi-Strauss, is Mauss's *Essai sur le don* (1924), known in English as *The Gift* (1967).

Lévi-Strauss saw in Mauss's essay a clear connection to the "science of semiology," conceived of by Saussure as a study of "la vie des signes au sein de la vie sociale" (1969, 33; orig. 1916). Mauss had shown in his essay that reciprocal exchanges of goods and services were not merely material transactions, but performed a communicatory function. Hence gift giving, as Lévi-Strauss observed, was part of the "life of signs in society," and the study of gift exchange belonged to semiology. Yet as Lévi-Strauss has pursued his broadly conceived semiological program, moving from marital rules, based on treating women as signs of integrative alliances, to myths that are said to have "no obvious practical function," he has tended more and more to privilege the internal logic of his "sign-systems" over their "life in society."[4] And one may argue that, in the process, he has lost touch with Mauss's original conception of exchange.

Mauss's study of a "necessary form of exchange" represents both a break with certain aspects of Durkheim's thought and the continuation of others. What is continued and developed is Durkheim's insistence on the necessity or social efficacy of symbolism, his deep appreciation for the role played by symbols in the life of society. From this perspective, *The Gift* is a quintessential expression of Durkheim's own lasting concern with the ideological integration of society. The break, on the other hand, is implicit in Mauss's central analytical concept, the "total phenomenon," which seems intended to resist and thwart the reduction of any one level of socially lived experience to another.

Mauss's model of exchange is based on the simultaneous presence of multiple aspects in any transaction. Other analysts (including Durkheim) might break up the total character of exchange, for instance, into ranked "religious," "social," and "material" components. But Mauss, in his persistent pursuit of that "fleeting moment when the society and its members take emotional stock of themselves and their situation as regards others," sought instead to capture and preserve the wholeness of social life, or, as he says, to "reconstitute the whole" (1967, 77–78).

Mauss's "others" include both the members of the group, tribe, or larger collectivity with whom one must somehow "come to terms" and also those invisible sacred beings, spirits or gods, the ritual allies of men, who "are the real owners of the world's wealth." Mauss does not develop this particular theme at any length in *The Gift*, yet the step away from Durkheim is evident and decisive. The "religious" is no longer taken as a mystified representation of the "social," but rather as one of several intricately interconnected aspects of exchange. One no longer goes "beneath the symbols" to find the social reality they express, for social reality is what is given in the totality of interlacing meanings conveyed by ritual practices. Thus

3

It is not *simply* to show power and wealth and unselfishness that a man puts his slaves to death, burns his precious oil, throws coppers into the sea, and sets his house on fire. In doing this he is *also* sacrificing to the gods and spirits, who appear incarnate in the men who are at once their namesakes and ritual allies. (1967, 14; my emphasis)

The critical point is made quietly and undramatically, in a statement that reflects back on Mauss's earlier, more "orthodox" essay on sacrifice, written with Hubert (1964; orig. 1899): "The connection of exchange contracts among men with those between men and gods explains a whole aspect of the theory of sacrifice" (1967, 13).

My concern here is with "connections" of this kind. My purpose is to preserve and convey the integrity, the wholeness, the total character of a set of ritualized exchange contracts that link persons with other persons, social groups with other groups, and human beings with the cosmos. In Mambai society these contracts are drawn out over years, so that the various partners in exchange relations are perpetually embroiled with one another, in the way that Mauss took to be characteristic of "total prestation."

The words "integrity," "totality," and "wholeness" are easily invoked, but to give them content is another matter. One assumption of this study is that indigenous conceptions of the whole are symbolically constituted. Different levels of exchange derive their unity from a system of symbolic categories. Eastern Indonesian societies are already well known in the ethnographic literature for the pronounced dualistic organization of their categorical schemes, as well as for a tendency to realize symbolic dualisms in social arrangements. Dual classification entails the ordering of symbolic categories into pairs of opposites, such as male/female, heaven/earth, above/below, outside/inside. Sets of dual categories are combined in particular contexts and used to represent diverse realms of experience. Whereas a principle of complementarity is signified by the redundant unions of opposites, an equally important feature of the classifications is categorical asymmetry. Typically, one element in any pair is marked as superior to its complement, and the differential ranking of complementary categories expresses hierarchical relationships.[5]

A major task for this study is to elucidate the internal logic and the social expressions of hierarchy. While conceding that the specific values of dual categories are relative to particular contexts of use, I argue that the Mambai system provides a principle for the absolute ranking of complements. This argument brings us back to indigenous

4

conceptions of the whole, by way of the temporal dimensions of symbolic schemes. To Mambai, the dualistic schemes that order social
arrangements also express processes of becoming. The model for
those processes, which we shall encounter in a variety of forms, is
the division of a whole into parts. Claims to hierarchical status are
based on this model and associate particular groups with images of
totality before division. By this same hierarchical principle, the ultimate whole, to which human beings as a class are absolutely subordinated, is constituted by the cosmic totality.

Other analysts of eastern Indonesian societies have observed
that the ubiquitous dualism of the classificatory schemes creates correspondences between the social and cosmological orders, to the
point where one is dealing with a single, comprehensive organization
of society and cosmos. It was van Wouden who first articulated this
insight in his study of eastern Indonesian social classification. But
van Wouden's analysis follows a route that leads from society to the
cosmos. He adapted Durkheim's genetic model and argued that symbolic structures were grounded in particular forms of social organization. Van Wouden took marital institutions to be the "pivot" of social
life in eastern Indonesia, and he claimed that social divisions among
marital allies were projected outward onto the world. By this analytical strategy, the intricate dualistic schemes that eastern Indonesian
peoples use in multiple social contexts could all be represented as
so many derivatives of forms of cross-cousin marriage.[6]

An alternate route, which I will pursue, runs from cosmos to society and follows closely in the tracks of indigenous conceptions.
The Mambai, who are my subjects, interpret social relations in terms
of obligations to the cosmos. They see themselves as privileged readers of a cosmological text, and this conception merits serious attention. To take an indigenous model seriously does not confine the
analysis to its terms, but it does imply a certain mode of transcend-
ing those terms. In this case, I will argue, we can best understand
the Mambai if we approach them as at once the creators and the
creation of their cosmological "texts" (I will explain the quotation
marks presently).

Translated into Durkheimian idioms, my point is this: Mambai do
indeed recreate their social order through ritual practices that bring
them into confrontations with one another, and also with their other-
worldly allies. But these practices are not to be understood by treating the second of those confrontations as a reflection of the first.
Mambai do not give meaning to their social life simply by enacting an
ideal image of society, but rather by enacting it in the context of an

ideal relationship to a cosmic whole. Theirs, in short, is a form of social life that takes the cosmos as both the primary referent and the modeling type of human action.

But this turn to indigenous conceptions of a cosmic "whole" raises another question, that of the systematic character of the system. Bourdieu (1977), has cogently argued for the need to distinguish between interpretive models and their object, that is, between the "system" constituted by and for the observer and whatever "system" is in fact required for individuals to generate culturally acceptable practices. Bourdieu's major point is that the former of these systems is the more highly systematized of the two, and this is so precisely because the observer is not called on to make his or her system operate. The observer's model is the substitute required by someone who cannot achieve competence through performance. In contrast, the members of a culture acquire a "practical mastery" of a "practical logic," by performing a variety of concrete activities in diverse contexts. They internalize a set of "generative schemes," used in and for negotiating particular situations. Inasmuch as there is a "system," from their perspective, it is best described as "a system of more or less integrated generative principles," and its products are characterized by a "fuzzy systematicity."

Bourdieu's points are well-taken, and one may add (as he suggests in another context) that informants themselves, in confronting and dealing with the observer, may also construct exceptionally systematized systems, which have a way of being presented later on as "the native model." In my own case, it should be stated at the outset that I maintained prolonged and intensive contact with two particular Mambai informants. These two men were remarkably skillful and also deeply interested totalizers of cultural schemes, and I will say more about our activities later. Although I will often draw on ideas that they conveyed to me, I do not regard these ideas as representing "the native model," nor do I wish to do violence to Mambai thought by attributing to it a degree of systematicity that it may not possess. I will, nevertheless, construct a system, one which I believe will allow us to make sense of Mambai social life. Moreover, I believe that the project of system building, if not the precise implementation, is consistent with a deep-seated Mambai orientation toward experience.

In their conversations with me, Mambai frequently drew upon cultural metaphors for the acquisition of knowledge that bear certain resemblances to our own conceptions of interpretive activity. The shared element is a common concern with part/whole relations. With some fervor, a number of persons gave voice to a conviction that all their various social and ritual practices were the partial expressions of an underlying whole, the bits and pieces of an original plenitude. Although most individuals simply directed me elsewhere to acquire full understanding, their persistent affirmations of the possibility came to dominate my field investigations, until it seemed to me too that the promised fullness lay just ahead of me, almost in reach, yet always deferred.

This ideally attainable whole that was held out to me is intimately associated with language and speaking. Mambai spoke of it as the "trunk of discourse," and they talked of a treasure of "words" that certain persons kept "inside their stomachs." In these images of a trunk that anchors speech and a hidden, hoarded verbal wealth, language is represented as both the vehicle and the content of the whole. Mambai emphasize, moreover, a particular use of language. The whole is said to consist of what we would call a narrative text—a story that runs "from trunk to tip," binding together the past and the present. One model for the acquisition of knowledge is the sequential unfolding of a full narrative.

In another Mambai model, a seeker of knowledge works from present experience and reinscribes observed events into their full context. The whole that motivates its partial expressions is conceived of as the union of what can be seen and what can be heard, and one reconstitutes it by putting together the multiple parts of which any event is composed. This idea of the whole composed of its parts is signified by the word *kdain*. The word may derive from *aia*, "tree," and Mambai draw on botanic imagery to explicate the concept. Thus *kdain* consists of the union of roots, trunk, branches, shoots, and leaves. And every action or object, Mambai say, is "with its *kdain*."

This concept was regularly invoked when I attended ritual performances and inquired into their significance or asked, as one says in Mambai, to know what a given ritual act "touches." My guides and acquaintances counseled patience and prescribed a fixed sequence. "First," I was told, "the eyes must see, and then the ears must hear." For one could, as Mambai often observe with satisfaction, take in everything that occurs in ritual practice and yet have received only the part, or the "tip," as they call it. But if someone with "words inside the stomach" would come forward, such a person could "explain and explain and explain until it reaches the *kdain*." This final goal might be translated as "meaning," but "totality" seems closer to the mark. *Kdain* is the totality that one constructs, the whole that one recovers from the parts. One could also say that it is the system which Mambai so obstinately insist underlies all their activities.

7

Even if Mambai had some precise object in mind when they instructed me to "look for the trunk" or to "arrive at the *kdain*," it would not be identical with what I will present in this book. Nevertheless, I have tried to construct this book in such a way that Mambai might recognize themselves in it, by telling what is in effect a kind of story, producing a narrative of sorts. This book is intended as my substitute for the perpetually deferred narrative text into which Mambai seek so anxiously to reinscribe themselves and their society.

PART ONE

Cosmos and Society

ONE

Ritual and the Social Order

1. The Life-giving Exchange

My focus throughout this study is a cultural conception of life that organizes Mambai representations of society and of the cosmos and finds its fullest, most powerful expressions in ritual contexts. The basic outlines of this conception may be simply stated. The Mambai conceive of life as a gift that requires a countergift. Life is not a free-floating vitality to be forcibly obtained, irrevocably possessed, but is rather the perishable product of a cycle of exchanges. What closes each exchange cycle and opens a new one is death, the final counter-gift. Death is at once a means of recompense and a technique of re-newal, or, put slightly differently, dying is conceived of as an obligation contracted through living. A principle of reciprocity integrates the two extreme poles of existence. Life and death are defined in this scheme as reciprocal prestations, complementary gifts which call forth each other in the dialectical unfolding of an exchange relationship.

Reciprocity between life and death structures the Mambai ritual system. All Mambai rituals are divided into the categories of "white" (*buti*) and "black" (*meta*). White ritual relates to agricultural fertility, black ritual has to do with the disposal of the dead, but the Mambai insist upon the complementarity of these performances. White ritual and black ritual are represented as the interdependent elements of a larger whole, which is evoked in the poetically stated premise of Mambai ritual life:

Buti ba rat	When white is not enough
Nor meta fe tlut;	Increase it with black;
Meta ba natou	When black is not sufficient
Nor buti fe naur.	Augment it with white.

These rhythmic alternations of white and black, of life and death, of receiving and returning, are the basis of a ritual system which will gradually reveal its "total" character as this study unfolds. At this point, let us note that the Mambai regard conceptually opposed forms of ritual activity as stages in a single project, the promotion of life through exchange. Ritual exchange involves both society and the cosmos, the human and the nonhuman, and Mambai move easily between these two levels of exchange. I, however, must follow them more painstakingly, tracing the multiple, overlapping manifestations of a unitary concept of life.

Mambai ritual is a technique of life-giving, to use Hocart's phrase, and Mambai society, like others analyzed by Hocart, is organized around the ritual promotion of life. In *Kings and Councillors*, his major comparative study of ritual and the social order (1970; orig. 1936), Hocart advanced the bold, suggestive thesis that social form in small-scale societies is related to ritually enacted conceptions of "life, fertility, prosperity." Ritual and the society that practices it thus "share a common structure," and Hocart treats ritual as the structuring term in this paradigm. The "quest for life," as he also calls ritual activity, is "a social affair," requiring the cooperation of many persons and groups; but in Hocart's model, the precise pattern of cooperation is derived from the rites themselves. Where Durkheim placed a represented social order anterior to its ritual representations (1965), Hocart argued for a society that "must organize itself for ritual," one that takes its form from the unfolding of the ritual process.

Social relations, in Hocart's model, are not merely "reinforced" or "strengthened" by ritual acts, as functionalism would have it. Language of "maintenance," "regulation," "restoration," and so on, assumes a preconstituted, analytically separable realm of "social organization," which is then said to be "transfigured" by symbols. Meanings, in other words, along with the rites that express them, enter into the social process only after the fact, to translate, enhance, and revivify an order that logically antecedes them. Fidelity to this construction leads to aporia, as Durkheim himself seems intermittently to have realized, whereas Hocart's approach avoids the abyss by defining ritually articulated meanings as constitutive of particular institutional forms.

Hocart's model of the social consequences of ritual suggests a perspective on Mambai society. So long as relations among persons and groups are seen as logically independent of ritual processes, it is impossible to *comprehend* Mambai society, in both senses of that word. To the Mambai themselves, all structurally significant relationships are inseparable from ritual obligations. The obligation is not something added to the relationship but rather constitutes it as a meaningful social form. To be involved with others is, in indigenous theory, to cooperate with them in the promotion of life; and where there is no such obligation, there is no involvement. It is no exaggeration to say that social organization in this society is ritual organization.

Social groups in Mambai society are defined and ranked by their complementary but unequal contributions to the ritual promotion of life. It is a cultural premise among the Mambai that life flows in one direction, outward from an origin point. This implies a division of persons into two categories: life-givers, who exercise ritual control over fertility (the senior lines of descent groups, the wife-giving sources of women, the ritual authorities of local communities, the Mambai people as a whole); and life-receivers, who must reciprocate with gifts and services for the benefits that they acquire (the junior lines of descent groups, the wife-taking recipients of women, the members of the community, all peoples other than the Mambai). Involvement with others takes the cultural form of dependency on others for life, and social obligations are defined in terms of life given, received, reciprocated, and renewed.

Such ties are not only thought but lived—in the little exchanges that organize domestic life; in the annual ceremonies that reunite scattered members of descent groups; in the formal prestations of complementary gifts and services transacted by affinal alliance partners; and in the presentation of material and symbolic gifts to the ritual heads of local communities, the "old mothers and old fathers" of their people. The hierarchical distinction between life-givers and life-receivers is continually recreated in social practices. It is in ritual contexts, however, that social distinctions resonate most profoundly with cosmology.

The social hierarchy replicates in complex ways the mutual but asymmetric dependency that the Mambai attribute to human relationships with the cosmic beings. The debt that is owed to the various social sources of life and well-being is also the debt that is owed by society as a whole to the encompassing cosmos. Social and cosmological obligations intermingle in ritual contexts, and Mambai themselves place the heaviest emphasis on the cosmic purposes of their rites.

Individuals employ a uniform idiom of reciprocity to account for their participation in any given ritual event. "We must make restitution," they will say:[1] and always what is reciprocated is identified as some previous gift of life and well-being. What varies, according to context, social status, level of knowledge, and other factors, is the precise source attributed to the obligation. Individuals are indebted to the parents who bore them, to the senior branches of their descent groups, to the groups that give women to their own, to the ritual guardians of their communities. But even as Mambai invoke particular social obligations, they will also speak of ritual in terms of a debt owed to "Our Mother who is rock/Our Father who is tree" (*it ina be hauta/it ama be aia*).

The problem for an interpretation of Mambai ritual is not to isolate the "real" motivation for prestations, but rather to apprehend overlapping obligations as multiple aspects of a life-giving exchange. If social collectivities must unite to repay and renew the cosmos, it is also the case that in so doing they reproduce their own hierarchical structures. Everything takes place as if the reproduction of Mambai society were at once the instrument and the outcome of a ritually secured cosmic balance.

2. Ritual and Society: Mythological Representations

Society must cooperate for ritual, yet Mambai hold their ritual duties to be older than the social groups which now perform them. The mythic origins assigned to ritual antecede the organization of society into the institutional divisions that obtain in the present. In the indigenous mythological model (which bears a certain resemblance to Hocart's analytical model), human beings divide themselves into groups, and these groups inherit ritual responsibilities already determined by the nature of the cosmos.

Mambai view the present order of the world as the product of a lengthy temporal process, which they often compare to the growth of a tree. Botanic metaphors play a pervasive role in Mambai thought, and we shall frequently encounter them expressing ideas of proper order and orientation, of complementarity and hierarchy, of unity and diversity. In the usage that concerns me here, past and present are disposed along an axis which is concretely embodied in the image of a tree. The tree is divided into lower and upper segments and stands balanced between below and above. In this imagery the past is associated with the "trunk" or "base" of the tree, with what Mambai call *fu*, a word that has the interrelated senses of "trunk, base, source, origin, beginning, cause." Recent and present time are classed together as *lau*, which refers to the top, tip, or highest point of any fixed and erect structure.[2] Metaphorically, *lau* is used to express the culmination or limit of a process, the end, outcome, or final result. *Ai-laun*, "treetop," denotes the crown of a tree; it is also used in reference to all of the tree's extremities, the crown, as well as the branches (*ota*), the young shoots (*sniki*), the leaves (*nora*), and the new buds (*diki*). Reaching upward and outward, the top of a tree branches off into multiformity.

A theme of complementarity is signified by the image of the union of tree trunk and treetop. But there is also an element of asymmetry implicit in the notion of a single trunk as the support of a ramified structure. Mambai concepts of time involve both complementarity and hierarchy. Present diversity is said to be anchored in an earlier uniformity, a distant trunk-time of origins, to which Mambai are profoundly attached. The other side of their attachment to the past is a conventionalized impatience with recent, present, or "tip-time." Many people would compare contemporary social institutions to the upper and outer part of a tree, and they warned me repeatedly against becoming entangled and lost amid the myriad, forking branches of their complex institutional life. "You must search for the trunk," they insisted, stressing that while the top of a tree is made up of many branches, these are all supported upon a single trunk. I came to take their admonitions seriously, and I directed my inquiries more and more to the "trunk" of the present social order.

At the trunk, base, or origin of things is the creation of the universe by the primordial male and female beings, Heaven and Earth. Their interactions, described in the next chapter, produce the world and its inhabitants, separate life from death, and generate perpetual tensions in the cosmos, to which Mambai ritual responds. Mambai also speak of this primordial past as the original Night (*hoda*) and distinguish it from a later period known as Day (*ada*), which begins in the mythic past and extends through the present.

The opposition between Night and Day encodes an important distinction between an earlier process of creation and a later one of regulation. During the mythic period of origins, the world and its inhabitants are created. The first ancestors of humanity reproduce and increase, and their progeny inherit from them ancient ritual obligations. During the Day the ancestor heroes establish a variety of social institutions, and so redistribute humanity into new categories. To each of these categories is assigned a role in the ritual process. But ritual obligations antecede these institutional divisions. Originating at the base of time, in the primordial night, obligations derive primarily from the structure of the cosmos, and only secondarily from the more recently differentiated structure of society. Or so at least it appears to Mambai, who often draw upon the metaphors of trunk and tip, night and day, to discuss the meaning of their ritual activities. Thus I have heard people airily dismiss the contemporary sociology of ritual performance as but the "tip" of ritual, in opposition to the unitary trunk.

In these mythological representations society has evolved over time, from a simpler to a more complex system, but the purpose of ritual remains fundamentally unchanged. By adjusting to new institutional divisions, ritual activity simply acquires new social classes of participants. In the indigenous conception, one might say, the purpose of ritual is not society; rather, the purpose of society is ritual.

3. Ritual Noise: Representations of Performance

Mambai rituals are composed of many elements. Any performance is a highly complex multimedia display. Minimally, all rites involve words, acts, objects, and places, but the rites that I shall examine later on also include percussive music. In fact, the playing of percussive instruments can symbolize the entirety of a ritual performance.

The term that Mambai most often use to designate ritual action is the verb *keo*. Strictly defined, *keo* refers to one specific and recurrent sequence within a performance, the beating of sacred drums and gongs in a formal procession. In this strict usage, *keo* is opposed to *beha*, a simpler mode of ritual performed without drum or gong. Although *beha* ritual involves various forms of speaking, it is classified as "silent" (*smera*), whereas *keo* implies that "things play" (*sauna haha*). "Silent" *beha* performances are considered less prestigious than those involving *keo*, and in the annual cycle of agricultural rites the use of drum and gong is a prerogative of particular social groups.[3]

Mambai also use *keo* in a wider sense to represent their ritual life as a whole. The statement "We *keo* rock and tree," the ubiquitous icons of Mambai religious life, comprehends a total system of ritual events. A reasonable, if unwieldy gloss of this statement is simply, "We perform rituals before rock and tree," or more suggestively, "We make ritual noise before rock and tree." Mambai also say that they *keo* a variety of objects, including spring water, rain, rice, corn, houses, and the dead. When any of these is verbally represented as the object of *keo*, the phrase designates a particular ritual event. For instance, *keo maeta*, literally "to *keo* the dead," refers to the staging of a mortuary ceremony.

Mambai have adopted the Portuguese word *adorar*, "to worship," and they sometimes use it interchangeably with *keo*. Thus they will say of their ritual practices both that they "*keo* rock and tree" and that they "worship rock and tree." At first, the identification of these terms may strike a Westerner as inappropriate, for *keo* has its referent in

16

what seems to be a technical activity, whereas we think of worship as involving a particular spiritual attitude of reverence. However, the ceremonial clamor that Mambai make over certain ritually marked objects also entails a particular attitude, one of respect, if not precisely of reverence. Moreover, Western religious traditions have also prescribed a form of strident, noisy worship as the correct expression of devotion to divinity. Thus we read in Psalms (97: 4–9):[4]

> Make a joyful noise to the Lord, all the earth;
> Break forth into joyous song and sing praises!
> Sing praises to the Lord with the lyre,
> with the lyre and the sound of melody!
> With trumpets and the sound of the horn
> make a joyful noise before the King, the Lord!
> Let the sea roar, and all that fills it;
> the world and those who dwell in it!
> Let the floods clap their hands;
> let the hills sing for joy together
> before the Lord, for he comes
> to judge the earth.
> He will judge the world with
> righteousness,
> and the people with equity.

In the psalm, man and nature together "make a joyful noise" before the Lord, whereas Mambai cosmology represents nature as silent, and human beings as the unique noisemakers. What concerns the Mambai in particular is the precise type of noise required, and while they too "sing praises," they also raise a deafening din of drum and gong. As in many other cultures, percussive instruments are used to establish contact with the other world. A connection between percussion and transition, which Needham (1967) has characterized as a universal feature of religious thought, occurs in Mambai ritual associated with concepts of reciprocity.[5] In Mambai thought the percussive sounds which circulate between this world and the other are at once a message sent and a gift offered to the cosmos. In effect, the underlying intent of *keo* is to exchange a ceremonially made clamor for life.

This idea of sound as a gift is based in Mambai conceptions of the cosmos, specifically, in a frequently invoked mythological opposition between silence and sound. The Mambai divide all things into two categories, "silent mouths" (*kuku molun*) and "speaking mouths"

17

(*kuku kasen*). The category of "silent mouths" includes all non-human creatures, animate and inanimate alike: rocks, trees, grasses, plants, animals, birds, insects, reptiles, fish, and the divine parents of this entire array, Heaven and Earth. The sole members of the second category are women and men who alone proclaim:

Aim kala kuku kasen	We are called speaking mouth
Aim kala lama kderen.	We are called articulating tongue.

The opposition is traced back to a mythological event. Once, Mambai say, all things spoke. In those days the ground cried out when people trod upon it, and trees and grasses screamed when they were cut. Father Heaven imposed a "ban" (*badun*) of silence on the world. By raising his hands, he removed the power of speech from all but his youngest, human children, who were then free to build their houses out of the mute, unprotesting environment. Soon afterward, Father Heaven and Mother Earth withdrew from human sight, each announcing in turn:

Au du ba kode sois	Already I descend with difficulty
Au sai ba kode sois	Already I arise with difficulty
Au kukun ba kase sois	Already my mouth does not speak
Au laman ba kdere sois	Already my tongue does not articulate
Au mudu sois	Already I am mute
Au toru sois.	Already I am motionless.

These events are not the stuff of antiquated narratives. To the Mambai, the silence of the cosmos is a central fact of existence, and a perpetual source of obligations. As "speaking mouths," human beings have a debt to pay, for their own material well-being is extracted out of the consenting bodies of their silent, elder kin. The "silent mouths" must die so that women and men may live, but the latter must make some form of restitution. Between silent and speaking beings, the proper relationship is one of exchange, and the medium of human restitution is ritual. Human beings offer to the cosmos the loudest sounds that they themselves can make, an extrahuman clamor pounded out on sacred drums and gongs.

We shall have to inquire more closely into the Mambai cosmos before we can fully appreciate the appropriateness of this noisy prestation. Here I note only that ritual activity is defined as an instrument for awakening the cosmic beings. One ritual language metaphor, "the dog barks/the cock crows" (*ausa noti/mauna foni*), identifies the sounds of drum and gong with the cries of the twin sentinels of the house who announce the new day.

On occasion, Mambai also note the aesthetic aspect of ritual performance.[6] A ritual, they will sometimes say, should be "beautiful" (*dadi*), and it should please the audience, composed of silent mouths. In such cases, where emphasis is placed on the spectacular and festive dimensions of ritual performance, the entire proceedings are defined as a prestation of sound and motion, an exciting multimedia display intended to rouse and delight a silent audience. In one of their own self-images, the Mambai are courtesans who speak, sing, play, and dance before a silent rock and a motionless tree.

4. Ritual and Daily Life: The Sacred in the Profane, the Profane in the Sacred

I have argued that Mambai conceive of life as the product of exchanges transacted in ritual contexts. By "life," I intend a general notion of fertility, prosperity, material well-being, or what Mambai sometimes call "the good bearing of women and the good bearing of men, the good breeding of pigs and the good breeding of dogs." This life or vitality is procured through collective rituals and then lived, or spent, one might say, over the course of everyday existence. In sociological terms, the promotion of life periodically reunites collectivities, which subsequently scatter again to get on with the business of everyday living.

These alternating rhythms of existence are related to the seasonal variation between rainy and dry periods, and evoke the situation analyzed by Mauss in his classic study of Eskimo social life, written in collaboration with Beuchat (1979; orig., 1905).[7] Mauss distinguished among the Eskimo two "successive phases of increased and decreased density, of activity and repose, of exertion and recuperation," which he defined as two "levels" of social life. These corresponded in his analysis to the oppositions between the collective and the individual, and between the sacred and the profane (78–79). His basic argument was that a conceptual opposition between winter and summer ordered the "twofold morphology" of Eskimo society and found expression in "the entire mentality of the group." Although Mauss insisted on the duality of Eskimo life, he stopped short of positing an absolute dichotomy and hinted that the two poles of existence might overlap. For instance, as an "appropriate" expression of the seasonal opposition, he quotes a fine Kwakiutl statement: "In summer, the sacred is below, the profane is on high; in winter, the sacred is above, the profane below" (77).[8]

In later chapters I discuss the morphological expressions of alternation among the Mambai. What need emphasis here are the continuities between opposed social states. At the so-called profane pole of existence, we find the scattered members of larger collectivities engaged in the very activities that are constitutive of ritual obligations—production and reproduction, which are thought to be made possible by ritual techniques. We find ourselves, in other words, not in a self-contained period, but in that extended interval between gift and countergift, to which Mauss himself would turn in a later essay (1967; orig., 1924). Always behind and ahead of the prosperity that ideally characterizes periods of dispersion is the obligatory return to an origin place to renew a source of life.

The relationship of the sacred to the profane may also be approached in terms of the analytical problem of identifying ritual activity. If, as Tambiah concedes, we can never separate ritual from nonritual events in an absolute way, in any culture, he goes on to argue, there are significant relative contrasts (1981, 116). Mambai themselves point us toward the culturally significant features of their ritual life in designating all nonritual periods as *ar-leta*. The prefix *ar* marks the future, and is used in counting forward from the time of speaking. Thus *ar-teul* means "three days from today," *ar-fat* means "four days from today," and so on. *Leta* has a number of meanings that merit our attention.

As a noun, *leta* denotes the outer veranda of a house, the area where guests are received. *Leta* is also used in conjunction with relationship terms, with the approximate meaning of "classificatory" relatives. *Nai leta*, for instance, includes all persons who stand as *nai* to ego, in distinction to *nai slol*, "direct, particular *nai*," which specifies the genealogical mother's brother.[9] A feature common to these two usages is the relatively undifferentiated, inclusive, or unmarked character of the concepts signified by *leta*. The inside of the house composes the private realm, which is marked off and reserved for the family, in opposition to the public, unmarked space of the veranda, where various types of people meet and mingle. Used as an adjective, *leta* denotes a class or category in distinction to a particular, marked member of that class.

By extension, *ar-leta* stands for the unmarked term in opposition to a variety of particular, marked ritual events. The distinction between nonritual and ritual time is between the absence and the presence of a quality, which in this case is literally a quality of markedness or boundedness. Where *ar-leta* denotes an undifferentiated extent of time, continuously unfolding toward the future, ritual time is marked off from ordinary time and has a disposition of its own. In ritual events, special restrictions obtain that are *relatively* absent from everyday life. I italicize the word "relatively" to emphasize the incompatibility of these conceptions with absolute distinctions between classes of events. What Mambai seem to intend are, rather, different degrees of formality that characterize particular situational contexts.

The relative formality of ritual events is subjectively experienced by participants, who think of themselves as voluntarily submitting to preestablished procedures, following, or endeavoring to follow, a fixed sequence of activities laid down in the past. From a comparative perspective, Mambai consciousness of external constraint is notably high. This is not to say, of course, that different enactments of the "same" ritual are identical, nor even that Mambai believe them to be so. Mambai do, however, repeatedly assert the ideal of a rigidly prescribed order of events, and when perceived deviations occur, it is not uncommon for the dubious segment to be reenacted in the "proper" way. For example, a sacrifice offered in the "wrong" place may be pronounced invalid and performed again, despite the material cost involved.

As will no doubt be apparent, such hyperformalization is conditioned by the presence of specialists who objectify the authority of tradition, and for whom competence in minute details is status-enhancing. But leaving aside, for now, the pragmatic aspects of performance, let us pursue the contrast between ritual and nonritual events at the semantic level.

Throughout this book I argue that participants emerge from ritual performances with a heightened consciousness of the meaning of their ties to one another, and in this respect the argument is certainly neo-Durkheimian. The weakness in Durkheim's approach, as many commentators by now have pointed out, was his failure to deal adequately with the semantic content of ritually awakened awareness, a failure which, in my view, is connected to his overemphasis of the opposition between the sacred and profane poles of social life. If any sense of unity persists in everyday life, and Durkheim claimed that it did, then it must be because individuals are able to connect their daily experience with ritual models of the social world. In other words, there must be semantic continuity, at the same time as there is a subjectively perceived contrast between two styles of conduct.

The contrast, as I have stated, is between the relative formality of ritual action and the relative informality of everyday life. Verbalization

21

is the primary means of formalization. Mambai ritual is characterized by its oratorical elaboration. While the physical settings of rites are integral components of performance, as are a variety of symbolically charged material objects, all such nonverbal symbolism is at least partly dependent on spoken words for its efficacy. In ritual contexts Mambai seem to be obsessed with the verbal categorization of sensory experience. Any subject that is implicated in the proceedings must be formally invoked in conjunction with its distinctive qualities, which are defined in turn by the contrastive qualities predicated of other subjects. Thus a trunk is anchored in the earth and a tip reaches out toward the sky, a woman sits in darkness and a man emerges into the light, to give but two examples of semantic parallelism in formal speech. Inasmuch as actual persons, places, objects, or acts also figure in a performance, they are always hedged in with words, signified by poetic formulae that index the particular subjects to semantic concepts. Relayed through poetic language, experience is ordered to a striking degree, as the systematic relationships among paired cultural categories are objectified in speech. Semantic meaning in no way exhausts the ritual uses of language, but the poetic function does, nevertheless, take precedence in formal contexts. In the unfolding of ritual discourse, a system of meaningful categories is projected onto events of speaking, or, to paraphrase Jakobson and Halle (1956, 76–82), the metaphoric axis of similarities is superimposed on the metonymic axis of contiguities.

The same categories are used in everyday life, but not according to such stringent combinatorial rules. So too, many of the activities that are performed or verbally represented in ritual contexts are characteristic of ordinary experience. In daily life, people nurse and cradle infants, draw water and gather wood, go into the house and out from it, walk toward or away from a center, lay down their heads and stretch out their feet, light the hearth fire and enjoy the shade, give food to boys and girls and scatter the leavings for pigs and dogs, embrace their mothers and bow to their fathers. What is done and said in ritual contexts is not foreign to the performers. Participants in ritual events do not enter some remote, spiritual realm that transcends their everyday concerns, nor do they encounter abstract principles of "authority" or "subordination." To a great extent, they do what they might ordinarily do, a fact which imparts a degree of realism to ritual events, but they do it with a difference. On the sacred ritual occasions when collectivities reunite, participants conduct themselves in formally prescribed and highly patterned ways, utilizing verbal and visual media to enact fundamental cultural conceptions of order. Through the unfolding of ritual processes, the implicit meaning of "profane" life is articulated and enhanced.

In sociological terms, the argument I have introduced relates to the structuring role of ritual in Mambai society. The Mambai are organized into a variety of overlapping groups based on various criteria of relatedness. When I turn to Mambai society, I will first treat ties between males which define groups that claim common descent. These groups are connected to still other groups by enduring alliances based on marital exchanges. They are also incorporated into larger communities disposed around named origin villages. What these several forms of relationship have in common is that they are uniformly enacted for ritual purposes: the differentiated parts of a descent group or "house" reunite to perform annual "white" agricultural ceremonies; when a death occurs within such a group, its members call upon their marital allies to participate in a series of "black" mortuary ceremonies; and, at a higher level of ritual performance, entire communities come together in designated villages for regionwide celebrations.

All of these rituals are divided into the two categories of white and black. What is striking is that white rituals, whether staged by an internally differentiated descent group or involving the higher-level ritual community, never mobilize relations of affinal alliance. Marital allies cooperate in the "black" disposal of the dead, not in the "white" regulation of agricultural processes, tasks which native poetry represents as complementary. Hence from a sociological perspective, we are confronted with a social division of ritual labor. But if we focus on cosmological symbolism, we find that this social division is suspended. When Mambai isolate the cosmic purpose of their rites, both the white and the black, they describe an undifferentiated community of speakers bound by obligations to a silent cosmos. White and black ritual, in this conception, appear as two moments in a single exchange transaction whereby life is reciprocated with death.

My guiding objective is to preserve what might also be called the "integrity" of these exchanges, by showing how social and cosmological obligations resonate together and mutually influence each other. My strategy is to begin with an undifferentiated concept of life as a gift, and then move outward, in two directions, toward the concept's interrelated institutional and cosmological expressions.

TWO

The Mambai and Their Land

The source of all things is the earth.
—A Mambai axiom

1. The Peoples of Timor

The island of Timor is occupied by two different language families, the one Austronesian, the other non-Austronesian, or "Papuan."[1] The majority of the population in western Timor speaks one of two Austronesian languages, Atoni or Tetum, but the linguistic situation is more complex in the east. On the eastern half of the island, fourteen distinct languages are spoken by ethnic groups that range in size from a few thousand to 80,000 members. With the exception of the Bunaq, who straddle the border between East and West Timor, the non-Austronesian speakers are concentrated in the extreme east of the island.

The linguistic situation reflects a long history of migrations and a convergence of peoples bearing distinctive cultural traditions. The island seems to have been a meeting ground for two major cultural influences, the one Indonesian and coming from the west, the other Melanesian and coming from the east. This history of diversity is reflected in Timorese oral traditions. Each of the peoples of Timor represent themselves as being descended either from original, autochthonous inhabitants of the land, or from ancestral invaders who are traced back to a mythic homeland overseas. Interethnic relations are represented in terms of a distinction between insiders and outsiders, although Mambai mythology, as we shall see later, introduces a subtle variation into this pattern.

The Mambai, who number over 80,000, are the largest ethnic group on the eastern half of the island.[2] Their language, also called Mambai, is Austronesian and it has close affinities with both Kemak and Tetum. It resembles the Atoni (also known as Timorese) and Helongese languages spoken in the west, in that all three share the phenomenon of metathesis, which Tetum and Kemak lack.[3] Mambai is more distantly related to the languages of Roti, Wetar, Leti, and Kisar and, less intimately, to those of Solor and of Sikka on Flores.[4]

The Mambai form a continuous and distinct ethnolinguistic unit, bordered by the Tocodede on the north, the Kemak, Bunaq, and

24

Tetum on the west, and the Galoli, Idate, and southern Tetum on the east. There are four major dialect divisions which the speakers themselves regard as mutually intelligible. The identification "we Mambai" includes at its widest the entire linguistic area.

2. Environment and Subsistence

The island of Timor is divided by rugged mountain ranges which run from east to west. This creates three major zones, a central upland flanked by two contrasting coastal plains. The northern coast is the most arid part of the island, while the southern coast is an area of relatively high rainfall and presents a more lush, tropical appearance. In the mountains the soil is impermeable and erosion-prone, and it undergoes desiccation during the dry season.

The Mambai are primarily a mountain people. At its broadest, the zone they inhabit spans central Timor, forming an arc from the northern coastal capital of Dili to the southern coast. Dili itself was formerly part of the Mambai domain of Motain, but its present population is ethnically mixed. The Mambai territory is divided into four administrative districts, Ermera, Aileu, Ainaro, and Same. My research was conducted within the district of Aileu, which has its seat some forty kilometers south of Dili.

Most of the Mambai territory is a mountainous terrain of hills and high river valleys. To the west, the landscape is dominated by the great Tat Mai Lau mountain range. Mount Tat Mai Lau itself, the highest mountain on Timor, rises to an altitude of 2,963 meters. It is an imposing, strikingly beautiful landscape, although often rugged and inhospitable. Great craggy mountains, dotted with strangely shaped rock formations, alternate with softer, rolling hills and open grasslands. The vegetation is a mix of grass savannah and savannah forest, the remains of a primary monsoon forest. The most characteristic species of vegetation are the acacia (*Acacia leucophloea* Willd., Mambai *hlala*), the white eucalyptus (*Eucalyptus alba* Reinw., Mambai *ai foia*) of the savannahs, and the black eucalyptus (*Eucalyptus platyphylla* Auct., Mambai *ai ura*) which dominates the secondary forest on the mountain slopes.[5]

The climate on Timor is governed by the tropical monsoons. These bring an alternation between a dry season and a wet season. The wet season is short and irregular, in opposition to a prolonged dry season. The east monsoon ushers in the dry season, which usually begins in the mountains in late May. The rains are brought by the west monsoon, and they may begin as early as October, or as late as the end of November. And there are years when the rains do not come at all.

Agricultural activity is organized around the rains. Mambai subsistence is based on the swidden cultivation of corn (*sela*), rice (*mea*), cassava (*samklesun* or *saima*), sweet potatoes (*sekar*), yams (*bala*), and several varieties of beans (*kasa*). Corn, root crops, beans, and vegetables are grown together on tiny swidden plots perched high on the hills. In the most mountainous regions south of Aileu, rice is also grown in mountain gardens. Elsewhere, the high valleys are given over to flat, dry rice fields.

The clearing and burning of swidden gardens begins in late August. Planting is timed to coincide as nearly as possible with the rains. The wet season is a time of intense garden activity, interlaced with the annual cycle of agricultural rituals. Rice fields are harvested in June, in concert with smaller ceremonies. Both sexes participate in agricultural work. Men perform most of the heavy clearing and burning, while women are responsible for the bulk of the daily weeding. Planting and harvesting are performed by both men and women.

Mambai grow a variety of vegetables such as lettuce, tomatoes, cucumbers, squash, turnips, cabbage, spinach greens, and peas. These are primarily cash crops, sold either at the weekly market held in the administrative seat, or in Dili. Individually owned orchards produce oranges, tangerines, pineapple, several varieties of banana, and mangoes, all of which are grown for market sale. The Portuguese have initiated extensive coffee cultivation in the district of Ermera and, to a lesser extent, in Aileu. Most Mambai in these areas own small coffee-holdings which produce the bulk of their cash income. The income brought in by cash-cropped vegetables and coffee is minimal, barely covering the yearly administrative tax, school fees, necessities of clothing, and ritual expenses. Mambai existence remains a subsistence one with corn and root crops making up the bulk of the diet.

Mambai herd water buffalo (*arabaua*), goats (*biuba*), sheep (*biub-malain*), and pigs (*haiha*), and raise chickens (*mauna*). Chickens, goats, and pigs are occasionally sold at the market, but most people keep their livestock for ceremonial exchanges. Buffalo are used for limited sawah treading in the valley rice fields, and the sturdy Timorese mountain ponies are used as mounts and packhorses. Other forms of animal husbandry are unknown.

In productivity, the Mambai territory compares unfavorably with other areas of Timor, such as the fertile southeastern lowlands and the rice-intensive northern plains. The southernmost reaches of the

Mambai zone enjoy the secondary rainfall brought by the eastern monsoon, and my impression from a brief visit there was that the area is agriculturally more productive than is the mountainous interior. The heartland of Mambai territory is strikingly poor. The soil is impermeable and subject to erosion, and much of the Aileu area shows signs of swidden deterioration. The eastern half of Timor has not experienced an ecological crisis of the same proportions as in the west, where population increase coupled with soil erosion has created what Ormeling (1956) calls "the Timor problem."[6] Nevertheless, life in the mountains is not easy, and the poverty of their land is an important element in Mambai representations of the ritual process.

3. The Order of the Land

Mambai life is bound up in the land with all its harshness, and their history, as they tell it, is the story of their relation to the earth. "It is the earth which is our base," Mambai say over and over, "the earth holds us." The most sacred of Mambai traditions are those that follow the origins of the earth in minute detail, projecting strange, agonistic tales onto the configuration of the land. For those who know how to read it, the landscape embodies its own history, inscribed once and for all during the Night of origins.

Mambai identify themselves as the original inhabitants of the land, and its guardians by right of birth. This collective self-image shapes their view of their relations to other ethnic groups. On Timor, where the several peoples identify themselves variously as autochthones or immigrants, the earthbound Mambai claim for themselves unique ritual obligations toward the rest of humanity. Thus Mambai ritual has a universal reach; it is performed for the benefit of the entire world, with all its inhabitants. In Mambai thought, they alone promote life for humanity as a whole.

This far-flung ritual community is described in idioms of consanguinity. Mambai say that there is but one mother, who is Earth, and one father, who is Heaven, and their children are scattered over the land and across the sea. As the eldest sons of these divine parents, the Mambai inherit inalienable ritual duties. Their task is to

Deiki it inan	Watch over Our Mother
Bale it aman	Look after Our Father
Boe nor it inan	Sleep with Our Mother
Ble nor it aman	Wake with Our Father.

27

According to this mythology of common origins, all the peoples of the world are descended from the primordial male and female deities and are kin to nonhuman beings. Mambai regard themselves as the eldest branch of humanity, those on whom all other peoples depend. Their unique status is also expressed in terms of a spatial model that situates them at the center of an islandwide cooperation for life. Other peoples are ranked and related to the Mambai on the basis of their relative distance from the symbolic center.

Two systems of orientation are used to order the land and its inhabitants. One system is based on the coordinates *hoha*, "interior," and *taisa*, "sea." These are aligned along a south/north axis that has an exceptional value in Mambai thought. The geographical contrast between the mountains of the southern interior and the expanse of the northern sea is projected onto space at multiple levels, including the land, the community, and the house. To Mambai, the symbolic geography of the land is the model for all other spatial structures and is itself conceived of in anthropomorphic terms. The topography of the land, high and mountainous in the interior and sloping northward to the coastal plains, is represented as a seated figure who faces to the north. There is a correspondence between localized places and parts of the body. The tallest mountains in the south correspond to the head, shoulders, and torso of a person; where the land begins its downward slope it corresponds to the lap and calves, and the coastal lowlands are the feet which tread back the sea. If east and west are added to the scheme, they correspond to a person's right and left arms. Mambai can incorporate any locality in Timor into the model represented in figure 1.

This system of orientation is most commonly used in its dyadic form, without reference to lateral symbolism. Any ritually significant object, such as a corpse, a tree, a mortar, is oriented with its head or top to the south and its foot or bottom to the north. Some people claim to orient themselves in this way when they lie down to sleep.

A second system of orientation is expressed as a four-point scheme based on the quarters. In this system, east is either "rising sun" (*lelo sain*) or "earth head" (*rai ulun*), and west is "setting sun" (*lelo dun*) or "earth foot" (*rai oen*). The "head" and "foot" of the earth are sometimes associated in ritual language with particular geographical points of reference. Thus east and west become

Mate Bian nor rai ulun	Mate Bian and earth head
Koban nor rai oen.	Kova and earth foot.

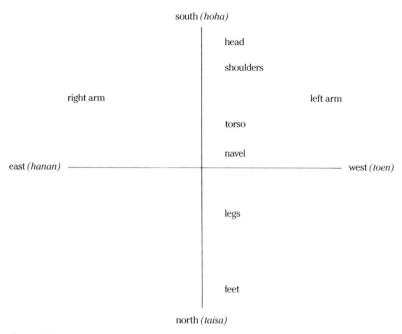

Figure 1: The orientation of the land

In accordance with the head-foot designations for east and west, it is possible to distinguish north and south as "left" (*toen*) and "right" (*hanan*) respectively. Here the assumption is that one faces to the east. However, Mambai rarely use the lateral symbolism, and they typically refer to north as "female sea" (*tais-hinan*) and south as "male sea" (*tais-manen*). People say that the northern Savu sea is "tame" or "calm," like a woman, whereas the Timor sea in the south is "wild" and male.

The equations east = head, west = foot are not associated with an anthropomorphic model of the land, nor are they used in orienting ritually significant objects. These equations are linguistic conventions for signifying the four quarters of space. The quarters are not internally ranked, nor are they associated with a congruent classification of colors or elements, as occurs elsewhere in Indonesia.[7] In certain contexts a distinction may be drawn between the east as the direction of the living and the west as the direction taken by the dead, but the four quarters viewed as a unit are equipollent. They are classified together as "outside" (*hoho*) in opposition to a center (*fusu*). In this center-periphery model, all the lands and peoples of Timor are subsumed under the category of "outside" and are opposed to a centerland occupied by the Mambai.

4. The Trunk of Discourse

Anthropomorphic models of space, formally encoded in paired body terms, are a common feature in eastern Indonesian cultures. There are, however, certain distinctive elements to the symbolic organization of space in Mambai culture. There is a discrepancy between the linguistic identifications of directional coordinates with body parts, on the one hand, and the anthropomorphic model of space, on the other hand. Ritually, east is signified by "earth head" and west by "earth foot," and yet, as Mambai insisted to me with some vehemence, the head and foot of the earth are symbolically located to the south and north respectively. This discrepancy is part of a coherent and conventionalized strategy of discourse which reflects more general attitudes toward the communication of sacred knowledge.

The anthropomorphic model of the earth is regarded as one expression of such knowledge. Mambai identify the seated figure with Mother Earth, who first gave birth to the land itself and then squatted on top of her firstborn to bring forth all her other children. These primordial events are included in a sacred narrative, the myth of creation, which Mambai call the "walk of the earth" (*raia ni lolain*). Mambai refer to all their origin traditions as "walks," and everything, from a particular foodstuff, to a social group, to the earth itself, is said to have its distinctive "walk" or origin path. Every walk, as the journey metaphor implies, unfolds in time and space. Indeed, mythic narratives largely consist of detailed itineraries, lists of place names ordered into spatiotemporal progressions. It is a narrative convention among the Mambai that all these walks originally unfolded in a sequential order. Together they compose a single, continuous story, the "walk of all things" (*sauna mret mret ni lolain*), a coherent narrative account of how the present order of the world originated.

Mambai also distinguish between the earlier mythic events that compose the story's "trunk" or "base," and later events that compose its "tip." Few Mambai claim to comprehend the story in its entirety, from trunk to tip, and indeed, there is a sense in which it can be said that no one comprehends the total narrative. There is, however, a notion of considerable importance to Mambai, which is that in order to understand the present fully, one must first understand the past. In Mambai idioms, one must "grasp the trunk securely in order for the tip to be erect." And it is a shared premise that the story of the past begins with the walk of the earth.

The creation narrative composes what Mambai call the "trunk of discourse" (*teora ni fun*), the base, origin, source from whence all other discourses derive.[8] It is located, Mambai will say, "inside the stomachs of those who know." These words-inside-the-stomach are contrasted to those that "leave the mouth" as the "trunk" to the "tip" of discourse. The opposition between internalized trunk words and externalized verbal display carries a distinction between the concealed essence of knowledge and the artful, oblique, branching expression of knowledge. This is not a distinction between truth and falsity, for the botanic idiom emphasizes the unity of the unspoken trunk and the spoken tip. In this metaphor public discourse is not, or not merely, a form of deceptive speech; it is also a culturally prescribed mode of indirect communication. Formal oratory works through hints and allusions, through oblique suggestions and conventionalized conceits, as a contorted, twisting index of the sacred words that compose its hidden trunk. To return to the materials that prompted this discussion, note the significant tension between the deceptive verbal identification of the earth's coordinates and the ubiquitous visual images of ritual objects positioned along a south-north axis. Mambai say that those with "words inside the stomach" will understand the full meaning of the rites.

I believe that it would be impossible to construct a coherent cosmogony solely out of the flood of oratory unleashed in ritual contexts. One can, however, assimilate a set of recurrent themes and relationships. One hears repeatedly of a meeting between Heaven and Earth that is followed by a separation; of the emergence of "dry land" out of the primordial "water and sea"; of a long dark night that ends in a sudden burst of light; of a narrow strip of earth that becomes "wide and broad"; of a creative collision between a rock and a tree; of an umbilical cord that "snaps and splits"; of a "black upper earth" that covers a "white lower earth," and so on, and so on. Formal ritual speech dances from one mythological image to another, shunning sequential narrative accounts of creation, but scattering bits and pieces of a story of life and death. And the more I observed and participated in Mambai ritual activities, the more I found myself forced into a pursuit of a coherent narrative. My interpretive activities came to take the form of a quest for a full story which, it seemed, would support, anchor, and unify the fragmented speech that I recorded.

Is there such a narrative text? Does a full account of creation exist? This may seem an odd question, especially as I shall soon present a narrative and return to it often in the course of this study. Yet the question of the narrative's existence, of its way of being in the world, this question must be addressed, even if it cannot be precisely answered.

The first point to be made is that Mambai themselves speak as if there were a full narrative. They insist that discourse has its trunk and tip, and that the trunk can, on appropriate occasions, be transmitted from a possessor to a seeker of knowledge. Fathers are said to withhold trunk-words from their sons until they lie on their deathbeds, and priests will jealously retain them until they feel that their lives and vocations are nearly spent, obliging their apprentices to make do until then with the unanchored "tip" of ritual knowledge. The unsaid words-inside-the-stomach are valued as treasure, wealth to be hoarded and stored like the sacred relics of an ancestral patrimony, and finally bestowed upon a designated heir. Mambai attribute to the act of communication the character of a communion, whereby the recipient inherits the essential self of the donor.

There is nothing particularly unusual about the removal of sacred words from ordinary conversation. More striking, perhaps, is their partial removal from ritual contexts, for a coherent narrative of creation is never recited in ritual performances. But what I find most characteristic of the Mambai is their brooding preoccupation with the hidden mysteries of creation. Mambai fret over the prescribed hoarding of sacred words. Their attitude toward the communication of sacred knowledge is ambivalent. Often they will accuse "those who know" of attempting to "shut in words," of appropriating for themselves a communal heritage of knowledge that ultimately belongs to the community as a whole. And Mambai sometimes voice a fear that this knowledge might someday be lost, buried beneath the dense, tangled branches of an increasingly rootless discourse.

It was this ambivalence, more than anything else, that came to shape my inquiries, for I was repeatedly instructed to pursue precisely those words that are most restricted in their circulation. I was told, over and over, by all those who showed an interest in my studies, that I had to begin at the beginning, at the trunk, with the walk of the earth. Often I was advised to abandon or at least postpone inquiry into more "recent" phenomena "of the day," that I might "come straight, go straight" in unswerving pursuit of the origins of the earth. "Menina must ask only for the walk of the earth for everything is tied into this," onlookers and critics would advise, as I prepared for an interview with some notable priest or elder.

My problem as an ethnographer was not to determine what questions to ask. Mambai readily and rigorously defined culturally valued subjects and furnished me with a series of symbolic cues. They told me to ask for things "of the earth" or "of the night," for the origin of "dry land" from out of the "water and sea." I was not to settle for things "of the day" or "of the tip," or for anything relating to the time when the earth was already "wide and broad." In effect, I was provided with a key to culturally significant cosmogonic events.

The difficulty, however, was to develop or stumble upon a method of procedure that elicited something more than the strained, awkward silences I all too often provoked. Indeed, it seemed at times that the more sophisticated I grew in my eliciting techniques, the less success I had. Everyone would solemnly agree upon the propriety of my questions and approve the order in which they were laid out. And then out of all this harmony would come the perennial refrain: "That is what we fear to say." And after that, silence.

Obviously, cultural boundaries played a role in such reticence. Traditions hedged in with proscriptions, their circulation rigidly restricted even within local communities, are not readily entrusted to a European stranger from overseas. Indeed, it was some time before I fully appreciated the precise nature and import of the cultural boundary between myself and the Mambai. Only slowly did I come to understand how Mambai collective identity is caught up in an idea of privileged knowledge about the cosmos, knowledge possessed by them alone. But then, what I found far more perplexing than their reluctance to share with me their most sacred words was their anxious insistence that I seek and acquire those words. Their recurrent admonitions, together with their concern and outrage over "words that did not touch," quite literally forced me to continue with an investigation that I would at many points gladly have abandoned.

At times my studies took on a circuslike character, with groups of onlookers hovering about the sidelines, waiting to overhear and evaluate a speaker, and perhaps also to learn from him. Such listeners would grow angry and break out into violent denunciations if they deemed the speaker's account of earth origins to be insufficient or ill-formed. "He jumps from trunk to tip, and his words do not touch," was the most frequent and bitter accusation.

What words should "touch" is the hidden trunk, the base conceived of as a narrative account of creation, which supports and unifies all other forms of discourse. This unspoken trunk is an idea that Mambai share about their discourse, and I would argue on the basis of my own experiences that it is the idea of a whole, and not any full narrative, that is held in common. By this I mean something more than that an oral tradition consists of all its variants, for I do not regard the notion of a system of permutable narratives as an adequate representation of Mambai cosmogony. Rather, under what I will call "ordinary circumstances" (and I mean these to include the repetitive rounds of ritual performances), the creation myth is embodied in what Mambai regard as its partial manifestations. These incomplete expressions are paired by cultural convention with a signified narrative which, I suspect, relatively few individuals are capable of producing in practice. But the *idea* of the unsaid whole, the unenunciated trunk that binds together the entirety of discourse, this idea is of immense value to Mambai. Insisting on the possibility of full knowledge is a way by which Mambai attempt to center their thought and their activities. Through the idea of the full story that links the past to the present, Mambai preserve, or endeavor to preserve, a promise of plenitude.

All this said, how am I to introduce the narrative text that I am about to present? To begin with, I must disavow any radical separation between myself and the text. The story I have to tell is not an object that I "collected." It was not lying about, waiting to be scooped up in the ethnographer's net, as one picture of ethnographic "discovery" would have it. Instead, I freely admit that I contributed to the production of a narrative, by participating in a lengthy process of listening and speaking, a long, twisting, and occasionally painful conversation, repeatedly interrupted by meaningful silences.

That process took over a year to unfold, and thus more than half of my stay with the Mambai was governed by a pursuit of one narrative. The pursuit involved me with many individuals and places, but most closely with my two guides, Mau Bere and Mau Balen. They belonged respectively to the villages of Hohul and Raimaus and they were widely regarded as being among "those who know."

Hohul and Raimaus are important, closely related centers of ritual activity, and it was in these two places that I conducted much of my research. I shall have more to say in a later chapter about the special status of Hohul and Raimaus within a larger community. Here it should be acknowledged that the account of creation that emerged out of my conversations with Mau Bere and Mau Balen embodies a view of the world as seen from the perspective of Hohul and Raimaus. Indeed, their narrative is a charter, in the traditional anthropological sense, for the ritual preeminence of these two villages, and I found that individuals affiliated to other villages would advance similar claims to status, while also acknowledging the precedence of Hohul and Raimaus. At this point, however, my concern is not with the sociology of narrative performances, but with the internal dynamics of a process of narration.

Mau Balen and Mau Bere did not recount the creation myth to me in any single sitting. The story was told in fragments, through sudden, excited, often unplanned confidences, hasty, tumbled chronicles that left speakers and listener alike shaken and uncertain. Toward the end of my fieldwork there were formal, planned transmissions, the kind of "parting gift" of words that many anthropologists receive from their closest informants. But before these came a variety of performances, some lengthy, others brief, some willing, others grudging, some alone, others in company, some premeditated, others abruptly triggered by an unwittingly astute query on my part. The settings were equally varied. We huddled in a crevice of a sacred mountain, with all the origin lands spread out beneath us; we perched atop a half-built house and talked until the wind came up and frightened us; we sat snugly around a table in a host of mountain homes, perhaps transcribing a taped chant, discussing a ritual sequence, or simply talking of this and that, until our words led us back to the Night of creation.

On my part, the learning process came to resemble a form of ethnographic detective work. I would pore over the various texts that I had transcribed and filter through my observations on ritual performances in search of clues that might at least generate new questions about world origins. Much of the time, I felt disoriented, confused, and not infrequently, resentful. Yet had Mau Bere, Mau Balen, or some other very brave, or very foolish, Mambai told me the creation myth from start to finish, early in my fieldwork, it would doubtless have seemed little more to me than an interesting cosmogony.

Instead, as things unfolded, I assumed something of what I take to be a Mambai attitude toward a narrative of origins that is ranked as the original narrative. Increasingly, as I sought to make sense out of ritual performances, it seemed to me that if I could only piece together the broken fragments of an underlying narrative whole, then everything would become clear, then I would understand ritual practices. And as my task was not to perform those practices but only to interpret them, my own need for a totalizing narrative was omnipresent. Now, however, having assisted in the making of such a narrative, I find that the interpretive task is only begun, and I have felt obliged to deconstruct my text before even presenting it. Indeed, I was tempted to withhold the full narrative entirely and offer only fragments, but that strategy became clumsy. And besides, it contravenes the Mambai insistence on wholeness, even if it accords with certain of their discursive practices. So I shall try to steer a middle course between narrative whole and partial performance. To this end, I will set out a narrative account of creation, but I will restrict my interpretive comments to a minimum, and readers are here forewarned against a sense of puzzlement and perplexity. However, in the course of this study I shall return repeatedly to the creation myth and use it as an interpretive model. The myth will tag us through the present work, never deciphered or decoded, but guiding us through Mambai social and ritual life, somewhat as my earlier quest after a narrative guided me through the events that I attended.

5. The Walk of the Earth

In the beginning there is a solitary being named Ina Lua. *Ina* is the Mambai term for "mother," which would indicate that the First Being is female. However, there are also suggestions that Ina Lua is hermaphroditic, and when mentioned at all, the First Being is simply called a "person" (*atuba*), without specification of gender. Whatever this person may be, it exists alone, in a shapeless realm, prior to the differentiation of above and below. In the midst of this primordial chaos, Ina Lua moulds (*lum*) a woman and a man out of navel lint, and shelters (*hoh*) them inside the hollow of its navel.

The man and woman are named Buis Mali and Seob Mali. *Mali* is a common element of Mambai personal names. *Buis* means "to pluck, to pick," as of a fruit or flower. *Seob* means "to pull apart, to tear up or rip open." The first couple are also called Ber Ulu and Lau Loer. *Ber* and *Lau* signify male and female names respectively. *Ulu* is said to derive from *lul*, "to roll up." It is used to describe the rolling of tobacco into a cigarette or of betel leaves to form a cone. *Loer* means "to open, to make wide"; it may refer to the act of adjusting a cloth around the body.[9]

These names, which are rarely uttered, have referents in narrative events. The import of rolling and widening will emerge in the course of the narrative, and the names of the great plucker and the great tearer relate to ritual conceptions of life. I shall refer to these figures throughout as the Mambai customarily do in their chants and in their ordinary discourse: Our Mother Earth (It Inan Raia) and Our Father Heaven (It Aman Leola).

Mother Earth is the first to quit the formless place of origins. Impregnated by her brother, she descends to an empty world and gives birth to the first "earth mound," which becomes the great mountain

Tat Mai Lau. The name is Mambai and means "highest, oldest ancestor." The mountain is brought forth at the center of a chaotic cosmos, or better, its birth centers the cosmos, orienting space around an origin point.

Mambai commonly refer to the mountain as Nama Rau, a name which I am unable to translate. In myth, the first mountain is also called Ama Lau, "Great Father." In ritual language Mambai avoid all these designations and coin more oblique references. In chants, the mountain is named with the formula No Bou Teten/Nau Sara Butin, "Tip of the Shading Coconut Palm/White Sheath of the Areng Palm." If these names have significance, I was unable to discover it.[10] The mountain is also known as Bebili Teten/Behaila Laun, "Tip of Bebili/Peak of Behaila," a formula which designates all ancestral origin villages and identifies them with the mountain. From here on, I shall follow what seems to be the most regular Mambai usage and refer to the mountain as Nama Rau.

The mountain is surrounded by whirling "water and sea." These represent the original birth fluid (*afi eran*), and they are increased through subsequent births. Mother Earth sits upon the summit of Nama Rau, with her back turned to the south, her feet stretched out toward the north. Sitting in this position, she gives birth to seven smaller earth mounds, which form a tight circle around Nama Rau.

Father Heaven is reunited with Mother Earth upon the top of Nama Rau. The mountain of origins at the center of the cosmos is the primordial nexus between below and above. It is the place where separate but as yet undifferentiated beings come together and are distinguished through the sexual act itself. Differentiation is expressed in idioms of transgressing boundaries, shattering the perfect, unbroken wholeness of the body. In ritual speech, the primordial union of Heaven and Earth is evoked by the image of a mutilating collision between a rock and a tree:

Hdis ni hauta	Smash the rock
Tbo ni aia	Crack the tree
Haut koa loren	Hollow horizontal rock
Ai koa sain.	Hollow vertical tree.

The cosmic union redistributes the cosmos and transforms the relationship of the deities into one of complementary opposition. Out of their union are born the parents of trees, rocks, and grasses. The ancestral trees and grasses leave their seeds for future progeny and

37

donate their bodies to Heaven and Earth, who use them to build the first house. Known simply as the Lone House (Fad Mesan), it shelters Mother Earth as she gives birth again to the first women and men.[11]

One pervasive image of complementarity is the opposition between outside and inside, expressed as a contrast between the open air and the house. To Heaven belongs the world of the exterior. He leaves his consort and their children inside of the Lone House, on top of Nama Rau. Then, late one night, Heaven descends through the roof of the Lone House, a terrifying, shining apparition. His human sons embrace him, and he confers upon each of them a distinctive identity and status, marked by the objects they receive as their share of the original patrimony. Then he vanishes again.[12]

Abandoned once more, Mother Earth wearies of the wind and cold upon the mountain peak. She leaves the Lone House and descends to Ur Bou/Ai Datu, a lower mountain to the north of Nama Rau. Here, she falls ill and dies.

Era kauk it Inan	Water shakes Our Mother
Nama bis it Inan	Chills take Our Mother
Ua maet ni Ur Bou	She dies in Ur Bou
Ua flair ni Ai Datu.	She flees in Ai Datu.

But the Mother's corpse continues to speak. Dead in Ur Bou, she calls out to Heaven and to her children and instructs them in the forms of black ritual, so that when the time arrives they will know how to *keo*. Then seven of the first earth mounds come and cover her body. She lays down her head to the south, stretches her legs to the north, and spreads her arms out to the east and west. Her subterranean movements spread out (*loer*) the narrow ball of earth in all four directions, pushing back the primordial waters a short distance. For seven days and seven nights Mother Earth lies beneath the ground. At the end of this time, her body remains intact and shows no trace of decay.

Usin ba broe	The urn is not rotten
Bian ba dome	The vessel is not decayed
Litan ba kdout	The skin is not broken
Ruin ba fo	The bone is not split
Kukun hi kase	The mouth still speaks
Laman hi kdere.	The tongue still articulates.

She arises once more. The myth goes on to tell of a strange funerary trek toward the north. Mother Earth drags herself along with her hands (*kdas*), supported by the seven earth mounds. Heaven follows her from on high. He sends his heart, Tat Kok (Old One Who Shows), to tunnel beneath the ground and point the way ("show the earth," *kok raia*). His breast disk, named Teut Rai (Weigh Earth), hovers above to smooth out and roll up (*lul*) the burial mounds. Heaven uses the disk as a scale, weighing (*teut*) the widened earth to determine whether they have arrived at the proper coordinates. The burial is repeated many times. But though the mass of earth grows wider with each attempt, the measurements "are not perfect/are not correct," and the corpse does not decay. The journey continues.

At last, the cortege arrives at the place now known as Raimaus. By this time, maggots have appeared in Mother Earth's flesh, but her body is still whole. She is buried in Raimaus, and the breast disk makes its calculations and finds them "perfect and correct." Mother Earth settles herself below the ground:

Teiki ulun man hoha	Lays down her head toward the interior
Fod oen man taisa	Stretches her legs to the sea
Mima toen man lelo dun	The left hand toward the west
Mima hanan man lelo sain.	The right hand toward the east.

At this there is a great sliding and tumbling of earth that bursts its confines and cascades outward to the four quarters. This last and most powerful thrust of the deity's head and limbs forces the earth into its present configuration of land hemmed in by sea. In the north, her feet firmly press back the waters, calming and controlling the "female sea." But the "male" southern sea, which is unrestrained, remains wild and treacherous.

Raimaus, the burial ground, is the perfect center of the widened land. It is called the "navel of the earth" (*rai fusan*). The identification has a double significance, as does the earth itself. Metaphorically, the shape of the earth reflects the seated figure of the Mother on Nama Rau; the entire land is described as her body, with Nama Rau as the head, and Raimaus, far below to the north, as the navel. Metonymically, the earth is shaped by Mother Earth's burial gestures and composes one vast, ordered tomb, with Raimaus situated directly over the navel of the corpse.

Great emphasis is placed on the concealment of the deity's body. Four of the earth mounds come and cover her, like a blanket, to keep her warm, and "tuck her in tightly." Their names are Fai Soma, Mod Tem, Moda Mau, and Lel Mau. The element *mod*, which appears twice in the list, means "to swallow" and is often applied to Mother Earth herself, as mistress of corpses. These four names appear only rarely in chants, but there are frequent ritual invocations of the earth in fours, as in the formulae "Four Secure Earths" and "My Four Mothers" (Rai Tama Fata; Au Ina Fata).

Tai Talo, the sacred banyan of Raimaus, is also planted over the grave to cover the body. The roots of the tree grow down into the navel of Mother Earth, who sleeps in the lower world. Like all things, Tai Talo nurses from the milk of the Mother. And now this milk is buried deep. The duality of the earth, as life-giver and life-taker, breast and tomb, reflects the condition of the Mother who is described as "half white and half black, half fresh and half decayed, half alive and half dead." Buried at the center of the earth, the corpse finally decomposes. Its putrescent flesh forms a layer of "black earth," which is invoked in ritual chants as "black chest, black upper earth." Beneath this black topsoil formed out of her own decay, the Mother remains whole and pure, and her white milk is undiminished by death and decomposition. In chants, this white, internal milk is addressed as the "white chest, white lower earth." From the "black earth," plants appear. These products of the Mother's death send down their roots into the white milk of the underground.

The fertile earth is now "wide and broad" (*mlua nor beka*), but it is not yet stable. Loose and formless, it slides constantly back and forth. Mother Earth calls out to Heaven from her grave. He returns to Nama Rau and gazes out upon the mountain called Us Luli. Located just below Nama Rau, Us Luli composes the "shoulder of the earth," which "lifts up" to Nama Rau as a person's shoulder lifts to touch the head.

Facing Us Luli, Heaven holds aloft his two arms in the gesture known as the "ban of the interior" (*badu hoha nin*). At this sign, the rocks, trees, grass, earth, plants, and animals all fall silent. Heaven leaves Nama Rau and proceeds to Us Luli, stopping halfway to erect an emblem of the ban. He plants a tree and suspends a solitary leaf from its branch. This structure is known as the *keora*; the sacred posts erected in every cult house are called by the same name and are described as "twigs" of the first *keora*. The place where Heaven erects the original *keora* is called Kru Keor/Sak Keor. *Kru* means "to sow" and *sak* means "to hang, to hang up, to erect." The name alludes to Heaven's act, which marks the boundary between the living and the dead.

Heaven arrives in Us Luli and appoints its four guardians.[13] They are to direct the rains and the winds, and to receive the souls of the dead on their journey to Nama Rau. Then Heaven removes his shoulder and collar bones and fashions them into the "tongs and hammer" (*karifi nor maknuta*). With these, he pounds the silent rocks into pieces.[14] Heaven blends the shattered rocks with earth to form a kind of paste, which he uses to bind fast the soft, formless land.[15]

Now the earth is declared "steady" (*tama*). At this time, the earth and the sky were close to each other, and many people say they were united by a vine.[16] The motif of a vine connecting earth and sky is expressed in physiological imagery. Thus many Mambai will identify the vine with the bound umbilicals of sky and earth. There are frequent ritual allusions to a navel cord, and in their chants Mambai priests repeat:

Do bail leola ni fusan	Cut the navel of the sky
Neur bail raia ni talin	Slice the cord of the earth
Leola oid sikati	For the sky to soar on high
Raia oid diau.	For the earth to sink down low.

Chanters will associate the act of separation with various places, often never identifying the site at all. But whoever goes to Raimaus will see, at the center of the village altar, an enormous hollow rock. A short distance outside of Raimaus lie three cylindrical stones that are identified as the upper, middle, and lower segments of the vine.

The motif of a cosmological vine also appears in prose tales as the focus of human mischief. In the context of earth origins, this prose version is explicitly denied and set aside. Yet the motif of a joined navel was a point where Mau Balen's and Mau Bere's accounts diverged from each other. Mau Balen said that when the First Being conceived in the upperworld, the placenta fell to earth and dragged the uncut cord after it. Alone with me, Mau Bere rejected the entire notion of an umbilical cord connecting the upper and lower worlds. In his final narration of the creation myth, he said that the only interconnected navels were those of the first earth mounds, the original mountains. These were tied securely one to another and never severed. Beneath the earth, the Mother holds fast to the end of the cord, to steady the land as a whole. When one hand wearies, she shifts to the other, and then the earth quakes.[17] Indeed, in chants the priests intone repeatedly: "Hold steady, steady, steady ooo ei!" Mau Bere insisted on his account with some vehemence:

If the navel were cut, this land would be water. It is the navels which pull one another. All those hills out there, it is the navels which pull one another. This navel, our Mother holds it steady. That is why they

41

trick, they say "the navel broke and arose here, the navel snapped and arose there." No! Our Mother holds the navel!

For Mau Bere, the great hollow rock of Raimaus is not the navel of sky and earth, but the navel-womb of the First Being, which came tumbling down to cover Mother Earth. He called it the "ancestor of all vessels."

It would be fruitless to seek to determine whether or not Mambai believe that the navel cord of the cosmos was once severed. The image exists and is ritually associated with the separation of sky and earth, a cosmological theme repeatedly invoked, but never explained, in ritual chants. The heavens are addressed as Three Wakeful Suns (Lelo Ble Teula) or My Three Fathers (Au Ama Teula). These titles are paired with those of the Four Mothers. Ritually, all these titles are often described as "polite" forms of address for Heaven and Earth, whose names may not be uttered. But in mythology the seven figures have their history. The Four Mothers, as we saw, are identified with the four earth mounds that cover the corpse. The Three Fathers, Eot Mali, Lua Mali, and Laif Mali,[18] names muttered only at critical points of ritual chants, are the remaining earth mounds that are carried aloft by the seven stars of the Pleiades to become the vault of the firmament.

Now that it is steady, the earth is ready to receive the ancestors of humankind, who remain clustered on Nama Rau. But the heavens are still dark and black, and the "walk" of the oldest Mambai houses begins in the Night of origins. The eldest children break pieces from the pillar of the Lone House and descend from the mountain to find a place to settle. These first ancestors arrive at length in Raimaus. There they sacrifice two water buffalo and two goats. Mother Earth teaches them to make drums out of the skins and tells them how to *keo*. When they do so, the Mother stretches her neck, and Raimaus itself splits in two. Half of it is carried due south to become Hohul. Beneath Hohul, the Mother's head rests in comfort. In folk etymology, the name Hohul is derived from both *ulun*, "head, first, eldest," and *hulu*, "hair."

Now that they have cleared the land, the ancestors desire to erect their houses. They begin to complain about the eternal darkness:

Leola sikati bail	The sky has even soared on high
Raia diau bail	The earth has even sunk down low
Hula ba tiar	Yet the moon does not beam
Nama ba ada.	The day does not shine.

Mother Earth hears. She removes her breast bone and it becomes the iron tinder stick (*aif taran*); she plucks a piece from her heart and it becomes the flint stone (*haut buita*); she rubs the grime from her forehead and it turns into tinder grass (*nau kutar*). She gives these items to her daughters, Soi Loko and Soi Lelo, and teaches them how to make a cooking fire. They light a great fire in Raimaus, a name which means simply "the earth smokes" (*rai masu*).

Now the ancestors begin to *keo* in earnest, in order to "wake" the columns of their house. In the excitement of the ceremony, the smoke from the new cooking fire wafts upward and stings Father Heaven's eye. The eye flies from the socket to become the globe of the sun, and it lights up the dark skies.[19] This ushers in the period known as the Day. In ritual language, the transition is marked with the proclamation:

Hula tiar sois	Already the moon beams
Nama ada sois.	Already the day shines.

The shining light of Day is the signal to those ancestors who still wait on Nama Rau to "divide and scatter" (*tol nor hai*). Each of them breaks a piece from the pillar of the Lone House and descends the mountain to wander, settle, erect his house, plant gardens, and procreate, until humanity grows as "wide and broad" as the land.

The many exploits of the original ancestors and their generations are related in a set of narrative traditions distinguished as *tata*, "ancestors," or *fada*, "houses." These narratives include lengthy genealogies by which Mambai descent groups trace their ancestry back to the Nama Rau figures and their progeny. Ancestral traditions include certain references to persons who spread out to the four quarters and there founded new lines. Mambai do not trace these distant lines beyond their founders. Installed upon the far reaches of the earth, the ramified lines are known only as the "children" of the quarters, and they are named for the lands on which they "sit." Thus they are called

Rai ulu anan	Children of the east (earth head)
Rai oe anan	Children of the west (earth foot)
Tais hina anan	Children of the north (female sea)
Tais mane anan	Children of the south (male sea)

The languages of these outsiders change over time. Unfortunately, I did not ask for an explanation of language drift, and neither Mau Balen nor Mau Bere offered one. What seemed to interest them most were certain events that draw the children of the quarters back to their forgotten homeland.

The children of the quarters have no fire. They eat their meat raw and their tongues are hairy. One day, the wind carries the smoke of a Raimaus cooking fire out to the quarters. The inhabitants set out to discover its source. Approaching Raimaus, they smell for the first time the scent of cooked meat. The masters of Raimaus are planning to *keo* for Mother Earth's mortuary feast, and the children of the quarters agree to help "pay for her fatigue." Garbed in ceremonial attire, they reconverge at Raimaus, bringing sacrificial water buffalo for a feast. In ritual language the visitors are identified with the footpieces made of goat hair and the headdresses made of cock plumes which male dancers wear on ritual occasions.

Biub-hulu anan	Children of the goat's hair
Maun-lai anan	Children of the cock's tail feathers
Ma it oid fu heua	Come so that we may blow the flute
It oid tau snaka	So that we may play the pipe
Heua oid lika	So that the flute may ring out
Snaka oid masi	So that the pipe may sound
Oid se kika	[For us] to open our ears
Oid ha mata	To turn down our eyes
Oid loet ina salun	To kill the female buffalo
Oid tar ama kakun.	To slay the male buffalo.[20]

In order to receive the visitors and their sacrifices, what Mambai call the "first table" is constructed. It consists of banana leaves, spread out in a great arc upon the ground. Baskets and bowls are fashioned to serve the feast. The guests seat themselves along the edge of the leaves and eat from the filled receptacles that are set out:

Oid so ni usin	To lap from the urn
Oid rak ni bian	To take from the vessel
Oid sium seita-boun	To receive the torch pole
Oid teh aif-nuban.	To accept the ember.

At the end of the feast, the children of the quarters carry their torches and embers back to their homes, promising to return to Raimaus for future rituals. But they forget their pledge, for they see little to fear or respect in the silent rock and tree of Raimaus. The rituals languish until the masters of Hohul acquire control over the winds, rains, and ravening diseases. With these new tokens, they elicit "fear and respect." At the sound of drum and gong, the children of the quarters return once more to *keo* their Mother and their Father.

6. Ritual and Mambai Collective Identity

Certain elements of this myth are so esoteric that, throughout, I shall have little to say about them. The references to the First Being are especially perplexing. From a substantial corpus of ritual chants, I have extracted only a sprinkling of allusions to any such figure, and even these are highly ambiguous. I do not conclude that an idea of the One is extraneous to Mambai thought; to the contrary, I suspect it has an absolute character and represents wholeness reduced to a single name. I am, however, largely unable to elucidate the idea. Cosmology and ritual share a common orientation. The First Being may hover in the corridors of creation, but it is Mother Earth and Father Heaven who have the most important implications for Mambai social and ritual life. And indeed, interpreting the meaning of the cosmic pair, composed of the woman and her roaming consort, demands enough (if not too much) rummaging through dense thickets of symbols. It is already a pursuit which leads into every crevice of Mambai existence.

At the moment, my purpose is a fairly narrow one. I am concerned with how Mambai draw on cosmogonic themes to create a distinctive collective identity based on ideas of ritual responsibilities and obligations. According to a conception that Mambai hold of themselves, what distinguishes them from all other peoples on the island is their unique role as ritual guardians of Heaven and Earth. And what binds other people to the Mambai, again in Mambai self-conceptions, is the fertility which the Mambai secure through ritual action. Thus all the peoples of Timor, the "children of the four quarters," are ideally subordinated to the Mambai within a ritual cooperation for life.

Within Mambai society, the ritual role of life-giver is assigned to particular social groups. But in opposition to the outside world, the figure of an ancient, immobile custodian of the cosmos represents the Mambai people as a whole. Adherence to this self-image does not presuppose mastery of a cosmogonic narrative. Individuals who make no claim to possess the "trunk of discourse," but who respond to the calls of ritual drums and gongs, assimilate a sense of the cosmic purpose of their rites. And they speak of themselves as the eldest people of the land, even while acknowledging that they, as individuals, are "like little children" who obey instructions received from the elders, for "it is the old ones who know."

The narrative that I have set out includes other significant themes. Expressed in the myth is an idea of original uniformity and lost plenitude that pervades Mambai social thought. The first peopling of the land follows a pattern based on symbolism of space and motion and realized in oppositions between the inside and the outside, the house and the open air, the center and the periphery, the static and the mobile, the enclosed and the unconfined. From an initial image of a group intact and undivided, its members clustered inside of the Lone House, the myth goes on to relate a process of migration and dispersion that scatters the original population to the four quarters of the land. Within this spatial model, the eldest representatives of humanity are those who remain behind to tend the origin place. They are represented as the motionless guardians of the center of oriented space, whose task is to reunite Heaven and Earth:

Lelo dun au ba la	I go not to the west
Lelo sain au ba la	I go not to the east
Tais hinan au ba la	I go not to the north
Tais manen au ba la	I go not to the south
Au deiki it inan	I look after Our Mother
Au bale it aman.	I watch over Our Father.

The ritual process ideally reverses the outward movement that disperses humanity, and the return to life-giving origin places closes humanity in upon itself. But between these two pulls, the centrifugal and the centripetal, there is a pronounced tension. Tension is expressed in the myth through the theme of a lag between the assumption of ritual status by the eldest people and the recognition of that status by the children of the four quarters. Reestablishing contact between life-givers and life-receivers appears as a central problem in the myth, and it is resolved twice over, first through the mediation of terrestrial cooking fire, and then again through the awesome power of celestial tempest.

The ideal relationship between the Mambai and all other peoples is based on exchange. Life and well-being circulate against material gifts and services. One metaphor for the relationship of ritual superiors to their dependents is the relation of parent to child. In this metaphor, which is based in the anthropomorphic model of the earth, the care of the earth is likened to the care of a body, in particular, to the

46

breasts and lap of the body, and the purpose of ritual is to produce milk. The ritual guardians nurture their "children," welcoming them with promises of milk:

Ma susu ni inkai ni susun	Come and nurse at my Mother's breast
Lele ni au aman ni fan.	Snuggle in my Father's lap.

Precisely how milk is produced in ritual is another matter, one which, Mambai say, should not concern participants from the outside. It is neither necessary nor desirable for the returning migrants to understand the cosmological conditions which keep the ritual guardians fixed in their place. Father Heaven has vanished into the upperworld, Mother Earth lies beneath the ground, and there is no need to say more as to their whereabouts:

Lelo dun ba eot	The west does not see
Lelo sain ba tad	The east does not know
Ba fe ni etan	Does not glimpse their body
Ba tad ni kalan.	Does not know their name.

What the visitors see are only the outward signs of ritual authority. Or, as Mambai often say, if they come and pay homage, it is because "they fear rock and tree."

Today the people of the four quarters bring no more water buffalo. In Hohul and Raimaus, and in certain other Mambai ritual centers, people recite the names of beasts sacrificed in ancient ceremonies and proudly boast of the great breadth of their horns. On ceremonial occasions, the people of the quarters are ritually summoned and addressed. Bowls are set out for them, and in certain climactic feasts Mambai participants are seated at a replica of the mythic table of banana leaves. But nowadays it is said to be rare for strangers from other parts of the island to return and acknowledge their homeland.

Contemporary dereliction in ritual duties is often attributed to lack of "fear and respect" for rock and tree. There is, Mambai say, nothing to be done. Their status rests on the display of sacred signs, a "silent rock and a motionless tree," and they themselves have no power to compel obedience. "Perhaps fire will burn their houses," Mambai remark, "but we cannot force them to come." Nor do Mambai think to reaffirm their status by revealing its cosmological basis. Mambai seem to prefer that other people remain ignorant, even if this means that those people will neglect their ritual obligations. For if to possess knowledge that others lack is to occupy a status that may be ignored, to disseminate hoarded knowledge freely is also to risk the unique status that it confers.

A small incident may help convey these attitudes toward the possession and communication of sacred knowledge. It happened when I was visiting another anthropologist, Shepard Forman, who was working to the east of the Mambai, among the Makassae. Mau Balen had accompanied me, on his own request. Early one morning I met him returning from a stroll, and wearing a look of suppressed excitement that I had grown to recognize. He greeted me and told me that he had been conversing in Tetum with an old Makassae man. He had asked the man to show him where the head of the earth lay. The old man pointed eastward to the Mate Bian mountain range. Mau Balen nodded and inquired as to the foot of the earth. The other pointed towards the west. Mau Balen then asked the old man if he knew where the navel of the earth lay. "That old fellow was at a loss!" Mau Balen exclaimed to me with a smile. "He didn't know at all about the navel." Then, in a more subdued tone, he told me that this was as it should be, for outsiders were not meant to understand the true shape of the earth.

7. Cultural Stereotypes

Mambai collective identity is defined in terms of ritual privileges and responsibilities. This self-assumed position is one that confines the Mambai to the background of islandwide affairs. They claim for themselves neither skill nor wealth, and they attribute these lacks to their prescriptive ritual tasks. Often Mambai will speak of themselves as "stupid" and "ignorant" folk, and they will wryly remark that the only thing they know how to make is a ritual.

Ritual performance is for Mambai the dominant symbol of their culture. The paradigmatic, culturally defining activity is to promote fertility and prosperity, which are unequally distributed. For Mambai are sharply aware of the poverty of their land, and they contrast it unfavorably to other parts of the island. Yet they do not interpret the barrenness of their own land as a sign of a failure of the ritual process, but rather view their relative poverty as a price that must be paid. Agricultural productivity can be interpreted in terms of the anthropomorphic model of the earth. Mother Earth's milk escapes those most closely connected to it, those who watch over her breast and her lap. For the milk flows outward, along the sloping land, and away to the four quarters of the island. Mau Bere once said to me: "So we Mambai sit poorly, and the milk runs, runs, runs out to the west, east, north, south, and so we are poor, and our crops do not thrive."

Utterances of this kind are not voiced in bitterness. The idea of sacrifice is deeply embedded in Mambai thought, and enmeshed in the idea of Mother Earth's life-giving death. Above all, Mambai take great pride in their unique ritual responsibilities to a suffering deity. It may seem a perverse pride, for it is derived from a task that in theory brings few material rewards to those who perform it, and that goes largely unrecognized by those who benefit from it. Yet when I think of Mau Balen's vivid pleasure when an old Makassae man's ignorance reassured him that his secrets were intact, I feel that a Mambai ethos was condensed in that brief exchange. Mambai are a people who look backward resolutely toward a past that they themselves may only vaguely understand, yet who seem, nevertheless, to find in that past a profound sense of purpose.

Mambai are acutely aware of the fact that they are looked down upon by the coastal peoples, and even by the local gentry, those of their own members who have "put on trousers." They feel that they are thought "stupid" and "backward," and indeed, they are widely regarded as ignorant, taciturn highland hillbillies—what Tetum speakers disparagingly refer to as *kaladi*, "hill people." Mambai call themselves *kaira* from the verb *kair*, "to scatter, to sow," probably a reference to the swidden pattern. "We *kaira* are stupid!" they will cheerfully and repeatedly affirm.[21]

Yet Mambai are also aware of an aura of mystery that surrounds them. On Timor many peoples impute to the Mambai esoteric knowledge and special ritual powers, and in this lingering awe, Mambai themselves take a somewhat hesitant pride. A local administrator has but idly to attend a Mambai ritual to breed a nervous certainty in the performers that he has come to ferret out their secrets. And when I first appeared upon the scene, countless Mambai asked me who had told me to seek them. They knew that I had been first to Laleia in the east, and they shook their heads and said it was little wonder I had not found what I wanted in those parts, and asked if the easterners had sent me into the interior to look for rock and tree; or was it perhaps my parents, across the water and the sea, who had directed my footsteps. And they told me come and *keo* with them and to search for words.

Ritual provides the lens through which Mambai view themselves as a people. It is a way of life, at once their responsibility and their privilege. Represented as a limiting, prescriptive function, one that confines its performers to a sedentary vigil over rock and tree, ritual is also the lever with which Mambai turn the tables on their "learned" (*matenek*) critics. For what the more sophisticated folk of the towns and the coast do not realize is that "stupidity" has its own meaning in the mountains, where social existence is oriented around the quest for life.

THREE

The Mythic Origins of Colonial Rule

Hauta luli	The rock is sacred
Aia luli	The tree is sacred
Baba luli	The marching drum is
Bandeira luli.	sacred
	The flag is sacred.

—A Mambai ritual chant

1. Insiders and Outsiders

As we saw in the previous chapter, Mambai locate themselves at the symbolic center of an islandwide ritual cooperation for life. Their place within this conceptual order is defined by the status that they claim for themselves as the original inhabitants of the land, the first to have descended from the cosmic mountain, and the people most closely connected to the divine creators of the world. Other peoples may wander away and forget their origins, but Mambai are those who wait behind and hold the cosmos together at its center.

The total story of world origins is regarded as privileged knowledge in Mambai society, and it is collectively attributed to the members of important ritual centers. What is held in common by Mambai is an image of themselves as the eldest folk on Timor, who are entrusted with unique ritual obligations that only certain persons are thought to understand fully. The figure of the one who comprehends and preserves the cosmos represents to Mambai their distinctive identity as a people.

The largest units that actually unite for the purpose of ritual exchange are local communities oriented around sacred centers. Hohul and Raimaus are two such centers. They stage rites that mobilize the community as a whole; and while the territory under their ritual authority is circumscribed, their claim to status is expressed in an idiom of universal domination. In each Mambai community, the life-giving ritual authorities are distinguished from other functionaries who maintain the public order. This institutional arrangement may be seen as an instance of a principle with a worldwide distribution, dual sovereignty or diarchy. To use Dumézil's concise formulation of the structure of diarchic ideologies, "sovereignty aligns itself on two planes, at once antithetical and complementary" (1970, 55).

Mambai political theory presents an intriguing twist. The power of local political leaders is held to emanate from other, more powerful sovereigns. These latter are the Portuguese colonial rulers, whose actual presence on Timor dates back to the mid seventeenth century, and who have had sustained contact with Mambai leaders at least since the founding of Dili in 1769.[1]

In Mambai models of political order, the institutionalized pattern of local communities is replicated at a global level as a functional division between the ritual, mystical, or spiritual authority of the indigenous Timorese and the political, jural, or temporal power of their Portuguese rulers. This division is mythologically represented as the product of an interaction between an elder and a younger brother. From the elder brother are descended all the peoples of Timor, with the Mambai as their eldest representatives. From the younger brother are descended the people whom Mambai classify as Malaia, a category that includes all non-Timorese, Europeans, Chinese, Africans, and so on. I use the term to designate the subclass of *Malai-butin*, "white Malaia" or Europeans.[2]

Mambai have not passively submitted to colonial domination. They have endeavored actively and creatively to make sense of their colonial situation by drawing upon preexisting symbolic categories. In the process of absorbing their colonial rulers into a cultural order, Mambai have produced a remarkably coherent and profoundly meaningful model of the world.[3]

The model is a variant of a widely distributed configuration which van Wouden noted in his comparative study of eastern Indonesian societies (1968). Van Wouden called attention to recurrent institutional divisions between ritual authority and political power. He also observed that these divisions were typically expressed as oppositions between insiders and outsiders, original inhabitants and foreign invaders, land and sea. Narrative traditions preserved in many eastern Indonesian societies trace the institutional division back to a founding event: the advent of a foreigner who displaces an original ruler.

On the island of Roti, for instance, the ancestor of the Manek or Lord is said to come from overseas and to engage in a contest with the Dae Langgak, the Head of the Earth. The outcome is that the Dae Langgak loses political power to the Manek, but he preserves ritual authority over fertility (Fox 1980, 109). On Timor, Belunese and Atoni traditions present variations on this pattern. The rulers of Belunese and Atoni realms are both said to come from different ethnic stock than their peoples. The founder of Wehali in central Belu is associated with a distant land overseas known as Sina Mutin Malacca (van Wouden 1968, 45–46). Both Belunese and Atoni traditions identify the Atoni ruler Sonba'i as the younger brother of the Lord of Wehali. To the Atoni, Sonba'i is an outsider. Myths tell of how he once defeated an original Lord of the Land, a chief named Kune, who retains ritual authority over the soil (Schulte Nordholt 1971, 262–274). Still another variation on the narrative pattern occurs in Bunaq traditions of the ancestors who come from overseas and subdue autochthonous "owners of the land" known as *melus*. Ritually, these *melus* are identified with the spirits of the deceased autochthones, and Bunaq regard them as the most powerful of all the "shades of the earth" (Friedberg 1980, 272–273).

The political structures associated with the narrative patterns also vary. On Roti, the symbolic opposition between outsiders and insiders corresponds to an institutional division of temporal power and spiritual authority, whereas the "outsider" rulers of Atoni and Belunese traditions become the chief ritual sacrificers of their realms. In these latter cases, the opposition to "original" inhabitants seems to express a distinction between two forms of religious cult. This situation has a parallel in certain Polynesian materials analyzed by Sahlins. What is common to all of these "stranger-kings," as Sahlins calls them, is not a specific position within an institutional order. Rather, they embody a conception of power as something originally alien to society. In all these political theories, Sahlins observes, "royalty is the foreigner" and "power is a barbarian" (1981a, 112).

It is precisely with regard to the extrinsic origins of power that Mambai political theory shows its originality. Strictly speaking, Mambai have no tradition of foreign invaders from the outside, nor do they have any real conception of a larger outside world which might encompass their own society. By Mambai theories of origin, the Malaia, who occupy the structural position of outsider-rulers, are not strangers at all, but are the returning younger sons of the land. The ultimate origins of the Malaia are autochthonous, their relationship to the Timorese is based on kinship, and their arrival on Timor signifies the return of the legitimate defenders of order.

These cultural features of the colonial relationship are often invoked in ritual oratory. The kinship tie figures prominently in ritual speech, and even a casual European observer of Mambai rituals is likely to hear that the white Malaia and the black Timorese are of common descent:[4]

Buti nor meta	White and black
Timor nor Fortukes	Timorese and Portuguese
Austali nor Alimau	Australians and Germans
Olandes nor Safones	Dutch and Japanese
Ro inan id	They have one mother
Ro aman id	They have one father
Mor buti nor meta	[Who] gave birth to white and black
Mor Malaia nor Timor.	Gave birth to the Malaia and the Timorese.

As the reader may suspect, there is a "walk" associated with the classification of peoples into white and black. Mambai distinguish it as the "walk of rule and ban" (*ukun nor badun ni lolain*), or as the "walk of the flag" (*bandeira ni lolain*). The flag is identified with the Portuguese flag, and its narrative "walk" provides a mythic charter for a total sociocosmic order. The story was entrusted to me with notably less reluctance than was shown by narrators of the walk of the earth. I received it, in part or in whole, from a number of people in different ritual centers.

Events relating to the return of the Malaia were the most willingly and frequently narrated. These unfold in the period known as the Day, and Mambai say that such matters are less "weighty" (*mdeda*) than those "of the Night." The origins of the Malaia and their flag date back to the Night of creation. Certain Mambai elected to reveal these origins to me at a time when there was considerable concern and anxiety over the prospect of decolonization—or, as one old man put it to me, over "this matter of our younger brothers going away." At that point, during the summer of 1974, many Mambai seemed to regard the idea of decolonization as a violation of proper order. Yet even over the few remaining months before my own departure, they had begun to accept the idea, and they were starting to look toward a political future that remained uncertain. The anxieties as well as the hopes that they voiced to me in this period shaped and were shaped by a mythic model of the colonial situation. I will present, in summarized form, one version of the myth.

2. The Walk of Rule and Ban

The walk of rule follows upon the primordial earth-walk and begins with the activity of Father Heaven. As sovereign god, Heaven's role is to articulate boundaries and divisions. He orders the cosmos by distributing signs of difference, and his first act is to divide his children into the opposed categories of silent and speaking mouths. The primordial enunciation of sovereignty removes the power of speech from Heaven's firstborn; it is called the "ban of the interior," or the "ban of rock and tree."

Meanwhile, Heaven's human sons assume distinctive physical characteristics. The youngest "draws white water" and "washes white/bathes clean," but the eldest "draws black water," which leaves him "neither white nor clean," in an unmarked state. Then Father Heaven, the great divider, distributes a patrimony between his two sons. To the eldest, Ki Sa, he gives the sacred rock and tree, tokens of the original ban and signs of ritual authority over a silent cosmos. Upon the youngest, Loer Sa, he bestows the book and pen, which Mambai regard as emblems of European identity. Heaven also deposits a variety of power signs inside the origin house. These compose what is called the "rule and ban" (*ukun nor badun*). Loer Sa steals all these as yet unspecified tokens and flees with them northward, across the "water and sea," to the land of Portugal. Henceforth, the stolen tokens are known as the "ban of the sea," and they are opposed on a south-north axis to the original ban of the interior.

Ki Sa is now left in the interior "with only rock and tree," the valid tokens of his authority over the cosmos. But when he displays them to the realm, women and men "neither tremble nor fear" (*ba rih/ba tmau*), meaning that they do not respond with the outward signs of respect for authority. Great emphasis is placed in the narrative on the image of a divinely appointed ruler whose orders elicit no response and who aimlessly "wanders and drifts" through a realm that does not recognize him. Soon the members of the realm begin to "stab and slay one another" (*sa ro/tar ro*). The textual expression for this situation is that "the rule is not heavy/the ban is not weighty." With his realm in chaos, Ki Sa resolves to set out in pursuit of a "heavy rule and a weighty ban."

He undertakes a long and arduous journey across the sea to Portugal. There he finds his younger brother shut up inside a house, fast asleep. Upon waking, Loer Sa receives obeisance from Ki Sa, and listens to a long and moving address. His elder brother describes his plight, and reminds the younger man of his obligations to the place he abandoned. He asks for some new token of status that will make his own realm "tremble and fear." Loer Sa responds by handing over a set of objects, promising that his descendants will return to Timor with the flag at a later date. In opposition to the flag, retained by the Malaia, the gift objects are equated with the flag pole (*bandeira ni rin*), and from this distinction Mambai fashion a suggestive metaphor for complementary governance: "Ours," they say, "is the base of rule, and the Malaia hold the tip of rule."

Ki Sa returns with his gifts to the interior of Timor. When he displays the new tokens, the realm responds with "fear and trembling" and hails him as the legitimate sovereign. Now his calls are answered, and the realm unites to pay homage to the sacred rock and tree.

Generations pass, but at last Malaia descended from Loer Sa return to Timor, with the flag flying from the mast of their ship. All the peoples of the land gather to meet them at the coast. Descendants of Ki Sa receive flags and other insignia of office from the Malaia, but they soon relinquish these tokens. Weary of command, they "surrender the rule" (*sra ukun*) to new indigenous executives who come from outside of the realm. By this act the original rulers renounce all worldly responsibilities toward the realm they founded, but they retain their ritual authority over the cosmos. The poetic expression for their renunciation of power is that they "sit down to look after the rock and to watch over the tree." The myth concludes with a description of the institution of a system of exchange by the Malaia and the ritual authorities. In this system harvest gifts amassed in the interior are delivered to the Malaia on the coast by the indigenous executive rulers. These gifts are reciprocated with prestations of raw rice, salt, and livestock. The transaction is represented as part of an exchange of services whereby ritual authorities promote the fertility of the earth, and the Malaia guard the boundaries of the fields and gardens.

Underlying the myth is an opposition between two orientations in space, which is manifested at the cosmic level in the theological pair. To Heaven, who orders the cosmos, belongs the world of the outside, and he has the open, unrestricted nature of a wanderer. To Mother Earth, who stabilizes and nourishes the cosmos, belongs the world of the inside, the dark, confined space of the house, and hers is the closed, restricted nature of one who waits at an origin place. From this follows a division of persons into two categories, those who wander away to the outside and those who are left behind by the wanderers. The myth links the opposition between outside wanderers and inside waiters to the division of the cosmos into those who speak and those who are silent. The younger brother appropriates power over "speaking" humanity and carries it away to the outside, leaving behind him an elder brother who is the custodian of a silent cosmos.

Loer Sa's theft of "rule and ban" projects the spatial polarity onto a south-north geographical axis and generates a new opposition between the "ban of the interior" and the "ban of the sea." These two terms stand in a relation of whole to part, for the ban of the sea is detached from its original source in the unitary cosmic law imposed by Father Heaven. Significantly, chaos erupts at this point in the narrative, associating the collapse of order with the theme of shattered unity and lost plenitude. In the political theory implicit here, ritual authority is inalienable (the elder brother keeps his rock and tree), whereas power over society is represented as a detachable, divisible, and transferable part of the greater whole. Originally contained within a moral order instituted by Heaven and subsequently appropriated by a usurper, power is first experienced in the interior as something lost, something missing. In the absence of power tokens, the realm fails to decipher the silent message of rock and tree, and when women and men neglect their moral obligations to the cosmic whole, the internal order of society dissolves. Chaos in the human realm poses a direct threat to cosmic order, and in these extraordinary circumstances, the guardian of the whole must act to restore order in the social part.

Ki Sa's quest and his encounter with his housebound, somnolent younger brother reverse the ordinary spatial orientations of the protagonists. The eldest becomes a wanderer, who recovers from the youngest a part of what has been lost. The transaction overseas subdivides power into two new complementary opposites, distinguished as flag pole and flag, base and tip. The imagery evokes a paradigm of objects that stand fixed in place and reach upward toward the sky. Like such axes mundi as the cosmic mountain, the world tree, and the origin house, the union of pole and flag expresses a hierarchical distinction between one who plants, grips, and steadies the foundations of a structure and one who keeps it upright and erect. This hierarchy of founder and preserver is enacted in the ensuing narrative events.

Once restored to their original source in the interior, the power tokens acquired overseas inspire the realm with sacred fear; they serve as the voice of an older, silent authority. The ritual sovereign now subsumes the initial opposition between power and authority. But Ki Sa's power is represented as the mystical power to command the realm's obedience to cosmic law. One phase of the narrative ends here, with an image of a ritually centered community, and of a jural power that is relegated to the outermost realm of space.

The final advent of the Malaia rulers signifies the return of the legitimate preservers of an already perfect order. The symbolism of the return emphasizes ideas of closure and containment. Symbolically associated with the perimeter of the land, and also with the doorway of the house, the Malaia take on the role of guardians of the threshold, and they assume the characteristics of fixity and immobility attributed to their ritual counterparts. When the Malaia move from sea to land, from beyond ordered space to the periphery of that space, a third term is interposed between them and the original ritual sovereigns, namely, the indigenous "outsider" figures, who assume responsibility for maintaining order within the realm.

At the two extremes of ordered space are the Malaia, who face northward toward the sea, and the original ritual authorities, who face southward toward the cosmic ban. When these two parties pivot to confront each other, contact is established through mobile local executives who act as bearers of messages and gifts. In the myth this scheme of opposition and mediation is associated with a system of tribute by which agricultural produce was channeled to the Portuguese during the colonial period. Although the tribute system no longer operates (it was abolished by the Portuguese in 1903), many Mambai speak of it often and somewhat forlornly; for harvest tribute, unlike the cash tax that replaced it, is comprehended as part of a total system of exchange.

3. The Social Distribution of Knowledge

The narrative that I have laid out embodies a view of the past as seen from Hohul and Raimaus, where Ki Sa is claimed as a founding ancestor. In Hohul there are material traces of Ki Sa's mythic quest. Loer Hoha, the sacred banyan of Hohul, is ritually addressed as the tree "of rule and ban," and it is traced back to the slip from Loer Sa's tree that Ki Sa obtained overseas. In ritual language the name of Loer Hoha pairs with Tai Talo, the sacred banyan of Raimaus, the tree "of women and men," which we have already encountered in the creation myth. The opposition between the two sacred trees expresses a distinction between aspects of the ritual function, to which I return in chapter 6.

In other ritual centers that I visited, both the Malaia and their flag figured prominently in the local origin traditions. What was not recited to me in these other places were the details of the original disappearance of the Malaia ancestor. Instead, tellers emphasized the return of the Malaia, and the subsequent distribution of new tokens of office. On one occasion, when I had asked a group of elders about the origins of the Malaia, I was told, after some reflection, that these were matters for Hohul and Raimaus to relate. This incident is worth pursuing further.

It arose in the context of a discussion about house structure. I had inquired as to the meaning of the three great central pillars that support Mambai cult houses. These pillars are oriented along a south-north axis, and in Hohul and Raimaus, they are identified with three mythic ancestors. From south to north, the pillar-ancestors are Au Sa, Ki Sa, and Loer Sa.[5] Au Sa, the eldest of the three (*maen-ulun* or "headman"), is the blacksmith who receives from Father Heaven the sacred "hammer and tongs, bellows and forge" (*karafi nor maknuta, toh-matan nor rai-inun*).[6] Ki Sa, the "middle man" (*maen-fusun*), we already know. Mambai houses are so constructed that the two southernmost pillars support the main room of the house. A central hearth crosses this room from east to west, dividing it into a southern and northern section. The southern section is called the *umolun* (from *molu*, "silent"). This is where the sacred house post (*keora*) is located, and it is where ritual offerings are made by the elders of the house. The northern section is called the "doorway" (*damata*), and young people are ritually seated in this area. The door itself is always on the north, and the house as a whole is said to face toward the sea. But the two innermost pillars, together with the sacred house post, are said to face southward toward the interior and to regulate the boundary between the silent and speaking realms.

The northernmost house pillar is identified with Loer Sa, the Malaia. This pillar is shorter than the other two and it supports the lowered veranda. Mediating between the inside and the outside, between the house and the open air, the veranda is the place where visitors are received. Within the structured space of the house, Loer Sa is the guardian of the threshold, who "looks toward the sea" and defends the house against external dangers. The threshold symbolism is consistent with the overall function assigned to the Malaia rulers, and in Hohul and Raimaus people readily expound on the significance of the house pillars.

But what happened in the other village was as follows. The group of elders who had convened to talk with me promptly identified the two innermost columns with Au Sa (their own ancestor) and Ki Sa. And what of the third pillar, I asked. A long silence ensued. I persisted (encouraged by Mau Balen and Mau Bere, who were with me), and the elders deliberated for some time among themselves. At length they conceded that they did not know about the third pillar. But neither Mau Balen nor Mau Bere would let the matter rest. They proceeded to deliver a wry, partly tongue-in-cheek lecture that ended with instructions to the elders to go away and reflect further on this matter of the third pillar.

The group broke up disconsolately, it seemed to me. Mau Balen,

Mau Bere, and I spent the rest of the afternoon alone together. The two of them were excited and talkative, commenting frequently, and in patronizing tones, on the ignorance of these elders. We dined, still talking about the incident. After dinner we received a visit from the elders. One of them came forward as spokesman and made a short, simple speech. The third pillar, he said, was "that youngest fellow, Loer Sa the Malaia," but they themselves knew only his name. If I wished to know more about his origins, the man concluded, glancing at Mau Balen and Mau Bere, I should "ask in Hohul and Raimaus."[7]

As this incident suggests, the full myth of the origins of sovereignty is regarded by Mambai as privileged knowledge, and it appears to be associated with particular social groups. However, while knowing the content of origin traditions is a conventional mark of status, it is not the case that such traditions are of no concern to other Mambai. The basic ideas that I have elicited from a complex, highly structured narrative are conveyed in non-narrative discourses and inform ritual events.

We should note, first of all, that the flag and marching drum are important in ritual as well as in myth, and their opposition to sacred rocks and trees is repeatedly enacted in ritual performances. Priests regularly recite sections of the "walk of rule and ban" in their chants, and, as I have already noted, the kinship of Timorese and Malaia peoples is a ubiquitous theme in ritual oratory. So too is the association of Timorese and Malaia with the basic opposition between the interior and the sea. Ritually, Mambai priests address a human community divided into an-hoha nor an-taisa, "children of the interior and children of the sea." Offerings to these two classes of persons are laid out on European porcelain and indigenous dishes of wood. These are distinguished as "the four white plates/the four black plates," white for the Malaia of the sea, black for the Timorese of the interior. United in a complementary opposition, the children of Heaven and Earth are said to feast together, collectively celebrating the fertility that only Mambai can promote.

In opposition to the Malaia, it is again the figure of the ritual guardian who embodies the wholeness of Mambai life and symbolizes the distinctive Mambai way of being in the world. Mambai also recognize and comment on the fact that few Malaia appreciate the import of indigenous ritual activities. The "children of the sea" attend Mambai rites in name but not in person, little knowing that their own material well-being depends on the activities performed by their elder kin. But then Malaia have their own task to discharge. They maintain the order of society with their "heavy law and weighty ban," thereby leaving Mambai free to address themselves to older concerns. In the repetitive rounds of their ritual activities, Mambai play out the unique communal identity which is so vividly and powerfully expressed in the myth of sovereignty.

That myth, I want to reiterate, was told to me with some urgency, at a moment when Mambai foresaw a threat to the existing order of the world. At that moment, the ideal complementarity of sovereign functions came into sharp focus, as did the mutual dependence of the cosmos and human society. I was told by various deeply concerned speakers that if the Malaia should depart in haste, without first ordering the realm and appointing a successor, there was real danger of a return to the mythic state of chaos. "Women and men," ran the grim premonitions, would once again "stab and slay one another," and the discordant noise of their strife would "disturb and agitate" the deities. So it was said, and at least the first element of that premonition has been tragically fulfilled.

4. Order and Transgression

Complementarity and order were never the full story of Mambai relations to their colonial rulers, nor did Mambai ever think that they were. There was a manifest tension between the collective representations of proper order that I have discussed here and the lived experience of subordination to colonial rule. That tension is openly expressed in Mambai discourse, and the form of expression is revealing of Mambai attitudes toward order. At issue is a particular cultural style of interpretation that reaffirms order in the very act of identifying transgressions. Mambai bitterly criticize Portuguese policies and conduct, in the context of insisting on the legitimacy of Portuguese rule. The result is what might be called a critique of the rightful rulers.

When the Portuguese, whether individually or collectively, commit acts that Mambai regard as violations of proper conduct, the perpetrators are said to have forgotten their obligations. Mambai often find occasion to levy such charges, and in so doing they enact among themselves their moral superiority to their heedless younger kin. By implication, the Portuguese truants are like small children whose hearts are still "whole" or "full." To Mambai, the "wholeness" of organs of perception connotes a state of unawareness and detachment, a kind of stupor that, as we shall see later, may be positively as well as negatively evaluated. Unawareness and neglect of obligations to kin, the Portuguese offense, is uniformly condemned by Mambai. My point, however, is that in reading European misconduct as lapsed obligation, Mambai critics recreate their own superior status as moral, knowing beings, and they also recreate an entire world of moral relationships. But the point is more eloquently and forcefully conveyed in a piece of poetic oratory that was once recited to me by Mau Bere and Mau Balen. Our topic of conversation on this occasion was the reciprocity between silent and speaking mouths. In this context, the abolition of the tribute system by the Portuguese was remarked on and condemned. "It was you (i.e., you Malaia) who ruined things," Mau Balen remarked. Then the two proceeded to recite in unison a long speech, which takes the form of a reprimand delivered by the elder brother to his younger Malaia sibling. Says the elder brother:

On fe haur-lolo	Yours is the shirt
On fe kambaia	Yours is the blouse
On fe rufia	Yours is the rupia
On fe fataka	Yours is the pataca
Oid ma oid fu snukan	Brought here to blow breath
Oid ma oid ret aban	Brought here to spit saliva
Snukan oid benu	For breath to expand
Mren oid tibe.	For the rattle in the throat to subside.
Aun fe bu-haluk	Mine is the seed basket
Aun fe nam-kruan	Mine is the garden-sower
Nor huit-bueta	With the yam bag
Nor daur-kaula	With the orange sack
Nor se ai huan dimundi, diabu.	With all manner of fruits.
Au mu, au nei on hail.	I eat, I give yours back.
O kikan mo	Your ears are clear
O matan ada.	Your eyes are shining.
O ma nor hatin	You come with the sharp thing
O ma nor blerin	You come with the pointed thing
Oid ma mri kout ni tatoi	To come stand guard in the portal
Oid ma mri kout ni salmata	To come stand guard in the doorway
Oid tauk rai ulun	To keep watch over the east
Oid tauk rai oen	To keep watch over the west
La hail ma kauk it ru inan	Lest anything should disturb Our Mother
Ma ro it ru aman.	Lest anything should agitate Our Father.
It ru maen ka	We two are elder brother
It ru maen ali.	We two are younger brother.
O fe nor hail hatin	It is you who is with the sharp thing

O fe nor hail blerin	It is you who is with the pointed thing
Nor hail tukan	And also with the banging thing
Nor hail leon.	Also with the flashing thing.
Ma fe au oid rih hail	You come so that I may tremble once more
Ma fe au oid tmau hail	You come so that I may fear once more
O ba kauk hail se au	You do not disturb me alone
O ba ro hail se au.	You do not agitate me alone.
O kauk hail, au kauk nor it inan	If you make a disturbance, I am disturbed with Our Mother
O ro hail, au ro nor it aman	If you create agitation, I am agitated with Our Father
Au met tirtei, o inan tirtei	If I too am lonely, your Mother is lonely
Au met malaka, o aman malaka	If I too am startled, your Father is startled
Kala bael hauta	Called rock
Kala bael aia	Called tree
Mudu man hauta	Motionless like the rock
Toru man aia.	Silent like the tree.
Beili des, fe des o	When there is hunger, it overcomes you
Mro al, fe al o.	When there is thirst, it possesses you.
Kleoka kal fe ol her o hlan	Maybe it is the rifle that you carry on your shoulder
Bolsa kal fe kles her o idan.	Maybe it is the gunbelt that you gird around your waist.
Tan la o fe beik	Because it is you who is stupid
O fe bodu.	It is you who is ignorant.
It ru mes lea	We two might simply converse
It ru had lea.	We two might simply talk together.
O ma nor hatin	But you come with the sharp thing
O ma nor blerin	You come with the pointed thing
Oid ma liu au man biub-rusa	To come chase me like a deer
Oid ma tau au man haih-huia	To come pursue me like a wild pig
Man au teora ba nei	As if I had no words
Man au kasen ba nei.	As if I had no speech.
It ru ba mes, ba mes la idua	If we two do not converse, we do not converse because of this
It ru ba had, ba had la idua	If we two do not speak together, we do not speak together because of this

63

It ru ba miku, ba miku la idua

If we two are not pledged, we are
not pledged because of this

It ru ba farenti, ba farenti la idua.

If we two are not kin, we are not
kin because of this.

The underlying theme in this text is reciprocity and its negation. The necessary interdependence of functions is stated at the outset and then asserted by negation, through accounts of transgressive acts. Transgressions are shown to recoil against the transgressor, since any disturbance within society threatens the life-giving cosmic relation of Father Heaven and Mother Earth. These ties of mutual functional dependency are at the heart of the elder brother's message to the younger. What I want to stress, however, is the position of that message within the text, where it is embedded in a prior enunciation of ideal complementary order. The language of the text affirms and preserves the order that the younger brother is accused of dissolving in practice. Transgression takes its meaning from this ideal order. By treating kin as if they were not kin, speaking human beings as if they were speechless animals, subjects as if they were objects, the younger brother reveals himself as one who has failed to comprehend the true relation that binds him, irrevocably, to the other. The bitter irony of the elder brother's reprimand lies in his claim that he has been treated as if he were mute, speechless, when his role within the text is that of master of words; the eldest alone speaks the whole, articulates the total order of things, and he recreates and preserves that order through his speech.

The tension in the poem is between the affirmation of an order that encompasses colonial rule and the moral condemnation of the rulers who disregard that order. From this tension the poem derives a performative force that would be lacking if the textual interlocutor merely berated the addressee, if his speech consisted in nothing more than a diatribe, a reciprocal denial of the humanity of the other. By insisting on the possibility of intersubjective communication, preserving through language an order which the other violates out of ignorance, the interlocutor advances his own claim to status. And so it was also, I should add, with the speakers in this event, who enacted that possibility and lived out their moral superiority by actually "speaking the whole" to a Malaia.

In public ritual contexts Mambai speak of the ideal order as if it were uniformly realized in practice. In private, they draw upon the same ideal of order to locate a threat from within—a threat that I would describe, in my own metaphor, as a loosening of responsibilities, a troubling slackness in social conduct that has its source in human ignorance. At the same time, there is an important sense in which the status of the one who knows is constituted by the ignorance of others. One might almost say that Mambai have created for themselves a collective identity that precludes general recognition.

Outsiders, from overseas or from the distant quarters of the land, may forget their obligations to Mambai, but within Mambai society the situation is different. Mambai talked *about* their relationship to other peoples, but they talk *to* one another. Among themselves, talk of ritual obligations and of a cooperation for life is embedded in an institutional order. Ritual exchange relations within Mambai society are lived as well as thought, and in the next three chapters I describe the various social groups that live them.

FOUR

The House as a Source of Life

1. The Concept of *Fada*

The term *fada*, "house," refers to dwellings and to social groups, or more precisely, the image of dwelling together in one place symbolizes ties that unite persons.[1] An additional and socially critical feature of this representation is that the ideal state of coresidential unity is associated with the past. House groups are composed of people who recognize a common source or origin place, to which they return only on specified ritual occasions. The idea of common origins provides the basis for ritual cooperation in the present.

To Mambai, *fada* connotes a concept of relatedness as a condition grounded in past events, a product of processes that have transformed earlier states. Oppositions between the closed and the open and between the full and the empty define the content of those processes. Mambai conceive of their collective history as a steady movement away from plenitude, a passage from unity to diversity. Corresponding to the time of original unity is the image of the closed house, full and intact, shut off from the outside world of motion and change. But the place of origins is also the site of dispersal, and the house corresponds in its open state to the present time of separation and division. Threshold symbolism connects the opposed states of the house. The doorway that alternately closes and opens has a double significance, marking both the spatial boundary between inside and outside and the temporal boundary between past and present. When the image of the closed house is projected onto social space, it evokes the earlier state of unity from which present divisions emerged.

To speak of the house is to assert or create ideas of unity before division and unity in division, of a primordial, undifferentiated whole and a whole reconstituted from its parts. Ritual action is the mechanism of reconstitution. Scattered house members reconvene at their origin places for ritual purposes, and dramatically re-present their

66

ideal unity and wholeness. But the dispersal of house members in everyday life is as fundamental to the system as is the ritually enacted idea of their original concentration, for it is the interplay of present separation and prior connection that creates the condition for hierarchy.

These remarks are explicated in what follows. I view the house system from what I take to be a Mambai perspective, as an aspect of their ritual life. The basic argument set forth in this chapter and the following one is further developed through the analyses of particular ritual complexes presented in part 2. Simply stated, it is that Mambai society is founded on an opposition between two modes of relatedness, which house groups reproduce in the totality of their ritual life. This opposition is personified in the deities, whose relationship to society is also reproduced through ritual action. As the ultimate recipients of all ritual services, Heaven and Earth are the primary metaphor of totality.

2. The Cosmology of the House

A crucial context for understanding the house system is the mythology of common origins, by which all living beings are descended from the deities and so participate to a degree in the nature of divinity.[2] Between human beings and the divine creators there is a special contiguity. Of all the "children of Heaven and Earth," only women and men are engendered inside the house, and their collective destiny is to repeat in multiple ways the processes of cosmic creation.

Just as all life forms derive from the deities, so do all houses have their ultimate source in the Lone House on the mountain, where Mother Earth brought forth the first ancestors of humankind. With the subsequent dispersal of the ancestors from the mountain, a process of separation and differentiation is set in motion. Continued over time in successive generations, it results in the multitude of differentiated house groups that make up the present social order. Mambai contrast the unity of the source to the multiplicity of its products. This contrast operates at multiple levels of the house system and provides the basis of social hierarchy. Its paradigmatic realization is in the relationship of the Lone House to all other houses, which correlates with the hierarchical relationship of the gods to humankind.

All of the houses founded by human ancestors are regarded as concrete tokens of an original type represented by the Lone House. Their resemblance to the Lone House is asserted in various ways. For instance, on the vertical axis any act of house-founding replicates the original conjunction of above and below. A wandering male ancestor comes to rest at the site where "heaven descends/earth arises." There he erects his house, which makes possible the reproduction of his line through offspring, as the Lone House made possible the reproduction of divine attributes in human form. But the relationship of ancestral houses to their modeling type is metonymic as well as metaphoric, for it implies a temporal order of succession that is also an order of status.

Antecedence is precedence in the house system, and the Lone House, the ultimate source of houses, is superior to its later replicas. There is a double aspect to this temporally patterned hierarchy of type and tokens. As the abandoned source, the Lone House is the part of a whole that remains after subtractions, but it is also the encompassing source, the part that stands for the original whole and represents the overarching unity of humankind. The type, in other words, both opposes and includes its tokens.[3] The distinctive logic of this scheme has implications for the definition of the human condition. Viewed from the perspective of outcomes, humanity is divided into hierarchically ranked houses, but viewed from the perspective of origins, the human condition is defined by unity. The idea of the encompassing source projects past unity onto present division, superimposing images of two distinct temporal states, one of which is privileged. Outcomes evoke origins, both metaphorically, by replicating on a lesser scale the earlier state of things, and metonymically, by their culturally defined status as parts detached from a greater whole. In their ritual life, Mambai recreate the whole in the part. At the highest level, they assert the encompassed unity of all human beings as the dependents of the gods, and at lower levels, they enact the hierarchical encompassment of one house by another.

Hierarchical relationships among houses are typically expressed in a botanic idiom that suffuses narrative accounts of house formation. When the first ancestors leave the mountain, each one "cuts a slip" from the central pillar of the Lone House, to "plant" later on at the site where he resettles. By this act he constitutes his new house as an offshoot of the original one. Mambai express this situation as an opposition between a "tip house" and a "trunk house," and "tip houses," as the botanic metaphor suggests, are prone to multiply. In each successive generation, the youngest offspring of house-founders take new cuttings from the paternal house pillars, to transplant yet again as the foundations of still other houses. These will stand as "tips" to their immediate "trunks" and to the ultimate "trunk house" on the mountain.

Botanic metaphors liken the process of house formation to the branching of a tree as it grows outward from a central trunk. The recurrent opposition between trunk and tip projects onto the house system a concentric model of space that also orders cosmogonic processes. Cosmogony tells of a world composed from its center, and the events of human history are the same in principle as those of world creation. Wandering men reproduce the cosmogonic sequence of condensation and dispersal, not only in their movements but in the permanent structure of their settlements. In a sense, it could not be otherwise. Inasmuch as the very space for migrations is defined by the cosmic center of centers, the effect of the migrations is to push back the perimeters of inhabited space, to extend the boundary of the settled "inside" at the expense of the wild "outside." From this perspective, to go out from an origin house is not to leave it, but rather to expand it.

The concept of the expansion of a unitary form is implicit in the imagery of botanic growth and stressed in the narrative caveat that departing men bear tokens of their center sources with them wherever they go. Appropriately, such tokens are detached from the central pillar of the origin house, its "leg" in the anthropomorphic model for house design, and denoted by the same term that is used of human limbs. The notion of a legged house connotes both fixity and mobility, repose and action. A house rests securely upon its trunk-leg, which roots the house firmly in the earth. But legs are also extended in motion for travel, and Mambai refer to narratives of house formation as the "walks of houses" (*fada ni lolain*). Alternately, to recount the history of a house group is "to relate [the story of] the house pillar." These narratives consist largely of strings of paired place names, recited in the order that they were visited by the house-founder in question, and composing his route from a starting place to a final destination.

Literally, it is of course the man who walks, and not the house pillar. Houses are fixed by nature, whereas men are mobile, destined to wander away, toward the periphery of ordered space. But if houses are mobilized by men, the latter in turn are fixed by houses, anchored in what comes before and lies behind, or inward, toward the center. Each such wanderer becomes a stable and stabilizing "trunk" to his own descendants, and in this way the house system "grows," extending farther and farther away in time and space from its original, encompassing source on the mountain.

As concrete tokens of the cosmic source, all houses are peripheral parts of an older and greater totality. This relationship is absolute and expresses the subordination of humankind to the paradigmatic house-founders, who are Father Heaven and Mother Earth. But the status of a house is also relative to particular social contexts of inter-action. Mambai fashion overlapping metaphors of hierarchy out of oppositions between trunk and tip, center and periphery, inside and outside, elder and younger, fixed and mobile, and they use these metaphors in asserting claims to relative status. The idea of the en-compassing source has multiple social realizations.

3. Manifestations of the House

While the term *fada* is occasionally used in an extended sense to re-fer to groups linked by marital ties, in what I take to be its primary usages it designates groups defined by agnatic or male-ordered de-scent.[4] From mythical times onward, men are represented as the founders and dividers of houses, and the unbroken continuity of a house over time is symbolized by lines of men that lead back to an ancestral house-founder. But as any such founder may well have origi-nated in another house, which ritually encompasses his own, the so-cial units designated as "one house" are of varying structural levels.[5]

The unity of a minimal house group has a number of signifiers. These include a physical structure, where rites are performed; a name that denotes both the physical house and the affiliated group, and that often alludes to an incident in the house's history; a succes-sion of male names, beginning with the house's founder, that is recited on formal occasions; a collection of heirlooms, including weapons and ornaments, that are represented as acquisitions of the house-founder and are stored in the recesses of the house; a set of cult practices known as *lisa*, comprising dietary restrictions and other observances inherited from the house ancestors.

Lisa, which I translate as "cult," may be used as an adjective modifying *fada* to designate the house as *fad-lisa*, "cult house." In many contexts Mambai use the terms *lisa* and *fada* interchangeably. Such queries as "What is your cult?" and "What is your house?" are likely to elicit the same response, which is the name of the cult house to which the respondent belongs. The house denoted in this way is not an everyday dwelling. It is the place of origins, where sacred heir-looms are kept, narrative history is recited, and collective rites are performed, the tangible link between a group and its past. The term *ria* refers to the places where cult houses are situated. As a gloss, I use "village of origins."[6] *Fada* and *ria* form a dyadic set in ritual lan-guage and are frequently combined in ordinary speech to express collective identities in an idiom of place. And indeed Mambai think of themselves as tied to particular localities, as being from determinate places that symbolize their status in relation to other groups.

But origin places are only intermittently inhabited. During the greater part of any year, a house group is dissolved into households, which are the residential and productive units. These range from extended families, composed of a man, his wife, their sons, their unmarried daughters, and their son's wives, to conjugal families that split off at the death of the paternal head. Typically, two or three households, related by agnatic kinship or by marriage, cluster together into small hamlets, which are grouped into villages for administrative purposes. Villages of this sort are designated by the Portuguese term *povoação*, or *pobsan* in Mambai. They are distinguished sharply from the *ria*, the village of origins.

Origin villages vary in size and scale, according to the status of the groups affiliated with them. Some are imposing stone-walled structures, perched high on mountain slopes and containing several interrelated cult houses. Others are little more than fenced enclosures built around small stone altars and rather ramshackle cult houses. All origin villages are practically deserted during ordinary time. They are visited only by an appointed "master" (*ubun*), who is regarded as the eldest member of the group. He tends the cult house and maintains a private residence near the origin village. But when a birth or a death occurs within the group, when it is time to perform the yearly agricultural rites, or when the "master" judges it time to rebuild the cult house, then the scattered members of the group return to their origin place.

The members of a minimal house group claim agnatic descent from a common ancestor, although precise genealogical connections are not preserved. Houses are ideally perpetuated through the affiliation of children with the father's group, a process which involves the transmission of names along agnatic lines and the ritual presentation of the child to the paternal cult house. Above all, however, the affiliation of children depends upon a series of prestations made by a husband to his wife's kin. In the marked cases where the requisite payments are not made, a man's children will be incorporated into their mother's house, and the man will have no agnatic descendants. Hence, as in other eastern Indonesian societies, a man does not perpetuate his house merely by begetting offspring. For the principle of descent to operate, it is necessary for a man to fulfill obligations to his wife's kin.[7]

An individual's same-sex agnates are classified as *kaka nor ali*, which are the relative age categories used reciprocally by same-sex siblings. An accurate if unwieldy gloss is "elder and younger people of my own house and gender." If the speaker is a man, he may prefix the term *maena*, "man, male," and refer to his agnatic kin as *maen-ka nor maen-ali*, "elder and younger men of my house." The equivalent for women, *hin-ka nor hin-ali*, is never used of house members as a collectivity, which suggests that a house is paradigmatically represented by its male members. More precisely, ties among house members as well as ties among houses that claim descent from a common ancestor are held to unite persons or groups of the same kind and are symbolized by relations among men. The notion of sameness is essential. The relative age categories *kaka/ali* entail hierarchy, but they also imply similarity. They are used in ranking persons or groups belonging to the same class as the speaker, same-sex siblings, agnatic kin, and agnatically related houses.[8]

Similarity of house members is also implied by shared cult observances, which are constitutive of differentially defined collective identities. *Lisa* denotes those practices that "we" do or abstain from doing, in distinction to the practices of "others." In-married women, a very special category of "others," are assimilated to the self in the idiom of cult. At marriage a woman is formally presented to her husband's cult house and "enters the cult of the man," taking on the observances specific to his group. Her identification with the husband's collectivity grows stronger over time, as she participates in its rituals, which will eventually include her own funeral. Nevertheless, her ties to her house of origin are never broken; she takes on a new cult and brings life to her house by marriage, but this life that she confers entails obligations to the house from whence she came.

Before turning to maritally established ties among houses, it is necessary to examine more closely the ties that are traced through men. These are activated in specific ritual contexts. In theory, no house is ritually self-sufficient. A minimal house group coordinates life-cycle rites for its members, but houses ranked as "elder and younger" cooperate in the local agricultural cult, performing roles that reflect and express their relative statuses.

4. Exchange Relations among Houses

Status in the house system is based on the process of formation of new houses out of old ones and is determined by the order of appearance of houses as differentiated units. Houses that claim agnatic relations to one another are ranked by their relative proximity to the common ancestor, from whose house they are all said to derive. That house stands to all its derivatives as elder (*kaka*) to younger (*ali*), or alternately, as "old mother/old father" to "child." In the ideology of the house system, younger houses, or more strictly, subhouses, should assist the eldest in its ritual undertakings. Such ritually interdependent houses are represented as "one house together," with the eldest defined as the encompassing part that stands for the whole.

In house narratives the relations between a whole and its parts are projected onto the sons of ancestral house-founders, and the act that creates division is the partition of a patrimonial inheritance. One variant of a recognizable pattern has the brothers agree upon the allotment of the patrimony. The eldest elects to remain behind at the origin place and tend *fada nor ria*. Mambai say that he "sleeps with the Mother/wakes with the Father." They stress his immobility, fixity, and constancy, attributes embodied in his self-defining activity, "to look after the rock/to watch over the tree." His younger brothers are characterized by mobility. They "set off toward the outside," taking with them not only their cuttings from the house pillar, but also a share of the sacred patrimonial wealth objects. These objects, which include weapons and metal ornaments, are referred to as *obrikisan* (from Portuguese *obrigação*), a token that commemorates an origin place. Divided and subdivided in successive generations, the wealth that an ancestral house-founder once amassed is dispersed by his descendants.

A variant on this pattern stresses an element of rivalry. There is reference to a quarrel between two brothers, usually having to do with some violation of ritual procedure.[9] In such cases, the younger brother is said to lay hold of the *saun-hot-hot, ber-ber/fil-fil, saf-saf*. Literally translated, this means "all-all, first-first things/however many, whatever kind," or, if the colloquialism is accepted, "the whole patrimonial kit and caboodle." For the younger brother is said to abscond with the entirety of the house's moveable wealth, leaving his elder brother "with only rock and tree."

In all the narratives that I recorded, a dualistic scheme distributes the statuses of elder and younger into opposed symbolic categories. The eldest is associated with the stillness of the interior, symbolized by the origin house where he remains, and by the sacred rock and tree over which he watches. Younger brothers belong to the world of the exterior. Active, mobile, restless, they traverse wild, open territories to settle at the fringes of inhabited space. In the botanic metaphor of house formation, the relationship of elder to younger houses is one of supporting trunk to the branching tip it supports, imagery that emphasizes both the asymmetry and the complementarity of the relationship. These categories are used in ritual contexts to represent the mutual but unequal dependency of participant houses. Rites unfold in concentrically structured space, at the *ria* of elder trunk houses that stand as center sources to their derivatives. Younger tip houses enact their subordination in returning with their sacra to the origin place, symbolically a movement from outside back to inside, where their "old mothers and old fathers" await them.

Note that the superordinate status of elder houses is not based on claims to possess sacred wealth objects. Narrative representations dwell upon the dispersal of patrimonial wealth, a process which, in the extreme case, leaves an origin place depleted, "with only rock and tree." It is true that these latter symbols connote a life-giving ritual authority, but I want to stress that such authority is defined as a remainder of a greater whole, the part left over after subtractions. As the part that stands for the original whole, a senior house evokes the past in the present, symbolizing by its relative emptiness an ideal fullness that once was but is no longer. According to the ideology of exchange, such a house is reciprocated for primordial acts of giving. Its status rests on its collectively recognized role as donor of the symbolic tokens of group identity, and of ritually secured life. This temporally conceived hierarchy is marked by the asymmetry of ritual offerings. Junior houses are expected to bring gifts of raw food, betal, and areca, the products "of the outside." These offerings are symbolically transformed by the hosts, who give back cooked food, along with the promise of renewed fertility that makes productivity possible.

Claims to the hierarchical status of a source are validated in practice by a house's ability to attract others to its seasonal rituals as junior dependents. Such claims are open to negotiation. Mambai speak freely of the capacity of junior houses to break away and constitute themselves as center sources to their own dependent derivatives. Centrifugal tendencies of this kind have been documented in related societies and would seem to be inherent in the indigenous models, which correlate increasing degrees of spatial distance with temporal remoteness from a source.[10] Among Mambai, the neglecting or forgetting of ties to an origin place are negatively valued acts, but they are also accepted as possible eventualities, most dramatically illustrated by the conduct of the Portuguese rulers.

What is asserted, then, is an ideal of immutable obligations laid down in the past, and that ideal is institutionalized by the annual cycle of agricultural ceremonies. The mythical sequence of condensation and dispersal is realized in the periodicity of ritual life as a perpetual alternation. Each year, the house cult of the rainy season reverses the outward flow of men and wealth objects and brings together what has been separated at localized places of origin. Such reversals do not exactly effect a return to the time of origins, for participant houses remain divided in the act that unites them, distinguished as elder and younger, trunk and tip, donor and receiver of life. The reunited houses commemorate their original state of unity, while simultaneously registering, in their hierarchical structure, the processes of separation and division.

5. Houses and the Deities

Houses, as we have seen, are hierarchically ordered, and their oppositionally defined attributes express the differential statuses of social groups. But houses also symbolize the opposed natures of the deities. As house-founders and house-dwellers, human beings participate in the life of the cosmos, reproducing their relationship to the gods through the same acts that reproduce social ties. Along with other similarly overdetermined symbols, the house condenses the fundamental conceptions of Mambai ritual life.

One point of departure is suggested by the narrative emphasis on the theme of the divided patrimony. Agnatically inherited heirlooms comprise a particular class of exchange valuables called *saun-lulin*, or *saun-lulin/saun-kesan* in ritual language, and glossed for now as "sacred objects."[11] These are regarded as inalienable, which means that they circulate only among houses of the same kind, those linked through males and ranked as *kaka nor ali*. Each house group stores its ancestral heirlooms in the recesses of its cult house, separate from the valuables that circulate in matrimonial exchange. Whereas the latter include textiles and female ornaments, the former class of valuables is represented by objects categorized as male, swords, spears, and the metal breast disks that men wear on ritual occasions. Each such object has its own name, personality, and history, and its acquisition by the house-founder is recounted in the house's origin narrative.

Mambai men, particularly older or high-status men, are extremely well-versed in this lore, which they distinguish as the "walk of sacred objects." Indeed, they seemed to me to be more concerned with the precise distribution of sacra over generations than with the genealogical connections among the ancestors who transport the objects from house to house. Whereas individuals would often give markedly different genealogical accounts of interhouse relations,

75

there was an equally marked tendency to reach consensus regarding the distribution of sacra.[12] Upon entering unfamiliar cult houses, my assistants would orient themselves by inquiring as to the names of the house's sacra, and not its ancestors. On several occasions, they went on to deduce genealogical connections from the sacra, reasoning that if an object which by tradition had once belonged to one of their own houses now resided in this other one, then it must have been brought there by some distant descendant of their own line.

Ritual obligations among houses are conventionally represented in terms of the transmission of sacra over time. Members of junior houses will say that they participate in the rites held by a senior house because their own sacred objects "first went out from that house," or conversely because objects retained by the senior house are "mother and father" to their own. Some people would personify sacred objects and describe them as so eager to participate in the festivities at their origin place that they set out on their own, dragging their human owners along behind them. Alternately, Mambai speak as if the primary ritual duty of a junior house were "to bear its sacred objects" back to their source. Aptly designated *obrikisan*, from the Portuguese word that means "to oblige, to compel," "to reciprocate, to thank," these sacred tokens of origins are really objectified obligations, the material traces of lasting ties among givers and receivers.

The tokens themselves are iconic of the nature of the ties. Fashioned out of hard, enduring metal, many of them phallic in shape, sacred objects connote a distinctive form of relatedness that persists over time. The moral qualities of faithfulness and constancy attributed to personified sacra express the same idea in another register. It is an idea of permanence, immutability, abiding order, of stability in change and similarity in difference, and it is socially realized in the unity of house groups bound by common agnatic descent. Agnatically related houses form a succession of fundamentally like units, each lesser than what antecedes it, but belonging to the same class and encompassed by its predecessor as an inferior token of a superior type. Such houses are conceived to be different versions of the same thing, distinguished by relatively higher or lower ranks, not by any fundamental contrast of essences. The whole is represented by particular parts, the acknowledged trunk houses, which are in turn subsumed by the Lone House.

This equivalence between the new, the different, the hierarchically inferior and the old, the same, the hierarchically superior gives to the house system a timeless character. Or more accurately, the passage of time is lived by house groups as a form of stasis, at once a recurrent return of the same in the different and a perpetual presence of the one that precedes the many. When the hierarchical structure of the house system is objectified in narratives or enacted in rituals, diachrony and synchrony become fused. Narratives portray the differentiation of houses as a diachronic process that replicates an anterior state of structure at progressively lower levels, while the ritual reintegration of houses into a structured whole evokes the diachronic process of house formation.

The ritualized interdependence of agnatically related houses reflects and expresses the idea of a static order, persisting unchanged over time. In theory, houses that were once united are never truly separated. Their relationship is immutable, indestructible, immortal, and is objectified in metal, masculine sacra. That such ties can lose sociological relevance is indicated by lapses in ritual participation, of which Mambai are well aware. But even when houses cease to cooperate, the ties that bind them are held to endure, unacknowledged, undramatized, but not thereby dissolved.[13] In a sense that will become clearer as this study unfolds, agnatic descent freezes time.

Both the represented idea of an immutable order and the objects and acts that represent it participate in the masculine principle of the cosmos. Swords, spears, and breast disks are invariably displayed in invoking Father Heaven, who is regarded as their originator. By one account, he fashions the primordial sacra out of his own bone; and in one of the more freely told episodes of the creation myth, he distributes the archetypal patrimony among his human sons. But if Heaven instigates the social process of differentiation, he is also its modeling type. In one of his manifestations, Heaven is the masculine principle of mobility that opens and extends the cosmos, the paradigm of the centrifugal orientation associated with younger sons. Yet he himself is greater than any part, and his defining function is the ordering of parts into a whole. Heaven's regulatory function is symbolized by concrete acts of binding and dividing. He creates the bones that give form to the formless earth, and he orders the human realm by bestowing differential identities on his sons. He is the personified principle of enduring order, who imposes differences and establishes connections. That principle is socially realized in the hierarchy of houses and objectified in the networks of sacred heirlooms. At the risk of oversystematizing these representations, agnatically inherited wealth objects would seem to be to the house system what the divinely fashioned bones of rock are to the earth, a metaphorical skeleton of metal that holds together the interconnected parts of a whole.

Yet to view the house system only in relation to the masculine principle would be to distort its cultural meaning. Indeed, in designating the social units of ritual action as "houses," Mambai implicitly make reference to the feminine principle of the cosmos. If Father Heaven personifies the qualities attributed to agnatic relations among houses, it is Mother Earth who presides over the house itself. Whenever Mambai speak of the goddess in her life-giving aspect, they depict her confined to the house, where she nurses her children and awaits her consort's intermittent visits. Father Heaven patrols open spaces, but to Mother Earth belongs the warm, dark, protected space of the house, the world of the interior, where human birth and growth unfold. She is the personified principle of life-giving immobility and constancy, a fixed point of orientation in a wider world of motion and change. Through its association with Mother Earth, the house assumes a manifestly maternal character.

From this perspective, an apparent inconsistency arises. All of the properties that Mambai attribute to the house in its maternal aspect are also attributed to senior trunk houses, associated with their male guardians. But this inconsistency is easily resolved by attending to the temporal dimension of symbolic schemes. The eldest son who stays behind at an origin place represents the procreative couple, the "old mother/old father" of the prior generation. In practice, the relational categories of elder/younger and parent/child are used interchangeably to rank house groups. An additional feature of the scheme is that the maternal role serves as a synecdoche for the "parental" house's relationship to its dependents. Hence there is a strong resemblance between the eldest male and the mother. Both figures are associated with the house and its life-giving routines, with fixity and immobility, with the steady trunk that anchors and supports peripheral branches. Together they embody the centripetal orientation that periodically reconcentrates dispersed individuals and groups.

At all levels of the house system, from the minimal units to the differentiated and ranked subparts of larger wholes, the alternation of ritual time with ordinary time is expressed in spatial terms, as an oscillation between going into and out from a house. By this symbolism, house members spend much of their lives "on the outside." Their daily routines take them to the zone of "palm tree and garden" (*naua nor nama*), and even farther outward to the "dense grasslands and forest" (*kur-lalan/ai-lalan*).[14] These zones mark what Mambai call the "outside and edge" (*hoho nor eha*) of inhabited space.

Mambai associate these movements in space with the stages of the life cycle, and they use the reciprocal obligations between parents and children as a metaphor for wider social relationships. When a house is represented as "old mother/old father," its scattered dependents are seen as grown-up children, who have gone off to toil in the outer realms and produce food for their weary parents. Emphasis is placed on the dangers of the outside, where wild spirits dwell. Known as "wild ears/wild faces" (*kika-hui/ahe-hui*) or "masters of the outside/masters of the earth" (*hoho-ubun/rai-ubun*), these bush spirits are opposed to the domesticated house sacra, which are referred to in this context as "tame ears/tame faces" (*kika-ai/ahe-ai*) or "inside lords" (*dat-lalan*). Here the sacra take on the role of nursemaids to house members. They are said to "follow behind" women and men, in order to protect them against the capricious attacks of the bush spirits. When danger arises, the diligent guardians "whisper in the ear/slap on the behind" (*sin ni kika/bas ni fere*), as a mother does to soothe and calm a frightened infant.

Verbal and visual images of parental nurturance are ubiquitous in ritual contexts. Reunited house members symbolically regress to a condition of infantile dependency, and they return "to nurse from the mother's breast/to snuggle in the father's lap" (*oid susu ni inkai ni susun/oid lele ni au aman ni fan*). The vulnerability of small children is a favorite metaphor for their condition. Like unformed infants who cannot endure exposure to the elements, women and men seek shelter within the temperate environment of an origin place, where sacred shade trees "push back the heat/sweep back the burning" (*seb-sak brusin/sar-sak banan*). Cult houses are metonymically represented as "the shading house/the warming fire" (*um-boun/aif-mamun*), a reference to rites of incorporation in which newborn children are symbolically heated at the sacred hearth.[15]

Other representations associate the house with nurturance and growth. It is described as an enclosed shelter and frequently likened to a woman who draws her cloth around her nursing children and "moulds" (*lum*) them with her milk. Nor are human beings the sole beneficiaries of the house's maternal qualities. Beneath the house, at the "base of the enclosure," the area marked off by the house pillars, pigs and dogs feed upon refuse that falls through cracks in the floor above. Mambai say that the various children of the house nurse in their own ways, some from above, some from below:

Hina nor maena susu	Women and men nurse
sai-sai	up-up
Haiha nor ausa susu	Pigs and dogs nurse
du-du.	down-down.

The house is also metonymically associated with women, who "follow Mother Earth" and preside over the inner realm of space. Symbolically, a woman's domain is the house, and she should not leave it. It is men as a class who venture outside, to work in the fields and gardens, to penetrate the bush and cut down virgin forest, to visit distant places, in short, to open up new spaces, while women, like Mother Earth, remain indoors with their children, waiting for the men to return. From this perspective, the overall well-being of the house is based on the same complementarity of male and female that sustains the cosmos as a whole.

As the fixed and life-giving center to the group that reunites there, the house is strongly associated with Mother Earth and with her human daughters. These latter, however, are unlike their divine prototype in one, socially critical respect. At the social level, the female vitality associated with a house always derives from elsewhere.

FIVE

The Renewal of Life through Marriage

Its trunk sits there. The little pieces of its tip go out
again and again. It has but one trunk. It is the bits of
the tip that are many.
—A Mambai description of marriage alliance

1. The House as an Alliance Group

Mambai use the concept of the house to speak of two processes of
dispersal that are realized in institutional forms. In the one case,
which we have examined, the agents are men. By dividing and sub-
dividing their houses, men create hierarchical relationships among
the differentiated parts of former wholes. In the second case it is
women who are dispersed. Their circulation among houses is effected
through marriage and creates relationships of a different nature, with
distinctive ritual expressions. My object in this chapter is to describe
and interpret the dualism of social ties.

Mambai marriages are largely private affairs, contracted with
relative informality by the individual partners. But these unions initiate processes that involve the groups to which individuals belong.
Any marriage establishes or renews an alliance between the group of
the woman and that of the man. Reciprocal but unequal exchanges of
gifts and services distinguish the parties in an alliance as wife-givers
and wife-takers (*umaena nor maen-heua*) and mark the former as superior in status. Great value is placed on perpetuating alliances over
time by repeating previous marriages. Mambai liken their marital destinies to the act of following a preexistent "path" (*dan*), a trail blazed
by the marriages of their ancestors. As in other systems of the alliance type, "marriage acquires a diachronic dimension, it becomes
an institution enduring from generation to generation" (Dumont
1968, 204).

A sociologically significant distinction between the marital "paths
of women" and the "paths of men" gives the Mambai alliance system
an asymmetric character. Asymmetry is encoded in the relationship
terminology, which distinguishes patrilateral and matrilateral cross-
relatives, and it is institutionalized by the marriage rule, which has
positive and negative expressions. For men, the prohibited category
includes the father's sister's daughter, and the positive injunction is to

marry a woman from a category that includes the mother's brother's daughter; whereas the prohibited category for women includes the mother's brother's son, and the prescribed marriage is with a man from a category that includes the father's sister's son.[1] At the level of the indigenous model, where the system as a whole is invariably represented from the wife-givers' perspective, the structural consequence of alliance is a unilateral circulation of women. This system may be included as a variant of the type known as "asymmetric prescriptive alliance" (Needham 1973a), "matrilateral cross-cousin marriage" (Leach 1961), "generalized" or "restricted exchange" (Lévi-Strauss 1949; transl. 1969), and "exclusive cross-cousin marriage" (van Wouden 1968).[2]

While Mambai speak of houses as the units in alliance relations, the structural level intended by *fada* in the context of marriage is lower than the encompassing whole. Alliances are ideally established and maintained by the differentiated subparts of a maximal house.[3] Hence two houses that claim common agnatic descent will ordinarily have different marital allies and may even stand in wife-giver/wife-taker relations to each other. In cases of the latter sort, Mambai speak of the parties as being agnates (*kaka nor ali*) "from one side" and affines (*umaena nor maen-hua*) "from one side." Should such doubly linked house groups interact in a ritual context, the two relationships are activated for discrete exchange purposes and are regarded as separable.[4]

If agnatic ties are held to connect fundamentally similar collectivities and are expressed by the relative age categories that distinguish same-sex siblings, ties of alliance connect collectivities regarded as dissimilar, and they may be specified in terms of the relationship between siblings of the opposite sex. The gender difference, in other words, connotes the disparate natures attributed to the partners in an alliance.

Categorized in terms of gender, the relationship of wife-givers to their wife-takers corresponds to that between a brother and the sister whom he relinquishes. As the house of the brother, wife-givers are male in opposition to wife-takers defined as female, but what needs emphasis is the temporal dimension implicit in the categorization. In alliance contexts, the idea of an original whole is projected onto the cross-sex sibling pair, the boy and girl, raised in the same house and later separated by their disparate marital destinies. Allied groups distinguished as brother and sister evoke this image of unity before division at the same time as they enact their complementary unity in division.[5]

Marital life replicates cosmological processes in its sequential patterning, recapitulating at the levels of domestic and group life what Mambai regard as the origins of their marital institutions. Let us remember that the time of origins is divided into two periods, Night and Day. Night is the period of genesis, when Heaven and Earth create the world and its inhabitants, while the processes that unfold over the ongoing course of Day relate to the differentiation of the social order. Marital institutions belong to the later period and bring about a transformation of the earlier, nocturnal order of things.

Originally, Mambai say, "the people did not know wife-giver and wife-taker." In those days, human beings imitated the deities, who are sister and brother as well as husband and wife to each other. So too did the first women and men pair, sister with brother, brother with sister, and they brought forth progeny out of unions that would now be regarded as incestuous. For the ancestors, sibling marriage was simply the natural course of things, though Mau Balen, in an idiosyncratically literal interpretation of cosmogonic symbolism, once remarked that it was too dark for people to notice who was coupling with whom.

That sexual practices were different in the Night is a collectively held assumption, and a widely known tradition regarding the origins of matrimonial regulations is often narrated in ritual contexts.[6] The myth tells of a certain brother who finished building his house and went with his sister to wash in the river. The narrative context defines their purpose. They intend to separate themselves from the marginal condition of house-builders, who observe prohibitions on bathing, hair-cutting, and sexual intercourse while the house is under construction. What occurs in the myth, however, is an arrested transition. Lured by tufts of his sister's hair, the brother swims upstream to where she is bathing and has sexual intercourse with her. Afterward, she complains to her kinsmen, who set off in pursuit of the offender, or in a variant, she herself pursues him across the land. All variants end with the beheading of the brother. His death marks the origin of the "ban of women and men" (*badu hina nor maena nin*), the marital proscriptions that Mambai observe to this day.[7]

Like the earlier "ban of rock and tree," imposed in the Night by Father Heaven, the new matrimonial ban is constitutive of boundaries. In describing the results of both bans, Mambai use the verb *ket*, "to separate, to mark off, to draw a boundary," which, significantly, is never used of the division of houses by men. What are separated by the matrimonial ban are the categories of wife-giver and wife-taker. In the myth, the incestuous brother is killed

Oid ket lar-hinan nor lar-manen	To separate female blood and male blood
Oid ket tbo nor nara	To separate sister and brother
Oid ket umaena nor maen-heua.	To separate wife-giver and wife-taker.[8]

Lisa, the cult prohibitions observed by house groups, are identified as a corollary of the mythic act of separation and are thus of later origins than the institution of the house itself. In other words, marital regulations impose a new difference upon houses. Similar from the perspective of origins, houses are dissimilar in the context of marriage, separated by boundaries that the concept of *lisa* connotes.

This dissimilarity is relative, not absolute, for any one house stands as wife-giver to its wife-takers and as wife-taker to its wife-givers. In theory, wife-takers may not give women back to their wife-givers, but the two parties ideally renew their alliance by repeating previous marriages in the following generations. From the temporal perspective that Mambai take on their alliance practices, matrimonial regulations are a cultural procedure for conjoining what has been separated, the wife-giving source and the wife-taking product of life.

2. Prescribed and Preferred Marriages: The Preservation of Alliances

The dual categories *umaena/maen-heua*, wife-giver/wife-taker, imply a triadic division of the social universe, both for the particular persons who unite in marriage and for the groups to which they belong. From ego's perspective, all socially relevant others belong to one of three mutually exclusive categories, which are distinguished in the relationship terminology. *Umaena* categorizes groups that have given women to ego's and includes the wife-givers of wife-givers, who are distinguished as *umaen-tkeun*, "neck wife-givers." Groups that have taken women from ego's are categorized as *maen-heua*, and their wife-takers are included as *ana hina nora nor laun*, "leaf and tip daughters." The category *kak-ali*, "elder and younger people," equates agnates with groups that share an alliance relation with ego's, for instance, the group of the mother's sister's husband, with which ego "shares a wife-giver."

Umaena is a compound of the Tetum term for house, *ume*, and *maena*, "male, man."[9] It may be glossed as either "male house" or "house of the man," where the man intended is the wife's brother. This individual represents the wife-giving house to its wife-takers, and he is specifically designated *umaena* by his sister's husband. Wife-givers are also associated with the category *nai*, foregrounding an idea of intergenerational ties contracted through women. An individual's *nai* are wife-giving or matrilateral relatives in the ascending generation, including the mother's brother, the wife's father, the mother's brother's wife and wife's mother (both marked as *nai hinan*, "female *nai*"), the father's mother's brother's son, and the mother's mother's brother (a "neck wife-giver"). Mambai distinguish the genealogical mother's brother as *nai slol*, "direct, specific, particular *nai*," and his special relationship to the sister's child provides one metaphor for marital alliance. In formal speech *nai* pairs with *tata*, "grandparent, ancestor," and wife-takers ritually greet their wife-givers as *au nai/au tata*.

Maen-heua, literally "new man," is the relationship term used by men for daughter's husband, sister's husband, and sister's child. It is the reciprocal of both *umaena* and *nai*, but when the latter term is used of wife-givers as a class, the reciprocal is the structural converse, *kai*. This category refers to wife-taking or patrilateral relatives in the ascending generation and includes the father's sister, the husband's mother, the father's father's sister, and the father's sister's husband and husband's father (both marked as *kai manen*, "male *kai*"). In-married women symbolize the status of wife-takers, who are ritually addressed by their wife-givers as *au tbo/au kaia*, "my sister/ my paternal aunt."

As the equations cited suggest, the prescribed marriage for men is with a *nai ana hinan*, "daughter of a *nai*," and for women, with a *kai ana manen*, "son of a *kai*." A voiced preference for marriage between the genealogical mother's brother's daughter and father's sister's son is one expression of Mambai concern for the repetition of past marriages. But other preferences within the prescription express the same concern in terms of the houses to which individuals belong and convey an idea of alliance as a relationship transmitted by collectivities from generation to generation.

Not all alliances are conceived of as inheritances from the past. Mambai are well aware of how alliances proliferate in each generation, as house members contract new marriages, only some of which are ever repeated. However, every house recognizes two other houses as its primordial wife-givers, the first of its marital allies in time and status. These two are distinguished from all other wife-giving houses as *nai fun* or *umaen-fun*, "wife-givers of origin, trunk wife-givers." The reciprocal category is *kai akin*, "paternal aunt from long ago."[10] Ritually, these primordial marital allies (and strictly speaking, only these) describe themselves as "sisters since the base of heaven/brothers since the rim of earth" (*tbo hoir lelo-fun/nara hoir rai-ehan*).[11]

Mambai represent the two wife-givers of origin as the "water buffalo of the mother and water buffalo of the father" (*arabau-inan nor arabau-aman*). "Water buffalo of the father" designates a house's earliest affines, those who by tradition gave a woman to its founder. The house of the "mother's water buffalo" is that which claims to have given a woman in the succeeding generation to a son of the house-founder. Images of anchorage and balance define a house's relationship to these primordial marital allies. Wife-givers of origin are described as "those who support the rock/those who steady the tree" (*ro fe seik-li hauta/ro fe dud aia*). Also known as the "underside of the interlaid stones," they are the base or foundation that fixes and sustains wife-takers from below. Symbolically, the original "trunk" givers of women are the source of all persons engendered in the wife-taking house, and they are linked through the daughters of their daughters to still other wife-taking houses. As Mambai say of marital alliance: "Its trunk sits there. The bits of its tip go out again and again." A wife-giving trunk house relinquishes its daughters, whose own daughters later marry out again, and so on over the generations, creating branching lines of maternal affiliation. The more distant an out-marrying woman is from an ultimate source group, the weaker the connection in both idea and practice, but the valued bond between primordial allies is ritually and socially preserved.

Trunk wife-givers and their *kai akin* interact in ritual events, of which the most important are mortuary ceremonies. Each party has formal obligations toward the other, and emphasis is placed on the life-enhancing role of the wife-givers. The ritual authority which these wife-givers exercise over their wife-takers has negative as well as positive expressions. Thus while all wife-givers are attributed power to curse their wife-takers, that of trunk wife-givers is held to be the most potent. Should they grow angry, Mambai say, they cause illness and misfortune among their wife-takers, who will die unless the aggrieved parties are appeased.[12]

Preferences within the prescribed category of spouses contribute directly to the preservation of primordial alliances. Marriages with women of the mother's and the father's water buffalo houses are equally preferred marital choices, distinguished as "to follow behind the mother" and "to follow behind the father." From the perspective of the houses involved, these marriages are even more highly valued than are marriages between genealogical cross-cousins. Marriages between primordial affines recreate the collective past of the allied

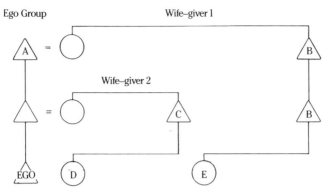

Figure 2: Preferred Marriages. Where A = male founder of Ego's line, then B = water
buffalo of father, and C = water buffalo of mother. Where the figure represents *any* three generations, Ego may marry either D or E. Marriage with D
is to "follow behind the mother." Marriage with E is to "follow behind the
father." Both D and E (MBD, FMBSD) are classed as *nai anan*. The two
marriages are equally preferred.

groups, and they mark or enhance the prestige of the individuals who
contract them. Most people, however, think more of their own close
relatives than of their house as a whole in making marital choices.
Egocentrically defined preferential marriages are also called "to follow behind the mother or the father," but at this level the referent of
the formulae is not a water buffalo house. For a male ego, "to follow
behind the father" means to repeat the paternal grandfather's marriage by taking a woman from the father's mother's house, ideally the
father's mother's brother's son's daughter. "To follow behind the
mother" means that ego repeats the father's marriage by taking a
woman from the mother's house, ideally the mother's brother's daughter (see figure 2).

All preferences are subsumed under the prescribed marriage
with the daughter of a *nai*. Categorically, there is no departure from
the rule. A man may seek a wife among "different people," those with
whom no previous alliance exists, but if he contracts such a marriage, the wife's group becomes *nai* to his own, and the alliance may
be perpetuated in subsequent generations. Before initiating a new
alliance, however, a man should get the consent of his mother's
brother, who is far more actively involved in the life of a sister's child
than are wife-givers of origin. The would-be groom is required to give
a goat to his mother's brother, in return for the "torch and fire" (a
roasted piglet and a cloth) that he needs to light up his search for a
"new path."

New alliances may entail uxorilocal residence, "to dwell with the wife's father." This is a low status situation for the husband. In such arrangements a man pays no bridewealth, but he is obliged to work for his wife's kin. He is represented as a domestic servant who "draws water/gathers firewood" (*soi era/hu aia*) for his wife-givers, tasks that are ordinarily associated with women. His low status is also expressed in spatial terms. He is identified with the "walls and veranda," the periphery of the wife-giver's house, a concise metonymy for his subordination. Finally, as already mentioned, such a man forfeits the privilege of perpetuating his own agnatic line, for his children will be affiliated to their mother's brother's house.[13]

The preferred and most common form of marriage entails virolocal residence and the ritual incorporation of the wife into the husband's house. A simple ceremony effects her "entrance" into the cult of the man, and she assumes his cult observances. In domestic life the new couple ordinarily resides with the husband's parents, if they are living. A young wife is subordinated to her mother-in-law within the extended household. At first she calls this woman *kai* (HM, FZ), and is addressed by her as *baki* (SW, BD), but the two gradually come to address each other as "mother" and "daughter." Over the course of the domestic cycle, a woman moves from the marginal position of a young *baki* to the elevated status of an "old mother," who ritually represents the cult house into which she married long ago. Nevertheless, she retains obligations to her own house of origin, and the ties between women and their sources organize ritualized exchange relations between marital allies.

3. Marriage and Death: Exchange Relations among Marital Allies

Marriages initiate formal exchange relations that unfold over the course of years, or even generations. All exchanges involve reciprocal prestations of complementary gifts and services. The exchange of gift items conforms to the gender categories that express alliance relationships. Symbolically "male" goods circulate against "female" goods, and groups are identified with what they receive. Wife-takers provide the male gifts (water buffalo, goats, horses, metal disks), and they are reciprocated with female gifts (pigs, cloths, coral necklaces, cooked rice).

Typically, the initial marital payments are materially simplified and linguistically devalued. As bridewealth, the husband and his close agnates may provide a goat or a horse, referred to as a "papaya

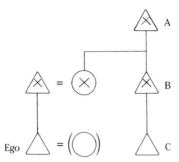

Figure 3: Inheritance of mortuary exchange obligations. C may hold a mortuary for A or B. If Ego's parents are dead he must "stand in their place" and attend the ceremony. C (here his MBS) will receive prestations which are dedicated to Ego's MB (*nai*) or his MF (*tata*). Ego is bound to make these prestations no matter whom he has actually married.

leaf." They receive in return a plain meal of cooked rice and pork that counts as "bitter coffee." The costlier prestations are deferred until future mortuary ceremonies.

Mutual assistance in the ritual disposal of the dead is collectively regarded as the paramount responsibility of maritally allied groups. This process has several stages, the most important of which takes place long after the deaths of those to whom the rites are dedicated. It often happens that a man who has pledged ritual assistance to his affines dies before the pledge can be fulfilled. Such a man's obligations are inherited by his eldest son, who "stands in his mother and father's place" at his allies' mortuary ceremonies. The son may be called on to sacrifice a water buffalo in honor of his maternal grandparents, or to attend a ceremony held by his wife-takers, where he will have to dedicate pigs and cloths to a long deceased paternal aunt (see figure 3). Particular alliance obligations are transmitted from one generation to the next, and while a young man is free in theory to initiate a new alliance, he does not avoid exchange obligations from the past.

"Time," Marcel Mauss observed, "has to pass before a counterprestation can be made. Thus the notion of time is logically implied when one pays a visit, contracts a marriage or an alliance" (1967, 34). Affinal alliances in Mambai society are framed by marriages and deaths. The interval between the initial gift of a woman and the deferred countergift of ritual respect to the dead is measured in terms of vitality given, received, and spent over the course of a lifetime. Wifegivers are life-givers, sources of reproductive vitality embodied in

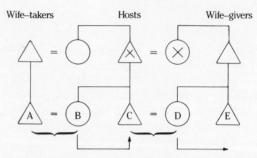

Figure 4: The sister-brother relationship as a model for mortuary exchange

women, and they are thought to be depleted by the loss of their sisters and daughters. A wife-giver's death marks the point of exhaustion, when life once given must be reciprocated and so renewed by the takers.

In the context of death ceremonies, sister and brother emerge clearly as the social focus of the alliance relationship. When a house group gathers for the final disposal of the dead, it always dedicates the ceremony to a deceased couple, a man of their house and his wife. The group is assisted by both its wife-givers and its wife-takers, who stand to it respectively as brother and sister, and to the dead as son and daughter. The sponsors will symbolically enact both these relationships over the course of the ceremony, facing their wife-takers as brother-son, and their wife-givers as sister-daughter. (See figure 4.) What is stressed in all exchange transactions is the exhaustion of the "old mother/old father" for whom the ceremony is held, and the symbolic purpose of all prestations is "to repay the dead for their fatigue." Prestations dedicated to the dead and negotiated by two pairs of marital allies project a composite image of the sibling couple, who were initially separated by the sister's marriage and are now reunited by the death of their parents.

From a sociological perspective, the purpose of the interval between marital exchanges and mortuary exchanges is the alliance relationship itself, secured through the total circulation of women, goods, and ritual services. Reciprocal obligations to attend death ceremonies held by marital allies are a form of delayed payment, imposed on both parties in an alliance relationship. The socially critical point is that payment must be delayed, that the maritally contracted obligations can only be fulfilled with the passage of time. Implied in any marriage is an element of imbalance that endures as long as the alliance, or better still, that constitutes the alliance. Imbalance, as Sahlins has suggested, is "socially of the essence" (1972, 222).

What also needs stressing is the mutual character of social imbalance, which precludes any notion of the "purchase" of a woman. Affinal gift exchanges are the price of an alliance relationship, and the price is paid by both parties. Material prestations are weighted in favor of the wife-givers and express the disparity between alliance statuses, but the maritally incurred debt is, and remains, reciprocal. The protagonists know that in contracting an alliance they are making pledges to render up something more in the course of future ceremonies for the dead.

During the protracted interval between two stages in an alliance, wife-givers and wife-takers remain embroiled with one another, enmeshed in open-ended, reciprocal obligations. Wife-givers may call upon their wife-takers for material assistance in meeting demands imposed by their own wife-givers; and wife-takers depend upon their wife-givers for ritual services necessary to their well-being. The temporal patterning of ritual exchange obligations prolongs and institutionalizes the mutual but asymmetric dependency of maritally allied groups.

4. The Conceptual Basis of Asymmetry: Botanic and Consanguineal Idioms

At the level of alliance ideology, asymmetry is a valued ideal. It is articulated in the prescriptive relationship terminology, institutionalized through the matrilateral marriage rule, and symbolically marked in the complementary prestations that define the unequal statuses of wife-givers and wife-takers.

Patrilateral marriages, which would reverse the direction of an alliance, are expressly prohibited. They are roundly condemned when they occur, and the groups involved take steps to prevent their repetition in the next generation. Collective sanctions are brought to bear on the offenders. A man who contracts a patrilateral marriage is stigmatized as someone who "desires the sister's daughter/cuts off the daughter" (*mlema ubun/baka anan*), thereby halting the outward flow of women. Should the marriage partners be close kin, they are open to accusations of witchcraft, for, Mambai reason, only witches would so willfully confound proper order. Even if their relationship is distant, they are ridiculed by their kin. Their disregard for marital proscriptions is likened to that of animals, who mate indiscriminately, in any place and with any partner, and who, where marriage is concerned, are the negative self-image of human beings. Symbolically located "outside the house," in the wild zones where animals couple, improper unions negate the humanity of those who contract them.[15]

Mambai often justify the prohibition on patrilateral marriage by reference to ritual exchange relations. These, they argue, would be confounded by marriage with a woman from a wife-taking group. Goats and pigs once received by wife-givers and wife-takers respectively would have to be returned to the donors, and such reversals in the directions of prestations are considered infelicitous. Conversely, social distinctions would be blurred, since each partner in the alliance would stand as both wife-giver and wife-taker to the other. "And then," Mambai ask, "who would eat goat and who would eat pork?" Terminological ambiguities are also stressed. Patrilateral and matrilateral cross-kin are distinguished as *kai* and *nai*, but patrilateral marriage would entail addressing *kai* (FZ, HM; FZH, HF) as *nai* (MBW, WM; MB, WF) and *nai* as *kai*. In such cases, Mambai say: "We do not see the *nai* clearly or the *kai* clearly, and this is not good."

All these criticisms of patrilateral marriage turn around the confusion entailed for the particular individuals and groups concerned. Yet such difficulties are not insurmountable in practice. Terminological ambiguities are resolvable by applying the relationship terms for parents to affinal relatives, and Mambai accept that circumstances often oblige groups to participate in ritual events from more than one "side." What is at stake in the condemnation of patrilateral marriage is a cultural ideal. The uneasiness that Mambai express over unions that reverse the flow of women has to do with fundamental conceptions of life and its promotion over time.

Implicit in the notion of the wife-giver of origin or "trunk wife-giver" is a botanic metaphor for alliance. As in the symbolism of house formation, the basic idea connoted by the image of a growing tree is the opposition between the unity of a source and the multiplicity of its products. In the context of marriage alliance, the privileged products of a source house are the women who leave it to bring life to other houses, and whose daughters are the means of life to still other houses, even more remote from the original source. Metaphorically, women pass over generations from the unitary base to the ever ramifying tip of a marital tree, moving upward and outward toward peripheral branches, twigs, and shoots as "daughters of leaf and tip."[16]

We know that similar botanic imagery is used to represent relations among houses linked through men and related as "elder and younger." I have argued that such agnatic ties convey an idea of immortality, of an enduring order that persists not so much over time as despite time, through the perpetual replication of a type in its tokens. It remains to specify the content of the opposition between these eternal agnatic ties and the life-giving connections traced through women. In so doing, we return to the point where we left off in the previous chapter, with the house that transmits to its members a vitality that it cannot engender by itself alone.

An alternate metaphor for alliance, similar in structure to the botanic metaphor, derives from ideas of sexual reproduction and identifies alliance connections with ties of blood. The Mambai theory of conception has one expression in cosmogony, in the theme of the cosmic division of sexual labor. Mother Earth, the female principle of vitality, is associated with instability and formlessness. She brings forth the soft, shapeless earth, which is then endowed with stability and form by Father Heaven, the male principle of order. Human reproduction is based on the same principles, and the cosmogonic process is replicated in the complementary contributions that women and men make to procreation.

As in many South and Southeast Asian cultures (see Leach 1961; Yalman 1967; Lévi-Strauss 1969; Fox 1971b), flesh and bone are identified as the respective products of maternal blood and paternal semen, or more precisely, of maternal "red blood" (*lar-meran*) and paternal "white blood" (*lar-butin*). The classification suggests that female and male contributions to the child are not thought of as different in essence, but as the same essence endowed with different attributes. This view is consistent with other statements that Mambai make regarding a process that, in its particulars, remains a matter of opinion. In other words, in asserting that there is a Mambai "theory of conception," I do not mean that Mambai hold to a uniform dogma. What individuals share are certain classificatory principles, from which they may construct variant representations of the procreative process.[17]

With considerable urging on my part, my two male assistants set forth a comparatively complicated model. They identified red blood as a substance shared by men and women alike, while asserting that white blood belongs only to men. Hence with respect to blood, men are marked and women are unmarked, or to reformulate my previous suggestion, the relationship is between the presence and the absence of a quality. However, my informants went on to add a twist characteristic of Mambai symbolism, with its insistent emphasis on complementarity. A man's white blood, they explained, is not self-generated, but derives from maternal milk consumed during childhood. Men convert a female substance into a male one, which is then empowered to transform a woman's red blood into a child. When white blood is injected into a woman through coitus, it "moulds" the red blood inside her stomach, causing the blood to coagulate and form a mass. Over the course of her pregnancy, the white blood gradually penetrates the soft, shapeless clot and hardens into the bones that give form to the child's body. At length, my informants brought the process full circle. In response to my still perplexed queries, they pointed out that a woman's milk, the substance said to "mould" young children, does not flow until she has lain with a man. That milk, they assured me, derives from male white blood left over from the "moulding" of the fetus.

By this model, to which I return later in regard to ritual representations of rain, paternal semen and maternal milk mark successive moments in a closed cycle of exchanges. These substances work at one level as tropes for gender identities, but they also connote the process of producing gender difference, of becoming male or female. It is difficult to imagine a more emphatic way of asserting the complementarity of the sexes than by representing men and women as the sources of each other's distinctive bodily fluids.

Milk, the male in the female, and semen, the female in the male, are dominant symbols in the agricultural rites performed by elder and younger house groups. Alliance relations are also regarded as life-giving, vitalizing, sustaining, but they are symbolized by blood, the maternal contribution to procreation, which connotes instability and formlessness. While house groups depend upon their wife-givers for the reproductive vitality embodied in women, these groups transform what they receive, as a man's semen gives shape and form to a woman's blood. In contrast to the division of houses by men, which produces lesser copies of an archetypal model, houses linked through women convert the same into the different. The theory of conception provides a metaphor for what is identifiable as an ideology of agnation, by which consanguineally related houses are held to "mould" a common substance in different ways, shaping their members to fit particular social identities.

When Mambai represent alliance relations as a flow of blood, they employ the categories of "female blood" and "male blood" distinguished in the mythology of marriage. The intent is to delineate two perspectives on the same vital substance, that of wife-givers, associated with the brother, and that of wife-takers, associated with the sister. "Female blood" is blood as wife-givers see it, carried further and further away from their house by out-marrying women (father's sister, sister, father's sister's daughter, sister's daughter, daughter's daughter, etc.), and it defines the category of unmarriageable women. "Male blood" is the same substance seen by wife-takers, coming toward them with in-marrying women of the mother's brother's and the mother's mother's brother's house, and it defines the category of prescribed spouses.[18]

To marry a woman from a wife-taking house is to reverse the outward flow and constitutes an "affront against female blood." By the same scheme, marriage between the daughter of a brother and the son of a sister effects the ideal union of male and female blood, a union that symbolically conjoins the brother and sister separated by the incest ban. Mambai understand the socially valued marriage as an oblique or displaced form of the prohibited marriage. They say: "The daughter of a brother and the son of a sister look upon each other as sister and brother."

In sum, wife-givers regard the immediate and eventual destinations of their women as "female blood," and wife-takers regard the immediate and ultimate sources of their women as "male blood." When Mambai represent the alliance system as a totality, they project blood imagery onto an imaginary space that is structured like a tree, oriented around a center source and forking outward along multiple paths. Neither at the level of ideals nor in their social practices do Mambai appear concerned with the eventual return of blood to its source. Rather, the indigenous model is of blood that "flows continually outward until it reaches its final bit," and no special value is placed on closing cycles of marital exchange.

What seem to preoccupy Mambai most are the vicissitudes of particular alliances, as these unfold in the interval between marriage and death. The death of a wife-giver represents in time what Mambai imagine as occurring somewhere in space: the utter depletion of a life-giving flow of blood. But if that flow does indeed come to an absolute halt, somewhere far beyond the horizons of the lived social universe, when the corresponding event occurs in time there are ritual means of renewing the flow.

Part 2 provides a close investigation of black mortuary rituals in their relationship to the white agricultural cult, and pursues in more detail the socially realized ideology of life that has been the focus of these chapters on the house. At this point, it is convenient to sum up the argument so far, and specifically, to objectify the content of the distinction that Mambai project onto their social universe.

Mambai conceptions of the house involve a scheme of oppositions that is socially expressed in the distinction between ties traced through men and ties traced through women. This distinction is critical to indigenous sociology and organizes the exchange relations among house groups. Its cultural meaning is defined by contrasts between the hard and the soft, the imperishable and the perishable, the immortality of bone and the mortality of flesh, which may be understood as concrete manifestations of the relationship between the static and the dynamic.

Alliance ties are vitalizing but perishable in nature, and they require renewal over generations. While following a preexistent marital path recreates the past, the important point is that the marital past needs to be recreated. "The paths of women and men wind here and there," Mambai say, and such paths may be forgotten. In that event, ties among houses loosen; if the neglect is chronic, the ties break. The alliance ends, and unless new alliances are contracted, the wife-taking house ends with it, "cut off at the base/withering at the tip." Mambai recognize this possibility.

Ties of descent traced through males are of a different nature. They endure even when neglected, they persist even when forgotten, and their capacity to last is symbolized by the quality of hardness. It is, I think, significant that Mambai do not ordinarily make use of bone as a symbol for the perduring nature of agnatic ties. To do so would be consistent with the theory of conception, which identifies bone with paternal semen. Yet when Mambai speak of houses linked through men, welded together into an ordered whole, the abstract notion of a form-giving framework is displaced onto sacred metal objects, which obliquely evoke the image of a skeleton by the references they make to Father Heaven. The enduring order that agnation connotes is imagined in what might be called a sublimated form, signified by objects that are not themselves metonyms of the procreative act, but are rather metaphoric of such metonyms. One effect of this symbolism, in my understanding, is to emphasize the radical dependency of male-ordered houses on their marital allies.

Admittedly, this last point is not a literal translation of Mambai statements, but I believe that it is in keeping with the spirit of their discourse, and that it conveys a premise implicit in their collective representations. To condense what I argue later in more detail, the house conceived of as a line of men is both immutable and sterile; the ties that a house contracts through women are both mutable and fertile. Social life is based on a complementary balance between a static male order and a dynamic female vitality.

Yet what characterizes Mambai thought is not only the insistence on complementarity, but also an equally insistent recognition of inherent antagonisms. The ideal balance of male and female effected through alliance has a temporal character. As but one moment in a dialectical process, complementary balance is always already a prelude to antagonistic separation. Anticipation of separation is built into the institutional structure of an alliance system organized around rituals of death.

Flesh and bone separate in the corpse, and it is in this ritualized moment that marital allies must choose anew between the incestuous and the social, between autonomy, isolation, sterility, and interdependence, solidarity, fertility. The choice is between denying obligations to others, and so destroying an alliance, or fulfilling those obligations, thereby renewing the life-giving ties. This choice, moreover, has cosmological consequences. Death ritual is Mother Earth's festival. It is she who receives decaying corpses in exchange for the life that she provides; and Father Heaven avoids her until that black transaction has been completed. Maritally contracted obligations to the dead are inscribed in a system of cosmological obligations, and withdrawal from alliance, with its rituals of exchange, poses a direct threat to the cosmic order. Cosmology impinges on social life in ritual, when maritally allied groups renew their ties to one another in the process of renewing the earth.

SIX

The Ritual Community

1. Models of Political Order

House groups are incorporated at a higher level of organization into hierarchically structured communities. Each such community is ordered around a pair of origin villages. These mark the symbolic center of the community and are henceforth designated ritual centers. Annual and periodic rites staged in ritual centers mobilize the community as a whole. Internally, the community is divided into ranked origin villages which have distinctive functions in the common cult. When the various members of the community unite at the ritual centers, they dramatically enact the ideal hierarchical order.

According to narrative traditions, ancestors of the ritual centers are the original sources of the power of rule and founders of the communities over which they now preside on ceremonial occasions. Tradition also relates that the founders relinquished political power to newcomers from outside the community. These latter became the active executives, responsible for the maintenance of jural order, while the old rulers retained ritual authority over the cosmos, or as Mambai say, "they sat down to look after rock and tree." The mythically represented succession of new rulers creates a diarchic division between active political leaders and passive ritual authorities.

As with the diarchy, so all connections to a ritual center are conceptually based on the past acts of the ancestors. Mambai regard the present order of their communities as the result of historical processes, which are acknowledged in narratives of community formation. By convention, the full account of a community's history is preserved in its ritual centers, whereas other members are thought to know only those events that directly involve their own houses. Hence ritual centers are defined as the unique custodians of the communal past. Special, encompassing knowledge reflects and in theory derives from the ideal status of founder of order, source of the power of rule that is now wielded by others. Narrative images of the distri-

98

bution of power express, at yet another level, the idea of a primordial totality and its division into parts.

The mythic origins of diarchic division mark the culmination of a protracted process. Although there is rarely consensus, even in the ritual centers, as to the precise sequencing of events, it is widely acknowledged that other houses also received titles and tokens of office from a community's founders and were thereby empowered to "rule" lesser houses. Title-holders and their subordinates comprise what Mambai now call the *reinu*, "kingdom" (from Portuguese), and recognize the dual sovereignty of ritual authorities and executive rulers.

The collectivity that unites at a ritual center is larger than the reinu, for it includes houses agnatically related to those of the center and, where appropriate, wife-giving and wife-taking houses. Mambai formally distinguish among these three forms of relatedness, using the term *kdi*, "to touch, to be in contact." Agnates attend a center's rituals as "people of one house," and their obligations are said to "touch upon elder and younger people" or "upon sacred objects." Ritual obligations of maritally allied houses "touch upon women and men," whereas those of the reinu are said to "touch upon rock and tree" or "upon the power of rule," phrases that evoke narrative traditions of succession to office. Where status relations overlap, as is often the case with alliance status and status in the reinu, Mambai discriminate between the different functions that a single house may be called on to perform in the course of a ceremony. If, for instance, the ritual authorities dispose of their dead or rebuild their cult houses, they call upon their marital allies at the same time as they convoke the reinu. Certain houses may have to participate in two roles, perhaps receiving gifts as wife-givers in one rite, and then offering their services as ritual subordinates in another.[1]

Ritual life unfolds at two levels, that of the local house cult and that of the more inclusive community. At the higher level, houses of the ritual centers are assisted by their *kaka nor ali*, who first perform their own small-scale versions of the annual agricultural rites, and then send delegates to cooperate in the common cult. In many respects, however, the status relation of a junior tip house to a senior trunk resembles that of the reinu to the ritual centers. The qualities of fixity and stability attributed to senior houses in the local cult are also attributed to ritual centers, and both statuses are associated with the regulation of agricultural and reproductive fertility. Moreover, ritual centers in the community cult are symbolically represented as "old mother/old father" to all of their dependents, irrespective of the precise definition of particular ties. In a variety of contexts described in part 2, the relationship of an encompassing house to its members is the trope for a community's dependence on its original founders and paramount ritual leaders.

It is not unlikely that the centralized and centralizing community cult developed historically out of the local cult, and that status relations between the senior and junior lines of houses provided a model for more encompassing political units. These higher-level units have the same double relationship to space that characterizes the individual house groups they encompass. In nonritual time (*ar-leta*), the community is embodied in a hierarchy of places, the deserted origin villages which are the community's ideal components. Whereas ritual functions in the local cult are verbally assigned to houses, at the level of the community cult, groups participate in the names of their origin villages. Disposed along a south-north axis, located at varying degrees of distance from the symbolic center, origin villages express the statuses of the groups that intermittently inhabit them. On ritual occasions the spatial model of hierarchy is dramatically enacted, as groups first assemble at their respective origin villages and then march in formal procession to the ritual center. The community, like the house, passes through cycles of condensation and dispersal.

To Mambai, the community is an abiding presence. Although it materializes in its ideal form solely for ritual events, its unity is symbolized by the permanence and fixity of its constituent origin villages. To outsiders, however, the significance of empty places is not readily apparent, and the ritual communities to which Mambai belong went largely unrecognized by the colonial administration.

When the Portuguese colonial authorities initiated administrative reforms in 1906 and gradually imposed a uniform system of administration throughout the province, they seem to have proceeded on the basis of a Tetum model. In some Tetum societies localized clans or *suku* occupy districts known by the same name, which are the immediate constituents of larger political units.[2] To this territorially based political hierarchy, the Portuguese added two purely administrative units, the *posto* and the *conselho*. The entire province was divided into conselhos or administrative districts, some of which were subdivided into administrative posts. The heads of both these units were appointed by the colonial government in Dili and were overwhelmingly of European or mestizo descent. Aileu, where I conducted my research, was elevated from a post to a district in 1973, and I briefly describe its internal organization.[3]

The colonial administrative system takes no account of the Mambai distinction between place of origin and place of residence. The latter determines affiliation to administratively recognized units. At the base of the administrative hierarchy, a number of residential hamlets are grouped into villages (*povoação*). Each village elects a headman (*ulun*), who represents the village to the next level of organization, the suku. A suku is composed of a set of contiguous villages, and its leader, the *chefe do suco* (Port.), is appointed by the colonial district administrator. Mambai refer to suku leaders as *Koronel* (from Portuguese) or *Liurai* (from Tetum).[4] They may also be addressed as *am suku*, "suku father" or "suku lord." The district of Aileu includes three independent suku; the remaining suku are grouped into three "kingdoms" (*reinos*, Port.), Aileun, Dai Lor, and Likidoi. Each of these higher-level units is headed by a functionary who is designated *regulo* in Portuguese, and is known as *am reku*, "kingdom father" or "kingdom lord" to Mambai. Kingdom rulers bear the Portuguese title of Dom, and they are represented in ritual speech as Liurai/Koronel.

This administrative pyramid bears little resemblance to what Mambai regard as their traditional system of rule. In effect, the colonial administration has projected a territorial model onto a system based on a genetic model. Village residents belong to different origin villages, and it is the latter affiliation that determines membership in the traditional community. The grouping of villages into suku, moreover, is a colonial innovation. Mambai speak of the suku as a "recent" thing, imposed by the Portuguese and led by chiefs whose traditional rank (the rank attributed to their houses) is in many cases incommensurate with the elevated titles that they bear as administrative functionaries.

While the "kingdom" heads are regarded by Mambai as legitimate rulers, their traditional realms are made up of origin villages, and not of suku. Mambai distinguish hierarchically ordered origin villages from the colonial administrative units by marking the former as *reinu akin*, "the kingdom of long ago," or *reinu antiku*, "the ancient kingdom." The antiquarianism is well placed, for colonial policies have undermined the coherence of the traditional community. Absent from colonial policy is any appreciation of the diarchic principle. Ritual authorities, who are the traditional counterparts of the executive rulers, go unacknowledged by the colonial administration, perceived, if they are perceived at all, as "religious" leaders. By an ironic twist that does not escape Mambai attention, the colonial government has largely ignored the very figures who claim responsibility for its presence on Timor.

It is of course possible for two systems to operate in different contexts and for different purposes. Used to balancing multiple, cross-cutting allegiances, Mambai have assimilated the colonial administrative system to traditional distinctions, and they balance two sets of demands as best they can. When suku and kingdom leaders call, one reports to one's suku meeting place "to stand before the state" and pay the annual tax; at the sound of the ceremonial drum and gong, one reports to a ritual center "to stand before rock and tree" and fulfill traditional exchange obligations. But between these two systems there is pronounced tension, and between the local representatives of the state and the representatives of rock and tree there is deep bitterness.[5]

2. Power and Authority: The Language of Opposition

Before describing the internal organization of Mambai communities, I want to take a close look at the symbolism of diarchic rule. Much of this will be familiar, for the relationship that Mambai have projected onto the colonial situation replicates the dual structure of community leadership. Categories of sovereignty are applied at two levels, to differentiate between the indigenous people and their foreign rulers, and to signify a functional opposition that is realized in institutional forms. At the level of traditional institutions, moreover, the categories recur in a range of contrasts. Ritual authorities are conceptually opposed to executive officers of varying ranks, and within the ritual plane of the system the recursion of complementary categories produces increasingly fine distinctions between aspects of ritual authority. Although these multiple contrasts are not identical in content, they are intelligible as variants of a basic dualism of sovereign functions, and not on formal grounds alone. Mambai themselves often speak as if all sovereignty were divided between two persons, whom I call the Ritual Lord and Jural Ruler. Leaving aside for the moment the complexity of the institutional situation, I want to focus on the symbolism of a single ideal relationship.

In treating an ideal prior to its institutional expressions, my interest is in the internal logic of dual categories. Diarchic symbolism provides a particularly rich field for inquiry. It is a highly elaborated subcode, contained within a wider code of oppositions that Mambai use to dichotomize forms of potency, and it needs to be understood in the context of the larger classificatory system. My specific concern in what follows is with the correspondence between cosmological and social dualisms, a correspondence that provides the basis for the hierarchical ranking of complementary opposites.[6]

The exercise of ritual authority is symbolically defined as a vigil without intervals or end. This notion is fundamental, and we have already seen how it shapes images of collective identity. What motivates the eternal vigil is an idea of a cosmos that depends on human intervention, but I focus here on the human figures who maintain cosmic balance.

Constancy is a defining attribute of the Ritual Lord. His task is one that requires unswerving devotion and renders him oblivious to temporal alternations.

Au hoda ba tad, ada ba tad	I know neither night nor day
Au usa ba tad, leola ba tad	I know neither wet nor dry
Au keo foro lelo	I *keo* over all the days that are past
Au noir sai ada.	I preserve the tradition for all the days that are to come.

Such faithfulness over time entails fixity in space. Mambai recurrently associate the Ritual Lord with the category of the inside, expressed by the house and the origin village where he is symbolically confined. In theory, the Ritual Lord does not move from the origin place. His qualities of fixity, stability, and constancy evoke the figure of the housebound woman, and the association with the female category is reinforced by the nature of his service to the community. As house members return to a house imagined in its maternal aspect, so too do the Ritual Lord's subjects come to him as children, to "nurse" at his breast, to find shelter inside his "shady and warm house."

Nor is it any ordinary woman whom he resembles. Supreme ritual authority is associated with images of blackness, darkness, and filth that evoke a founding mythological event: the ordeal of Mother Earth when she endures death and decay. The Ritual Lord represents himself as one who dwells in nocturnal darkness, who dresses in tattered clothes, and who exposes his naked body to "refuse and dust." Although he never assumes the name of the deity, he speaks of himself in terms that also connote her primeval condition.

Au kala saun-lun	I am called refuse
Au kala rai-fafon	I am called dust
Au kala hli-teten	I am called surface of the hearth
Au kala rauf-laun	I am called end of the ash

Au kala muda	I am called darkness
Au kala meta.	I am called blackness.
Au du ba kode	I go down with difficulty
Au sai ba kode.	I arise with difficulty.

But Mother Earth is not the only model for the Ritual Lord's confinement. He also likens himself to the objects of his vigil, the silent rock and the motionless tree. His most common title is "Koronel Rock and Tree," and he is often addressed by his subjects as "My Mother Rock/My Father Tree." When he emphasizes his physical incapacities, he compares his restricted condition to that of his charges. Ritual speech is laced with similes of this kind.

Au du ba kode	I go down with difficulty
Au sai ba kode	I arise with difficulty
Au mudu man hauta	I am mute like the rock
Au toru man aia.	I am motionless like the tree.

Sacred rocks and trees are ubiquitous icons in ritual performance. Speeches and invocations are addressed to them; they are the recipients of all sacrificial offerings, and their right to the first portion organizes ceremonial feasts. Before women and men may partake of a sacrifice, offerings must be consecrated to rock and tree. A defining duty of the Ritual Lord is to oversee the distribution of shares in the sacrifice, making sure that the silent mouths precede the speaking mouths. The verbs that denote this transaction are also used to describe the feeding of an infant. They mark the maternal character of the Ritual Lord and also of his sacred charges, who symbolically release the remainder of the sacrifice for human consumption.

Au hoit man hauta	I spoon food to the rock
Hoit hail ma	It is spooned back here
Au fa man aia	I hand food to the tree
Fa hail ma.	It is handed back here.

Recurrent verbal and visual identifications of the Ritual Lord with his silent elder kin lead from an association with the female to an image of the lord as the eldest, the "old mother/old father," whose passivity and constancy are more a function of age than of gender. To a people enchanted by origins, the Ritual Lord is the "old one." He is the guardian and preserver of a past that composes the base or trunk of the present order, and he himself embodies the past in the present.

Descended from the original founders of the community, devoted to the ritual duties that they received and handed down, he expresses his claim to status in idioms of seniority and age. Lord of Night, Lord of Rock and Tree, Old Mother and Old Father, he is the original, eldest authority, and his eternal vigil is the sign of the community's fidelity to its past.

Metaphorically, the Ritual Lord is to the community what the cosmos is to all humankind. His manifestly female character as dark, nurturing life-giver stands for the totality of male and female that makes life possible. But Mambai are more concerned with contiguities than with resemblances, and the Ritual Lord must create at the cosmic level the unity that he embodies at the social level. Rotating the horizontal axis that runs from inside to outside establishes a vertical axis that runs from below to above and cuts through the center of ritual space. At the center, Mambai thought places, not the solitary female, but the life-giving couple. In this model the Ritual Lord is the mediator who conjoins separate spheres. Poised between below and above, he brings complementary opposites together, a task that is expressed by the metaphor of tending to a tree:

Au fe se fu	I look down upon the trunk
Au ktar se lau	I gaze up upon the tip
Au du nor it inan	I go down with Our Mother
Au sai nor it aman.	I arise with Our Father.

Less obliquely, he calls upon "Heaven to descend/Earth to arise," and to meet at the center of space.

Opposites also meet and are combined in the Ritual Lord's nature. He symbolizes both an ancient couple (a combination of male and female that is itself sexless) and a newborn infant. This latter representation figures prominently in ritual oratory. Drawing on images of birth, performers liken themselves to babies who have just emerged from the womb:

Au sbein koho	My brow is soft
Au fusan lara	My navel is bloody
Muira her au sbein	There is oil over my brow
Lara her au matan.	There is blood over my eyes.

The metaphor of a child expresses the type of intelligence that is attributed to the Ritual Lord. In his detachment from worldly affairs he is like an ignorant child who has yet to be educated, and the same terms are used of both conditions. Says the Ritual Lord:

Au ulun hi tema	My head is still whole
Au kikan hi benu.	My ears are still full.

States of "wholeness" and "fullness" are signified by the terms *tema* and *benu* in Mambai. *Tema*, "whole, intact, entire; unopened, closed," refers to an object that has not been penetrated in any way, something from which no part has been removed or extracted. Foot, calf, and thigh form the "whole limb" (*fa tema*); the full moon, a task not yet begun, an unopened container with all its contents are also described as *tema*. *Benu*, "full, filled up, overflowing," signifies a quantity that can be reduced but not decomposed into parts. Thus *benu* can be used of a container filled to the brim, a raging sea, a river that floods its banks.

Predicated of organs of perception—eyes, ears, heart, head—*tema* and *benu* are metaphors for psychological states. The focus is on the relationship between the person and the outside world. Wholeness and fullness connote a state of closure, a turning inward, an imperviousness to external influences. Such states have multiple values. Thus *tema* is opposed to that which is broken up or fragmented (*rahu*), and also to that which is hollow (*koa*). A child is ignorant because its "heart is still whole, not yet in pieces" (*huan hi tema, ba rahu hei*); knowledge of sexuality makes women and men "hollow," and the phrase *matan tema*, "unopened eyes," has the double sense of virginal and stupid. *Benu*, predicated of both the head and the ears, connotes a person who is filled up from within and cannot receive messages or stimuli from the outside.

These usages are integral to the cultural meaning of the ritual function. With his "whole head/full ears," the Ritual Lord is impervious to worldly concerns, existing in a kind of stupor that is positively valued. He is stupid and ignorant with respect to the outside world, where he defers to other authorities, but he is imbued, filled to the brim, as it were, with knowledge of another sort, embodied in the instructions handed down by the ancestors.

The ancestors, however, are dead and gone. Only their teachings remain as traces. These Mambai liken to a trail that leads backward in time, and the Ritual Lord "follows the grass track/retraces the footsteps" (*tuir ni kneora/dad ni oe haita*) left behind by the ancestors. Mother and father of his community, he represents himself as an orphan who continually calls out to his cosmological parents. But if they indeed hear him and respond, the only sign is the fertility of the earth.

Au in her lelo dun au ba eot	I see not my Mother in the west
Au ama her lelo sain au ba tad	I know not my Father in the east
O hunan fe au	Your orphan am I
O lakon fe au.	Your lost one am I.

In this the Ritual Lord symbolizes the human condition. The deep and mournful theme of Mambai cosmological thought is that all women and men are orphans, their Mother hidden somewhere beneath the earth, or enclosed in the "House of the Dark Rock," their Father wandering somewhere above on the "outside and edge." Year in and year out, the "orphans" gather to *keo* before a rock and tree, in answer to the Ritual Lord's summons. His task, reduced to its structural outlines, is to bring together what has been separated.

The Jural Ruler is his counterpart in all respects. In contrast to "Koronel Night," who sits in darkness, the Jural Ruler is "Koronel Day," whose rule sheds light over the land. He is also known as the "beaming moon/shining day" (*hula tbiar/nama ada*), and as the "child of the star/child of the sun" (*hiut-anan/leol-ana*). In another metaphor, he is associated with a tall shade tree that rims and shelters the realm, as the vault of heaven rims and shelters the world.

The Jural Ruler resembles Heaven in function as well as imagery. As the active, vigilant, male sentinel of the outside, he reproduces Heaven's regulatory function at the level of the community. Thus he defends the outermost boundaries of space, and one of his symbolic roles is to "tred back the sea so that the water may not overflow and the sea may not rise up." By nature he is alert, perceptive, open to the world, observant of everything that passes within his realm. In formal contexts he is addressed as "he who has the nose of a dog/he who has the eyes of a cock" (*ua fe inun ausa/ua fe matan mauna*), a metaphor based on the acute senses attributed to the animal guardians of the thresholds of the house. Particular emphasis is placed on his fleetness and mobility. His vigil requires perpetual motion, and his portion of ritual sacrifices is the leg, "so that he may walk."

By tradition his ancestors come from outside of the realm and take over responsibility for maintaining order in the community. The original rulers bestow upon him the "flag and marching drum," as token of his "heavy rule/weighty ban." In contrast to the silent rock and tree retained by the Ritual Lord, these tokens speak out to the realm and elicit the outward signs of respect for authority. The Jural Ruler's subjects "tremble and [show] fear" in his presence, and when they quarrel, they submit their disputes to him for judgment. The activity that is paradigmatic of his function is that of a lawgiver. His primary responsibility is to "place justice" (fois sustisa, from Port. justiça), an expression that evokes his ritual counterpart who "places rocks" (fois hauta), that is, lays out offerings. Another expression for settling arguments is "to cut words," and the Jural Ruler is the great divider. Reduced to its structural outlines, his function is to separate terms that are inauspiciously joined: the sea and the land, the opponents in a confrontation, the tangled words of a dispute.

At one pole of the diarchic opposition, a dark, silent, life-giving authority is embodied in a figure associated with both femaleness and age. Immobile, restricted, dull, the Ritual Lord withdraws from the world of motion and change to devote himself to an eternal vigil over rock and tree. At the other pole is the bright, assertive power of an active, mobile, male newcomer. The sphere of the Jural Ruler is the outside world, a world of fluid boundaries and shifting relations, of conjunctions, boundaries, transgressions, and separations.

A relational similarity between two complementary oppositions is clearly apparent. The opposition between the Ritual Lord and the Jural Ruler is analogous to the cosmological opposition between Mother Earth and Father Heaven, and this analogy is supported by a number of direct resemblances.[7] The female deity, who vitalizes and stabilizes the cosmos, seems to be closely associated with the Ritual Lord, while Father Heaven, who upholds the order of the cosmos, shares common attributes and functions with the Jural Ruler. Mambai, however, do not make these particular comparisons, nor do they explicitly articulate the analogy. In certain contexts, however, they represent the division of sovereign functions as a contrast between female and male.

I would hazard a general statement with regard to the use of gender categories to express political statuses. Mambai seem to emphasize the sexual contrast when they wish to stress the jural or political inferiority of the Ritual Lord. When ritual authorities emphasize their unfitness for active political life, or when they affirm their subordination to the temporal power of jural figures, then they will say that they are "like women who sit in the house" and equate their "stupidity" with that of a housebound woman. The metaphor is drawn from the routines of domestic life where, according to Mambai men, "the man rules the woman." But significantly, in my view, Mambai do not asso-

108

ciate the diarchic opposition with any specific form of male/female relationship. The two sovereigns are not represented as sister and brother or mother and father, nor is there a tradition of affinal alliance between their respective houses. The deities, in contrast, are both sibling and spouse to each other, and their union is the source of life.

When emphasis falls on the spiritual superiority of the Ritual Lord, then Mambai seem to veer away from sexual symbolism and they represent the ritual function in terms of seniority and age. Jural figures pay homage to ritual authorities by addressing them as "old mother and old father," and any ritual performance creates, through multiple registers, a powerful image of the Old One, who reunites male and female. As the eldest, the Ritual Lord represents the cosmic totality, in opposition to the Jural Ruler who stands for but one part of the whole.

If we begin at the cosmic level, we arrive at similar conclusions. Father Heaven has a complex personality. As the founder of cosmic order, he institutes a moral law that regulates the universe. As the consort of Mother Earth, he is the potent genitor who also gives form to the soil. In cosmological symbolism the regulatory function is a metaphorization of male procreative power, and the vehicle as well as the tenor are attributes of the deity. In diarchic symbolism the regulatory function that identifies the Jural Ruler with Father Heaven is relatively detached from the root metaphor of genital potency. The ideal maleness of the human lawgiver is imagined in a sublimated form, and it is encompassed by the life-giving function of the Ritual Lord who conjoins male and female.

Any diarchic structure has what Dumont calls a "double aspect" (1970b, 65). It is constituted by the combination of spiritual superiority/temporal inferiority with temporal superiority/spiritual inferiority, and also by the ranking of these two aspects of the relationship. That is, a hierarchical principle also determines "in an absolute fashion" the relationship between spiritual status and temporal power. In Mambai conceptions, as in the lofty theory that Dumont extracts from the Brahmanas, spiritual status has an absolute value. The relation of the spiritual to the temporal is, in Dumont's concise phrase, one of "mutual but asymmetric dependency."[8]

The culturally specific principle of hierarchy is articulated in the mythology of rule, "the walk of rule and ban," as Mambai call it. Without reviewing the mythological foundations of order in any detail, let us recall that order has its ultimate source in Father Heaven's primordial "ban of the interior." Political or temporal power, identified with the "ban of the sea," appears as a part that is split off from the original, undivided, and encompassing whole. When the ancestors later set off on their quest overseas, they acquire what is in effect a part of the part, and it is this power, embodied in regalia of office, that they eventually surrender to newcomers from the outside. As donors of power tokens, the original lords legitimize their successors. Henceforth, the newcomers preserve the order of the human community, whereas the old lords retain the ritual function of upholding the encompassing order of the cosmos, and so participate in the exercise of the original "ban of the interior." These relatively involuted representations of sovereignty are based on the same temporalized structure that we isolated with regard to the house. Like the eldest line of a house, the Ritual Lord is the hierarchically superior part that stands for the original whole.

3. The Organization of the Community: The Jural Plane

In the Portuguese administrative system, Aileun is the name of one "kingdom" within the administrative district now known by the same name. I write the latter as "Aileu." The kingdom of Aileun is administratively divided into three sukus, Seloi, Liurai, and Haut Bos. Each suku has a chief, the *chefe do suco*, who is subordinated to the ruler or *regulo* of Aileun.[9] But in the eyes of the local population, power and authority are also distributed among origin villages now contained within the administrative unit. Aileun itself is one such origin village, located within what is now suku Liurai. This same suku also contains a pair of origin villages called Hohul and Raimaus. Within suku Haut Bos is another pair, Er Hetu and Kai Kas. Each of these pairs composes what I call a "ritual center" and is responsible for communitywide ritual events. All four of these origin villages acknowledge Aileun as the Liurai/Koronel, or what I have called the Jural Ruler. In this model, Aileun is the political pivot between two paired centers of ritual authority.

"Aileun," Mambai often say, "is not in Aileu [that is, not in the seat or vila of the administrative district]. It is in Bandeira Fun." This name means "base of the flag" and it designates the administrative meeting place for suku Liurai. Just outside of Bandeira Fun is the origin village of Aileun. The name means "twisted tree," an allusion to a withered tree located in the village which has deformed branches that grow inward toward the trunk. The tree is sacred to village members, who say that it represents the folded arms and chest of the village founder, one Dom Bau Meta; a round rock that resides in the village cult house is identified as this same Bau Meta's head. The cult house itself is symbolically divided between two groups named Mau Leu (literally, "twisted fellow") and Bar Tai. The former group is traced back to Bau Meta, and it has no living representatives. The cult house is tended by members of Bar Tai, to which the present ruler of Aileun belongs.

A man from Bar Tai gave me one account of the origins of his house.[10] He identified the ancestors of Bar Tai as the two youngest of seven brothers. Six of these brothers left the eldest behind in a distant origin place and wandered off in pairs "to search for gardens and palms." The four eldest of these arrived in the valley of Seloi, where they scattered to found their own individual houses. The last two, Mau Hutu and Mau Rai, came to Aileun and encountered Dom Bau Meta. At that time Bau Meta was the ruler (Koronel) of Aileun and, according to a widely disseminated prose tradition, he had precedence over his traditional rival, the coastal ruler of Motain.[11]

Having no sons, Bau Meta "seized" the two strangers, or in other words, he gave them his daughters in marriage and persuaded them to reside "with the wife's father." He also relinquished to them the office and title of Koronel. After Bau Meta died, the elder son-in-law took charge of his wife-giver's cult, accepting the "spoon and plate" (*snura nor bika*) used to make offerings to the ancestral rock and tree. Mau Rai, the youngest of the original seven, "carried [the office of] Koronel" (*oid Koronel*).

Strictly, the title Liurai/Koronel belongs solely to Bar Tai, but all of the migrant ancestors are classified as "Koronel ni tatan," ancestors of the Koronel. The houses founded in Seloi by Mau Rai's elder brothers are collectively designated "Koronel Seloi." Each of these houses is ranked below Bar Tai, as Maior or Kafitan, yet Mambai also say that the houses are "alike" or "identical" (*hanesa*), and should circumstances require, any one of them might legitimately "carry the office of Koronel." Thus status adheres to titles which, in theory, circulate among agnatically related houses.

Only the head of Bar Tai is addressed as "Dom" or "Am Reku," and he is formally responsible for the maintenance of order throughout his territory. From time to time he makes official visits to outlying villages, but he is not precisely the eternal sentinel of symbolic representations. He maintains a local police force (*folisi*, Port.) to patrol the kingdom and report to him on his subjects. One of the functions of the police is to protect the "kingdom horses" (*kud-reino*). These horses belong to the Dom and are kept at his disposal, to be used by him and by colonial administrators who tour the kingdom. The police are also empowered to seize wrongdoers and bring them before the Dom for judgment. Disputes, usually related to theft or adultery, are also brought to the Dom by the disputants themselves.

In practice, many of the duties formally assigned to the Dom are distributed among those above and below him in the colonial administrative hierarchy. Above is the colonial administrator of Aileu (the district), to whom all local leaders report for weekly consultations, and who in theory arbitrates serious local grievances. Below are the suku chiefs who are responsible for the maintenance of order within their own subterritories, although the Dom is empowered to intervene in suku affairs. The formal administrative hierarchy materializes in the enforcement of colonial directives. For instance, if the administrator of Aileu requires the populace to assemble for an official function, such as the yearly census, the order passes from him to the rulers, to the suku chiefs, who instruct the village heads to alert the villagers.

Other calls to assembly move in a different direction, summoning the rulers of Aileun into the presence of the Old Koronels, the lords of rock and tree. A representative from Aileun (the actual Dom's elder brother in cases that I witnessed) attends major ritual events in the four ritual centers and formally enacts the ideal diarchic relationship.

4. The Distribution of Ritual Authority

Each of the four ritual centers contains a set of named cult houses. The total number of these houses varies from one village to another, but each village includes one house that is classified as the "Old House" (Fad-Main) and is associated with Mother Earth. The Old House is the "mother house" of a ritual center. Those affiliated to it trace descent to the original village founder and they compose the leading descent group of the village. Strictly speaking, their house alone bears the title of "Koronel." In the ideal, the master of the Old House presides over ritual events. This is the case in Hohul, where the master is a very old man, to whom special ritual knowledge is widely attributed, and whose name and figure evoke to Mambai the village as a whole. In Raimaus, however, the head of the Old House surrendered his public ritual responsibilities a generation ago to the head of a lesser, "younger" house. Sons of this latter man continue to officiate at ritual performances, although they defer to the "old master" of Hohul.[12]

Whereas the title of "Dom" or "Am Reku" always adheres to a particular person from the ruling house of Bar Tai, there is no unique embodiment of ritual authority. Moreover, while supreme ritual authority resides in theory in the Old House, the situation is fluid in practice. Particular ritual roles and responsibilities are formally assigned to specific houses, but, as the Raimaus case indicates, there is considerable flexibility regarding their actual distribution at any one moment. Thus the superior status of the Old House may be enacted by men who in fact belong to a younger, agnatically related house.

We must also distinguish between publicly and privately performed ritual roles. By "public roles," I intend the duties discharged by those whom Mambai call *kuka*. The word, derived from *kuku*, "mouth," foregrounds the verbal aspect of the role, and this is the unmarked sense. However, it applies to men who officiate at ritual performances in various capacities. I translate *kuka* as "priest."[13] Mambai distinguish different kinds of priests according to the particular activities that they perform. *Kuk-kdein*, "sitting priests," are those who sit to prepare the offerings, as opposed to those who stand to make invocations and to present the offerings. "Standing priests" identify themselves with ritual authority in formal discourse and momentarily assume the role of Ritual Lord. However, various individuals will enact this same role in the course of any one performance.

"Private" ritual roles are discharged by the "masters" of the village cult houses, who may or may not be priests as well. These persons observe a number of special prohibitions associated with their houses and they receive special portions of the sacrifices. Unless they are also priests, such persons remain in the background of ritual performances.[14]

The position of house master is transmitted from father to eldest son, and Mambai regard it as inalienable. In the case mentioned previously, for instance, the old head's son became house master even though public roles had passed to another house. There is also a tendency for sons of priests to follow their fathers and become priests themselves, but this is not obligatory. Mambai speak of priesthood as a vocation that is open to all male members of a ritual center.[15]

What needs emphasis is that ritual authority is not circumscribed by public or private offices. It is paradigmatically embodied in houses and origin villages, rather than in offices to which individuals may lay claim. The language of authority is singular, and officiating priests represent themselves as what I have called the Ritual Lord, a person charged with mystical power over the cosmos. But Mambai seem to think of the village itself as the "person" designated, and ritual status is shared by all village members. Typically, if an individual wants to associate himself with the ritual function, he neither claims a particular office nor invokes his house, but rather identifies himself with the origin village as a whole and says, "I am Raimaus" (*au Raimaus*), or "I am called Hohul" (*au kala Hohul*). Divided into ranked houses when viewed from within, the village of origins unites to confront the outside world, and all of its members represent themselves as "masters of the house/masters of the origin village" (*fad-ubun/ri-ubun*).

These confrontations take place at collective ceremonies that activate three types of relationship to a ritual center. Houses that claim agnatic relations with any of the center's houses participate as *kaka nor ali*. I discuss these agnatic connections in later chapters on ritual performance. Other relationships to a center are traced back to particular mythical events that give rise to two types of ritual subordinates, Dat Raia and reinu. The former are represented as the domestic servants of a ritual center; the latter compose its realm.

Dat Raia (from Tetum *dato*, "lord") may be translated approximately as "custodians of the soil." The title belongs to certain origin villages located at the periphery of a ritual center. The ancestors of these places are represented as the original inhabitants of the land, who receive the founder of the ritual center. In all cases that I recorded, Dat Raia are also wife-givers to the Ritual Lord.[16] But their stressed role is "to show the land" (*kok raia*), that is, to direct the lord to the place where he will settle. Dat Raia clear the ground for him, and when he is ready to erect his house they send carpenters to carve the house pillars.

Ritually, they retain these functions. Dat Raia are responsible for the maintenance of the ritual center. Should a branch fall from one of the village's sacred banyans, only a Dat Raia may remove it.[17] When the members of the ritual center rebuild one of their cult houses, Dat Raia attend to clear the ground and to supervise the construction, and only Dat Raia carpenters may handle the ceremonial tools. At all *keo* ceremonies, Dat Raia are responsible for cooking the sacrificial meat. They are most commonly addressed as *kosineiru*, "cook" (from Port. *cosinheiro*).

Each of the four ritual centers also presides over a cluster of outlying origin villages which compose what Mambai call a "kingdom of long ago" (*reinu akin*). The "kingdoms" of Hohul and Raimaus and of Er Hetu and Kai Kas overlap, so that certain origin villages participate in ceremonies held by both members of one or the other pair. Symbolically, the division between Dat Raia and the kingdom is a division between inside (*lalan*) and outside (*hohon*). As domestic servants Dat Raia look after the inner realm of ritual space, while the heads of the kingdom patrol the outer territories. In this model the community composes a series of concentric rings oriented around a ritual center.

Narrative traditions preserved in each of the four ritual centers trace the formation of a kingdom to the distribution of sacred staffs of office by the ancestors. These staffs or sceptres are known as *uaia*. Each one has its own name, and they are said to have been given to the ancestors by the Malaia. Their new recipients, the heads of outlying origin villages, are ranked and paired as *Alferes* and *Kafitan* (from Portuguese). Upon receiving the emblems and titles of office, the Alferes and Kafitan establish control over other origin villages, which are said to acknowledge their authority because "they fear the sacred objects" (*ro tmau saun-lulin*).

The staff-bearers are at once authorities who "rule and observe the kingdom and the domain" (*uku nor blei reinu nor tahek*) and sentinels who serve the ritual centers from whence their authority originally emanates. In one cosmogonic tradition their ancestors are birds, who relay messages between ancestors remaining on the mountain and a vanguard party that goes ahead to found new villages below. In a common ritual formula, the Alferes and Kafitan "tend to the road and the bridge," the passageways connecting separate points. In space they represent movement and transition. Their role is to mediate between the ritual center and its kingdom, and they convoke the villages under their authority in the name of the ritual center:

Ro fe deiki luron	It is they who look after the road
Ro fe bale dambata	It is they who watch over the bridge
Ro fe inu-ausa	It is they who are dog-nosed
Ro fe mata-mauna	It is they who are cock-eyed
Inan kau, ro fe flik	[When] the Mother calls, it is they who hear
Aman kau, ro fe tad	[When] the Father calls, it is they who know
Oid ma konta	To come and account
Oid ma farti.	To come and report.

The titles of Alferes and Kafitan are held by individuals who enact the mediating role on ritual occasions—when members of the ritual centers perform the yearly agricultural rites, when they dispose of their dead, or when they rebuild their cult houses. In the past, Mambai say, these same two officers performed another, critical function: they supervised the collection of harvest gifts and presented them to the ritual centers. This tribute system no longer operates (a point of considerable importance, to which I return shortly), but traces of it are preserved. When the Alferes and the Kafitan lead the kingdom in a grand procession, to assist in whatever ritual event is underway in the center, they bear with them the gift items that ritual authorities traditionally received from jural rulers.

It is possible to describe the relation of the Alferes and Kafitan to the ritual center as an instance of diarchy, for it includes several features characteristic of the Mambai pattern. Ritual authorities are defined in narrative models as the donors of tokens of office, and their relationship to the recipients is based on familiar oppositions between inside and outside, immobile and mobile. But the office assigned to the Alferes and the Kafitan has no jural content. These officers are not represented as lawgivers, and they have no special duties or prerogatives in daily life. Their role is limited to ceremonial contexts, where they serve as the messenger or herald who establishes contact between the parties in an exchange. The asymmetric complementarity of ritual and jural functions, however, is realized inside of the ritual centers.

5. The Dualism of Ritual Centers

Mambai communities are characterized by the linking of ritual centers in pairs. Each member in a pair is defined in relation to the other, and a principle of recursivity generates additional dichotomies at various levels. According to context, Mambai may either emphasize the divisions internal to a center or, alternately, merge the differentiated parts into a unified whole. In the former case the recurrent application of dual categories projects onto ritual space what Mambai regard as the temporal order of sovereign functions.

The formal relationship between Hohul and Raimaus is one variant of a temporalized structure, with certain unique features of content that reflect distinctive origin traditions. The categories of elder and younger differentiate houses in Raimaus from others in Hohul and serve as a trope for the tie between the two origin villages. It is common for Mambai to designate the villages as "elder man Raimaus/younger man Hohul." Narrative traditions present the pattern of house division in its strong form. There are frequent allusions in ritual speech to one Nun Loko of the house Nunu Fun in Raimaus and his younger brother Mau Loko, who fled to Hohul with the patrimonial *saun-hot-hot/ber-ber* and founded the house called Haih Nua. A chanter has only to call out "Nun Loko, Nunu Fun/Mau Loko, Haih

Nua" for Mambai to be reminded of the relative emptiness of Raimaus, which was left "with only rock and tree." Another narrative tradition that also enters ritual oratory links the relative fullness of Hohul
to the acquisition of "rule and ban" from overseas. Raimaus's status
as the unmarked term is evident in these narrative schemes. The elder village is defined by its lack of qualities that are added to the
younger Hohul. To Mambai, this is a contrast between silence and
voice, the mute and the articulate. As the eldest, Raimaus connotes a
primordial silent authority, derived from the "ban of the interior" and
associated with rock and tree. Hohul is marked in contrast as the
possessor of power tokens that inspire sacred terror, tokens that
speak out to the beholders and compellingly assert the status of the
possessor. The same mythical opposition is condensed and conveyed in the paired names of two sacred banyan trees, Tai Talo in
Raimaus, tree "of women and men," and Loer Hoha in Hohul, tree "of
rule and ban." While the distinction is awkward to phrase, it is
roughly between an older, relatively passive power of increase that
emanates from the southern interior and a younger, relatively active
language of command that is recovered from the sea.

The categories of elder and younger recur with a somewhat different meaning in the system of relations that defines the component
houses of each origin village. At the symbolic center of each village is
a pair of houses differentiated as male and female and associated
with Father Heaven and Mother Earth. Together they form a complementary whole, and they are opposed to a third house which they
encompass. The third is symbolically male and has the status of the
youngest. In formal speech it is represented as "house of the beaming moon/house of the shining day," or "house of rule and ban." In
ordinary speech it is colloquially designated *fad-loban*, "little" or "junior" house. Its junior status is also marked by temporal categories,
and Mambai often contrast the two older houses, which "appeared in
the Night," to the younger house, which was founded in the Day.

In Raimaus, where the Old House of the Mother is named Nunu
Fun (Base of the Banyan) and the Father's house is Fad Fusun (Center
House), the younger house is named Mau Nunun (Banyan Fellow).
The Father's house in Hohul is called Ba Boe (Sleep Not), and the
Mother's house, Haih Nua (Pig's Lair), is symbolically divided into
two houses. The junior side is called Dil Bauk (a name that I cannot
translate), and it represents the third term in the scheme, equivalent
to Mau Nunun in Raimaus. Hohul people tend to be somewhat vague
as to the precise relationship of the Mother's house to Dil Bauk, but
Nunu Fun and Mau Nunun are consistently classified as elder and

younger men. There are various accounts of their precise genealogical connection. In one version that I recorded, Mau Nunun is founded by descendants of Nunu Fun, who return to their origin place after generations of wandering on the outside.[18] My assistant Mau Bere, who is from Dil Bauk, gave a similar account of his house's origins. Other members of Hohul say that Haih Nua and Dil Bauk were originally wife-giver and wife-taker, but now "look on each other as elder and younger people" and no longer intermarry.

What Mambai agree on is the relative status of these houses. Both Mau Nunun and Dil Bauk bear the title of Maior, while the Mother's house is ranked as Koronel. Symbolically, junior houses are the active, younger, male executives of ritual centers, and they represent the center to the outside world. They are identified in narrative models as the original repositories of power tokens that were later given away to others. The past is commemorated on formal occasions. Visiting rulers from Aileun are ceremonially received in Mau Nunun and Dil Bauk. The metonymy "grass mat and pandanus mat" characterizes the junior houses as the place where the rulers rest and refresh themselves before proceeding to the houses of the Mother and the Father. In the following allusion to Mau Nunun, the junior house is represented as the waiting room where the rulers may put aside their traveling gear:

Kud-kusin ni leu-hatin	Place to put away the saddle
Raisa ni sak-hatin	Place to hang up the bridle
Oid liuf kena	To fold the loincloth
Oid liuf mala	To fold the cloak
Kena be tita	So that the loincloth may not be wet
Mala be broe	So that the cloak may not be rotten
Oid rei sikoti	To hang up the whip
Oid rei uai-mauna	To hang up the cock-staff
Oid kof mima hail	To clasp the hands again
Oid dad oe hail	To stretch the feet again
Oid tut-ulu man o inan	To bow the head to your Mother
Oid tah bei man o aman.	To pay respect to your Father.

The names Er Hetu/Kai Kas are used as a shorthand to designate four origin villages organized into a structurally similar system. By tradition Er Hetu is the first and eldest of the four, and Er Hetu ancestors receive tokens of "rule and ban" from the Malaia. Soon afterward, the Old House of Er Hetu is divided by two younger brothers, who transfer the tokens to an origin village named Ai Leta. Er Hetu is now left "with only rock and tree," and the tokens of rule are kept "on the outside." In the next generation, these tokens are transferred once more, to a village called Ai Roma. When a man from Kai Kas resides uxorilocally at Ai Roma, he becomes the guardian of the tokens of rule that first went out from Er Hetu. The relationship of Er Hetu to Kai Kas replicates at another level the relationship of the female Old Houses to the junior houses in Hohul and Raimaus. Ranked as Maior, Kai Kas pivots between the older Er Hetu and the younger rulers of Aileun, to whom it now stands as "grass mat and pandanus mat."

Whether encoded in systematic relations of houses or of origin villages, a scheme of oppositions divides the ritual plane into complementary but unequal components. At the inner pole of the center are the passive "old mother/old father," the manifestations of the ritual function in its unmarked, encompassing form. At the outer pole, mediating between the inside and the outside, are the younger, active, male executives who ritually represent the center to the present holders of power. The political implications of this scheme cannot be overemphasized. Mythically structured space asserts the status of original founder of order, a status to which all ritual centers lay claim. The meaningful order of synchronically related places projects the past onto the present, evoking an earlier state of things, a time when the founding authorities kept their executives close by their sides, and when the now empty waiting rooms were filled with power tokens that the ancestors had acquired from the Malaia. System expresses history and keeps history alive.

Previously, I noted that the ruling house of Bar Tai claims to have succeeded to the political office vested in the now extinct line of Dom Bau Meta. But it is also acknowledged in Bar Tai that this Bau Meta was himself a newcomer and that, in a more remote past, power belonged to the lords of rock and tree. Members of Bar Tai do not claim to know how these ancient figures lost or renounced the power of rule. Nor, for that matter, is there any consensus among or even within the ritual centers. In Hohul and Raimaus, in Er Hetu and Kai Kas, traditions are preserved of how power passed from their ancestors to Bau Meta's house, Mau Leu. Strictly speaking, of course, these claims are inconsistent, but they do not ordinarily come into direct contact. When they did, in my own experience, Mambai saw no inconsistency, regarding it as perfectly plausible that the same Bau Meta might have acceded to office twice, under different circumstances.

Events relating to the transmission of rule are encoded in narratives categorized as the "walk of the Koronel" (*Koronel ni lolain*) or the "walk of rule" (*ukun ni lolain*). Mambai professed a marked willingness to recount and discuss these narratives, which contrasted sharply to their ambivalent reluctance to relate the earlier "walk of the earth." Their readiness to tell the story of rule was accompanied by (or perhaps generated) a relatively high degree of variation. The particular circumstances under which an original lord was said to "surrender the rule" often seemed a matter for speculation. Narrative performances had an almost improvisational character, and rarely did everyone present at any one sitting agree on all the details. In various performances that I witnessed, the following accounts were given: an original ruler is tricked in a series of contests where the stake is political power; he marries incestuously and thereby renders himself unfit to rule; the young pretender spies on him, and he abdicates out of "shame" (*moe*); or, in what I found to be the most persistent motif, the original lord grows so old and weary that he "no longer wants to rule," so he "sits down to look after rock and tree."

Mambai would sometimes remark on such variations (especially if I prompted them to do so), but without evincing much concern. Yes, the conflicting details were no doubt puzzling, but they were of no great importance. "Each one has his own words," as Mambai say, and it is the way of words to "twist about." Yet I have seen men leave a room in silent rage rather than listen to what they deemed an inaccurate account of earth origins. With regard to the transmission of rule, however, it seemed to me that what was important to Mambai was not how the event had come about, but rather the idea that it had somehow occurred.

If Mambai do not worry over the precise content of these traditions, the temporal patterning of sovereign status injects a sense of disquiet into political life. The ideal relationship between the ritual centers and Aileun is one of complementarity and cooperation. Yet oral traditions, transmitted in tales and daily rumors, convey a bitter, nagging theme of conflict and rivalry. At the root of the conflict is an ancient privilege of the ritual centers.

6. The Tribute System

The "kingdom of long ago" is well named by Mambai, for what they identify as its primary function is no longer discharged. "In former times," Mambai say, the origin villages under the authority of a ritual center were required to present harvest gifts to the center, in exchange for the ritually secured well-being of their crops. Although the villages of the kingdom also owed other forms of ritual service, my informants regularly identified this tributary relationship as the referent of the assertion that a ritual center "rules" (*uku*) its ritual dependents. "What they rule is only the sacks," I was told; in other words, ritual centers once presided over the collection of harvest gifts.

Harvest tribute is known to Mambai by the rubric *hiura nor kaula*, "wax and sack." *Kaula* denotes the great bags that are used in transporting rice and corn after the harvest. *Hiura* is the term for wax and also refers to native-made candles. Apparently wax was one of the traditional tribute items, although I am not completely clear on this point.

In 1903 the Portuguese colonial administration abolished the indigenous systems of tribute in kind and substituted a cash head-tax levied on all adult males. Each year the entire population of an administrative district is required to gather in their suku meeting places for purposes of census-taking and taxation, a fact that accounts for much of the hostility that Mambai feel toward the suku. Whereas the tribute system was given meaning by a traditional ideology of reciprocity, the cash tax has no such legitimacy and it is widely resented by the local population.

Tribute has its own mythology, based in the ideal reciprocity between silent and speaking mouths. Mambai often allude to the mythology of tribute. The story begins with the sudden apparition of Father Heaven inside the Lone House, on the top of the mountain. Some of Heaven's children fled in fear of his gleaming presence. Those who squirmed through cracks in the floor and the walls became the vermin of the earth and the birds of the air. They are silent mouths, but they too are our brothers. After a while, these creatures grew hungry and they went weeping to Father Heaven. He told them to seek help from their younger, speaking kin, and he authorized them to ravage the gardens should humankind refuse to help them in their distress. Upon learning of the plight of the birds and mice, the Timorese and the Malaia agreed to institute the tribute system ("to make the wax and the sack"), so that their hungry, silent kin might share in the harvest. The task of distributing harvest gifts devolved upon the "dog-nosed/cock-eyed" lord of Motain, who could detect the nests of the vermin and see to it that they received their portion.

What Mambai now describe as their traditional tribute system has its historical referent in a local variant of an administrative system by which tribute in agricultural produce was delivered to the Portuguese in Dili. I alluded to the mythological model of this system in the context of the mythology of the flag. The model appears to be the product of an adjustment between a colonial system of administrative control that dates back to the late eighteenth century and an older model of precolonial exchange relations that linked rulers on the coast to those in the interior.[19]

The version of the model presented in chapter 3 relates to the exchanges governed by Hohul and Raimaus, and the same basic model orders the relation of Er Hetu and Kai Kas to their realm. In each case, the system of exchanges unfolds on a south-north axis. The flow of harvest gifts begins in the outlying origin villages under the authority of the Alferes and the Kafitan. These officers deliver the gifts to their ritual centers, where a great celebration is held. Next, the active executives of the centers are said to transport the harvest gifts to Aileun. As the pivot between two pairs of ritual centers, Aileun receives gifts from both pairs and is entitled to extract a share of the revenues. Then the fleet, mobile rulers of Aileun, those who "go down to the sea/go up to the interior," deliver the amassed tribute to Motain on the coast. Motain also extracts a share, sees to the birds and the mice, and presents the remainder to the Malaia in Dili. After this the counterprestations begin. Motain reciprocates with prestations of rice, salt, lime, wax, and livestock, to be delivered by Aileun to the old lords of rock and tree in the interior.

The total system of exchanges is seen by ritual authorities as an index of their status. As the ultimate sources of the bountiful harvest, it is they who make exchange possible, and the final countergifts are interpreted as an enactment of the hierarchical ideal. At all major ritual events the Alferes and the Kafitan now present a symbolic tribute known as *isi Liurai/telo Koronel*, "Liurai flesh/Koronel egg." This consists of a palanquin laden with the gift items traditionally sent by Motain. Yet such ritual survivals do not conceal from Mambai that the tribute system has lost its total organizational form. The abolition of the "wax and sack" is a recurrent theme of Mambai discourse and assumes mournful and sinister overtones.

Mambai do not blame the Malaia for the abolition of tribute. Instead, they accuse the rulers of Aileun. In all four of the ritual centers, I was told repeatedly that Aileun had somehow tricked both the Malaia and Motain into substituting the head-tax. Many informants suggested that the Aileun rulers found it easier to expropriate cash than agricultural produce. But now the mice and the birds go hungry and they ravage the fields and gardens, so that the harvest is diminished and men too suffer.

I repeat here a section from a long poem recited by a young priest of Kai Kas. He had come to see me on the eve of my departure from Kai Kas. He looked unhappy and nervous. He said that there were a few words yet, the words he had received, he did not know if they were true or not, but he wanted them to "enter the book." The speech he recited alluded to the institution and abolition of the "wax and sack." This is the closing passage:

Bui id fe neo	It was one woman who deceived
Maua id fe dobo	It was one man who tricked
Oid koil-hula au oid klai ia	That here I search for the seed basket
Oid koil-baka au oid klai ia	That here I search for the seed carrier
Muan oid ba nei	That there is no food
Enun oid ba nei	That there is no drink
Hutan oid ba nei	That there is no clothing
Fitan oid ba nei	That there is no covering
Au oid kala hli-teten	That I am called hearth-top
Au oid kala rauf-laun	That I am called ash-tip;
Au keor man mauna	I crow like a cock
Au foru man ausa.	I bark like a dog.
Tul-li ni Hiur Kait Mau	Pull down on the wax called Kait Mau
Fali nor Ai Ber Bonu.	Hold with the tree called Ber Bonu.
Hiura oid hu	The wax is lifted away
Aia oid lako	The tree is lost
Au oid fein ni hoda	So that I attend throughout the night
Au oid knan ni ada.	So that I wait through the day.
Au in her lelo dun au ba eot	I see not my Mother in the west
Au ama her lelo sain au ba tad,	I know not my Father in the east,
Au fe kiak tus-tus	Though truly I am poor
Mleuk, au ba mleuk	Forget, I do not forget
Au fe dere tus-tus	Though truly I am stricken
Sau, au ba sau.	Release, I do not release.[20]

The issue of the tribute system is also said to concern those responsible for its abolition. Less than twenty years ago, an Aileun ruler accused an individual affiliated to Raimaus of attempting to "grab the lordship" (*hau Koronel*) by reinstating the old tribute system. It is commonly believed in the ritual centers that the present Dom and the suku chiefs still harbor such suspicions.[21] Ritual performances in both Raimaus and Hohul are laced with emotional insistences on the ritual leaders' lack of interest in wordly affairs. But at the same time members of these origin villages speak bitterly of the lost prerogatives to which the very space that they inhabit silently attests.

Dramatic legends, told in the conventional folktale form (*maer*), have sprung up around the tribute institution. In Raimaus and in Hohul, Mambai speak hauntingly of Dom Felis, the "son of God" (*Maromak ni anan*) who wanted to build a "church" (*fad-kreda*) in Hohul and restore the "wax and sack." Arrested by Aileun on false charges, Dom Felis survived fire, water, and burial alive to wreak a most un-Christian revenge upon his errant people. Many people believe that Dom Felis will come again and complete his mission.

Antagonism between the ritual and the jural functions takes shape around the tribute system. Accusations, counteraccusations, rumors, and legends accumulate and feed an anxiety that permeates ritual life. So deep runs the fear and distrust that the priests repeatedly assert in every ceremony:

Au ba keo saun mosun id | I do not *keo* a thing which plummets down
Au ba noir saun dlesun id. | I do not teach of a thing which surges up.

These lines allude to the story of Dom Felis and they amount to a protestation of innocence. For the crime of which Dom Felis was unjustly accused by Aileun is known as a thing that "plummets and surges."

The birds and the mice still go hungry. Mambai return over and over to this fact. I have heard individuals from both sides of the diarchic divide voice their concern for the plight of the silent mouths. That particular groups have pragmatic interests in the restoration or abolition of the tribute system is apparent, but concern over tribute is not reducible to those interests. The content of Mambai response to tribute and taxation has a cultural basis. Their distress is motivated by a meaningful situation, as opposed to a brute happening, and arises out of an act perceived as a violation of a code of reciprocity.

1. The sacred origin lands

2. A cult house

3. A white altar rite (Raimaus). Women prepare areca and betel for the reception of the deities.

4. A white altar rite (Raimaus). A priest (seated) invokes Father Heaven at the altar post. Another priest (standing) wears a headdress of cock's tailfeathers, symbolic of Father Heaven.

5. A white altar rite (Raimaus). While men chant before the altar post, older women and young people gather at the edge of the altar.

6. A white altar rite (Hohul). After the priest (seated, holding staff) concludes the invocations, two men prepare to receive Father Heaven upon sacred spears. The man on their left is a Dat Raia.

7. A white altar rite
   (Raimaus). A priest
   makes offerings to
   the hollow rock.
   This act concludes
   the sequence of
   offerings and is
   followed by a
   communal meal.

8. The meeting at the
   spring. Women
   prepare baskets of
   rice for the recep-
   tion of the shades.

9. The meeting at the spring. Men invoke the shades of the dead at the sacred spring.

10. A house-building ritual (Hohul). The elders of Hohul wait at the altar place to greet the members of their kingdom.

11. A house-building ritual (Hohul). The Kafitan (foreground) and Alferes lead the kingdom members to the altar, in a formal enactment of hierarchy. Their folded arms and lowered eyes are ritual expressions of obeisance.

SEVEN

Divinity and the Social Order

1. Levels of Understanding

In the last three chapters I have introduced the social groups that conduct ritual exchange relations, and in part 2 I will examine the exchanges transacted in three different ritual events. In this chapter I return to the cosmic beings whom Mambai identify as the ultimate sources of life and recipients of ritual prestations. That identity is objectified in cosmogonic narrative, as we saw in chapter 2, but the full "trunk story" of creation is marked as the special possession of a select few and is socially restricted in circulation. If, then, Mambai understand their ritual life as an obligation to the cosmos, nonelites must have access to other forms of cosmological knowledge. It is to such relatively unrestricted forms of knowledge that this chapter is addressed.

My guiding intent is to comprehend the social consequences of ritual events in terms of the meanings that those events convey to participants. Bracketing for a moment differential levels of understanding, the fundamental problem is the relationship of symbolic categories to social action. Durkheim argued that rites reproduce social structures, but his model of the symbolic mechanisms of reproduction is inadequate and gives the impression that meanings are merely added on to raw social forms.[1] Conversely, certain forms of structural analysis have a tendency to underemphasize the sociology of ritual action in favor of its logical functions. Ritual then appears as a mechanism for objectifying an abstract system of categories, defined solely by their internal relations of opposition and correspondence. The approach taken in this study is intended to mediate between those two extremes. Rites, as I understand them, project symbolic categories onto lived situations, onto concrete persons, places, objects, and acts. When symbolic schemes are instantiated in the unfolding of ritual processes, participants renew their understanding of the ties that bind them to others. In short, what are reproduced and strengthened in ritual performances are meaningful relationships.

Our relatively rapid review of the Mambai social order has isolated one recurrent principle. Indigenous models of the house, of marital alliance, and of the community express in different ways the idea of an original source of life, and this idea orders exchange relations at multiple structural levels. In my presentation I have repeatedly called attention to the structuring of time implied in obligations to a source. Periodic returns to localities construed as origin places keep the past alive in the present and define its content. On ritual occasions Mambai commemorate prior situations that are shaped by asymmetric transactions between superior life-givers and inferior life-takers. Those founding exchanges are represented as the basis for ritual cooperation in the present. Life-takers must reciprocate for what was previously received, and in so doing they express and recreate their dependence on social sources of life. The asymmetry of exchange relations is the basis for hierarchical status in a system that ranks primordial givers over primordial receivers.

Trunk houses, wife-givers, and ritual centers embody a past of varying depths—not, however, the past as it originally was, but the past as it comes down into the present, marked by a history of divisions and subtractions. Representations of the empty or depleted source are critical to the Mambai ideology of exchange. Although unequal, the dependency of givers and receivers is also mutual, and a source requires the complementary services owed it by its subordinates. Symbolic emphasis on the dependence of givers upon receivers accounts for a distinctive tone of Mambai ritual life. Life-givers dwell in ritual speech upon the ordeals they have endured, to the point where superior status is culturally associated with sacrifice, suffering, and privation. How seriously people take such oratory at any single moment is difficult to say, for it becomes a highly stylized convention to invoke one's own past abnegations, and Mambai are not without an ironic sense.

But where the cosmos is concerned, suffering and restitution are profoundly significant matters to Mambai. That the cosmic givers of life in turn rely upon their human children is a fundamental premise of ritual action. From this premise, moreover, much of the social efficacy of ritual derives. Rites iconically associate cosmological ordeals with the hardships that human life-givers endure. One effect of this ritually constructed resemblance is to enhance the meaning of social ties.

Resemblances between cosmos and society are implicit in the categories that Mambai use to represent exchange obligations. It is not simply that duties to the cosmic beings are formally identified as paramount. It is also the case that those duties evoke the totality of reciprocal duties among social groups. All of the symbolic oppositions that I have isolated in the preceding chapters are condensed in the figures of the female and male powers who stand as mother and father to the world that they create.[2] In the very process of acting out their ties to one another, Mambai are referred back by overdetermined associative paths to their primary obligations to the cosmos.

The tendency to emphasize these founding obligations is most pronounced in the ritual centers, where status is based on a represented responsibility to the silent world. In the centers one meets exceptionally skilled hermeneutes who are predisposed to read rites as cosmological dramas. My companions were men of this sort. I do not regard them as "typical" Mambai, nor were they in their own estimation or in the regard of their fellows. On the contrary, it was because of their special knowledge that I was told to contact them. It is also true that my close and protracted relationship with Mau Bere of Hohul and Mau Balen of Raimaus led me to privilege the cosmological aspects of Mambai ritual—to the point where I sometimes found myself impatient with the social interests manifestly at stake in any performance. My two guides would often consign ritually enacted status relations to the period they called Day, and they would remind me that Day followed after Night. And so, both by the instructions I received and by personal dispositions of my own, I was drawn backward, inward, toward the primordial purpose of ritual events.

To dismiss the cosmological aspects of ritual as the esoteric concern of specialists would be to ignore what Mambai say about their rites. That rites influence the cosmic order is a collectively held, publicly enacted assumption. Their precise mode of influence is represented as privileged knowledge. By epistemological principles that Mambai apply at various levels of social reality, to understand a phenomenon is to know how it first came into being and assumed its present form. Inasmuch as rituals have their origins in cosmogonic processes, they are fully intelligible only to those who know the "trunk" story of world formation. Membership in a ritual center is defined as a necessary but not sufficient criterion for knowledge of this type. Even men who publicly preside over ritual events may portray themselves as ignorant of the ultimate purpose of their acts, without, however, questioning the nature of that purpose. Those who, whether by convention or by their own self-presentation, are not qualified to relate the creation myth consistently define their own understanding as a mere "tip" or part of a greater, encompassing whole. "This thing," Mambai say of any ritual practice, "is with its *kdain*," the word that I have glossed as "totality."

If the cosmology of ritual is culturally of the essence, to ignore the sociology of performance would be equally misguided. To read Mambai rites solely as cosmological dramas would be to project onto them a spiritualism that may satisfy our own nostalgic yearnings, but tells us little about Mambai ways of being in the world. Mau Balen, Mau Bere, and a few others like them could afford to displace the immediate social realities of performance and focus upon the cosmological trunk. On the one hand, lack of interest in worldly affairs, including the worldly aspects of staging a ritual, is itself a culturally recognized index of status. On the other hand, and thinking now more in terms of semantics than pragmatics, they chose a course most appropriate for Mambai, which was to elucidate the social part of ritual by the cosmological whole, and not, conversely, to elucidate the whole by the part. To them, the connections between cosmological and social realities were natural and self-evident. They lived those connections in performing an array of practices, whereas I have had to map laboriously, and no doubt at points with a somewhat heavy hand, a system of cultural categories that integrates different realms of experience.

2. *Icons of the Deities*

When Mother Earth lay dead, her flesh at last approaching putrescence, Father Heaven recoiled from the stench of decay. "Set my place apart!" he cried. So the Black House was built, and the corpse of Mother Earth was laid out there and readied for burial. But Heaven would not come near. He withdrew to his own White House, where the smell of death did not reach.

When the woman sank down into her grave, Heaven wandered away into the upperworld. The earth and the sky drifted far apart, for the black, ugly, naked body of his consort repelled Heaven, and he no longer desired her nor wished to dwell with her.

Each one took on a separate task. Mother Earth nourished and sheltered her children, folding them tightly in her arms and satisfying them with the cool, white milk that remained untouched by decay. Father Heaven traversed the world each day, accompanied by his messenger the wind. Wherever he went, he inquired into the affairs of his children, the silent ones and the speaking ones. If they quarreled or did wrong, he saw and took note and devised ways to punish them. And if they suffered from hunger or thirst, this too he observed and remembered.

He needed his consort's aid, but he could not permit her to enter his own house. And so they agreed to meet in the Black House, where her corpse had once lain. And now, late at night, when all the children are asleep, Mother Earth lights the two hearth fires of east and west to cook food for her man. Then Heaven descends through the roof of his White House. He crosses over to the woman's abode and eats the food she has prepared. They sit together and talk. He reports to her if any of her children lack nourishment and wither beneath his fiery brilliance. He counts all the children of the land and measures their needs. Then Father Heaven and Mother Earth lay their heads together and they stretch their legs together, and the mat swells and the bed oozes.

In the morning, the children awake and fog hangs over the land. By early afternoon, the rains begin to fall.

I have constructed this text out of comments made by various persons in a variety of contexts. The connection of divine sexuality with rainfall was established several times over, in relation to certain key segments of ritual discourse that I deal with later on. The story of the construction of the Black House and of the meetings that take place within it was told to me, in hushed and furtive tones, soon after I had begun to visit ritual centers. Whenever I inquired into house symbolism, someone would relate or allude to the narrative events of house origin. The idea that the deities are spatially disjoined recurs repeatedly in Mambai discourse, both in formal ritual speech, and in ordinary language conversations. "Our Father and Our Mother," Mambai soberly explain, "have separated (*ket*) from each other. They reside apart."

This situation is materially manifested in the separate houses of the Father and the Mother that are maintained in the ritual centers. I will discuss the symbolism of the opposition at some length, but first I want to reflect on the role that the houses play in the communication of sacred knowledge.

Whenever Mambai talked to me about the houses of the deities, they seemed to speak in a temporal mode that might be called a "perpetual present."[3] Admittedly, this is an intuitive impression, for aspect is not marked in the Mambai language. It is, however, the case that when Mambai narrate the myth of world origins they typically use such formulae as *berbera*, "in the beginning," or *ni fun*, "originally," which they do not use in speaking about the meeting of the deities inside the Black House. Speakers seemed to treat that event as something imminent, about to occur that very night, or perhaps occurring even as it was spoken. Such speech acts foregrounded the immediate, ongoing reality of an interaction that began long ago in a primordial past.

The houses themselves are one visible trace of that past and are regarded as tokens of the mythical types. The type of all Black Houses originates to receive a sacred corpse. And yet, when Mau Balen and Mau Bere narrated the walk of the earth, they made no mention of any house. If I questioned them, they would contrive to locate the construction of the Black House within the narrative sequence, but if I kept silent, then they took Mother Earth to her final resting place below Raimaus without alluding to any internment of her corpse. My conclusion is that although a skillful narrator can incorporate the symbolic values of the Mother's house into cosmogonic narrative, sacred myths are not necessarily consistent with other symbolic forms.

What I am getting at has to do with different modes of communicating sacred knowledge. Myths of origin compose one level of verbal communication, and they have a privileged position as the "trunk" of discourse. But we know that relatively few Mambai claim to possess the trunk, and even fewer, in my own experience, can in fact create coherent narrative accounts of creation. On the other hand, all Mambai inhabit and become familiar with the mythically structured space of the opposed houses. This lived-in, meaningful space conveys knowledge that many people organize into narrative sequences—not into a grand creation story, but into episodic accounts of the domestic relations between Father Heaven and Mother Earth.

The houses of the two deities function as what Bourdieu calls "structural exercises," lived experiences in which the relationship between the human body and inhabited space provides a form of "structural apprenticeship" (1977, 88–89). Through practices performed in the opposed houses, individuals internalize fundamental principles of cosmology. One learns, for instance, to associate Mother Earth with death and decay by enduring long vigils over the corpses that are laid out in her house before burial. And the mourners confront Heaven's antagonism to death in the strict prohibitions that ban them from his house so long as they are polluted by the dead. Some may detect behind these observances an original, founding event; for others, it may be enough to know that the dead who belong to the Mother are abhorrent to the Father.

My point, then, is this. In Mambai culture, as we have seen, re-strictions are placed on the circulation of cosmogonic knowledge, and original "trunk words" are cherished as hoarded treasure. But we need not assume from the unequal distribution of sacred knowledge that the ordinary participants in ritual performances are ignorant pawns, who blindly follow poorly understood instructions. The rela-tively esoteric doctrine that specialists can assemble is comple-mented by more mundane images of cosmic order. The somber themes of creation flit through Mambai thought in homelier dress, embodied in material structures, and in the storylike musings that these structures provoke.

We shall see later on that ritual performances include highly styl-ized dramatic enactments of the meeting between Heaven and Earth. Key ritual icons also give expression to the ideal union of the celes-tial male and the terrestrial female. On the other hand, there are rela-tively few objects that could be described as images or effigies of the deities, that is, as icons where the resemblance is based on shared qualities.[4] Mambai describe Heaven and Earth as "resembling people" (*man atuba*) in appearance, but they do not ordinarily fash-ion anthropomorphic images of the deities. The few that came to my attention are carefully sequestered and imbued with mystery. Long before I went to Hohul, I was told that I would see there images of Our Mother and Our Father. I also met with a sinister tradition concerning a "statue" of the Mother that was said to be locked away inside a cof-fer.[5] A similar statue of the Father, many people told me bitterly, had been lost by the Hohul ancestors under mysterious circumstances.

When I did go to Hohul, I saw the upright forms of a naked man and woman, carved in bas-relief upon the southwestern wall of the Father's house. I was told that one must avert one's eyes to avoid looking directly at the figures, "because they have no clothes."[6] The statue that is supposed to be kept inside the coffer was never shown to me; talk about the missing statue, referred to as the "body of Our Father" (*it aman ni etan*), wove through my visits, conveying a mourn-ful, bitter sense of loss, which puzzles me now as it did then.

From the intensity of the responses they elicit, it would appear that such images are more than artistic imitations of the god and god-dess. In ways that I do not pretend to understand, they may be thought of as mystically connected to the figures they represent. Per-haps for that very reason, they are kept hidden, and rumors spring up around them. This uneasiness before images of the divinities is in keeping with the wider etiquette of ritual life, where whatever has most value is concealed or expressed obliquely. Not for the Mambai a

"magical" manipulation of potent images through display. If the sequestered icons are indeed held to possess a mystical efficacy, then
theirs is a power which acts in private rather than in public.

3. The Houses of the Mother and the Father

Permanent and public representations of the deities are embodied in
the paired houses maintained in the ritual centers. These houses are
distinguished as the "house of the white" (*fad-buti nin*), which belongs to Father Heaven, and the "house of the black" (*fad-meta nin*),
which belongs to Mother Earth. I shall frequently refer to them as the
White House and the Black House.

Considered as an isolate, each of these houses forms a poly-
semous sign system. As are all ritually significant houses, each is oriented along a south-north axis and "faces" northward. At one level of
interpretation, the house composes a complex model of the correspondences among the human body, the landscape, and the cosmos.
On a vertical axis, the house mediates between below and above,
and the rites for its rebuilding are organized around an opposition
between the pillars and the roof. The patterns made by criss-crossing
roof beams are also attributed sexual significance, and the divisions
of space inside the house are symbolically associated with particular
categories of persons. I will leave all these matters to one side, however, to deal solely with the contrastive symbolic values signified by
the opposed houses. As a pair, the houses form a complex iconic representation of the relations between their master and their mistress.

Like all symbolic objects in Mambai culture, the houses are
hedged in with words. Each one is associated with a set of titles and
poetic formulae, but while I shall make use of these verbal classifiers,
I would stress that they are juxtaposed to the physical reality of the
houses. There to look upon and to enter, the houses have a concrete
and immediate presence that is central to their meaning. They exhibit
the relationships that they represent. The deities themselves vanish,
and while they return periodically, they are never seen. "My Father
has gone up to the sky/my Mother has gone down to the earth" (*au
aman sai her leola/au inan du her raia*) is the mournful refrain of
ritual chants, the orphan's lament. The closest that one can draw to
the lost parents is in approaching the houses of white and black. For
Heaven and Earth are nowhere so "visible" as in the contrastive characters of their homes.

The sexual identities that Mambai attribute to the houses are signified by their distinctive roofs and roof ornaments. The maleness of

140

the White House is marked by its conical roof. Viewed laterally, the thatched house resembles a bulging triangle capped by a crosslike ornament of bamboo.[7] The shaft of the roof ornament is rounded at the top, and the ends of the cross-piece turn upward to form a crescent. Mambai describe the roof ornament as the "hat" (*tudan*) of the house, and they liken it to the ceremonial horned headpieces (*fil diun*) worn by men, which have the same crescent shape as the roof ornament. *Fil diun* are worn over a kerchief, which is tied so as to form long, stiff wads on either side of the head, and I have also heard Mambai compare the male roof ornament to a kerchief.

The Black House is recognizable by its elongated, flattened roof and ornament of the same shape. Viewed laterally, the house has the appearance of a quadrilateral, with the short side uppermost.[8] The roof ornament, which runs the full length of the roof, is a flat wooden board, carved into knobs at either end. It too is described as a "hat," and it is also compared to the wooden combs that women wear in their hair.

Whereas the sexual characters of the houses are signified by resemblances to human dress codes, white and black enter into the system by another route. There is nothing in the outward appearances of the two houses that distinguishes them as white and black. These qualities are ascribed to them by convention.[9] One signification of the opposition is a narrative sequence of events: Mother Earth, blackened by death, is banished to a separate house, so that Heaven's abode may remain white and pure. But the meaning of the opposition is not necessarily dependent on any image of primordial events. The male house is treated in a way considered appropriate for things categorized as white, while the corpses received into the female house categorize it as black. In other words, the immediate interpretant of the opposition is a distinction in ritual values, which in turn signifies the distinctive relations of the two deities to human beings.

This last is also implied in another lexical distinction that Mambai draw between the two houses. They categorize the White House of Father Heaven as *fad-lulin*, "sacred house," but the Black House of Mother Earth is distinguished as *fad-lisa*, a "cult house." In most ritual centers this distinction is sociologically significant. Cult houses belong to designated social groups, and the group affiliated with the Mother's house in a ritual center precedes all others in status. But the Father's house is ordinarily detached from the social hierarchy. It is also designated as the "house of God," or simply as the "God house" and Mambai often introduced it to me by specifying that it was not a "cult house," but rather a "sacred house."[10]

The term *luli* is used in a variety of ways that provide clues to the significance of its contrast with *lisa*. In ritual language *luli* pairs with *kero* and *kesa*. *Kero*, "forbidden," is an adjectival form of the noun *keora*. The latter term denotes the ritual house posts, which are said to face toward the original "ban" imposed by Father Heaven. The term *keora* is also used of the signs that an owner places in his orchard to ward off thieves. *Kesa* comes from *kes*, "to measure, to mark off," and various articles used to mark off ritual space are included among a house's sacra. Hence in both these formal ritual uses, *luli* is associated with words that connote notions of boundaries. As a provisional gloss, we may assign to *luli* the double meaning of "sacred" and "prohibited."[11]

Mambai use *luli* in reference to objects and places. A sword, spear, ornament, gourd, staff or plate, a rock or a tree, a mountain, a grove or a plain may all be described as *luli*. In such usages *luli* denotes particularized, named members of a given larger class. For example, not every rock or tree is considered *luli*. "One rock is like another rock, one tree is like another tree," Mambai say enigmatically, "but some are called *luli*." A person can, in effect, sacralize ordinary objects by bestowing on them names and ritual roles.

It is ritual treatment which renders something *luli*, and it is in performance that the elements of sacredness and prohibition are most evident. In nonceremonial time (*ar-leta*), movable sacra are kept stored away in the house, and the sacred rocks and trees of the origin village are given a wide berth by casual visitors. In ritual contexts, the sequestered articles are brought out for display. Together with the rocks and trees, they become centers of activity and are the objects of oratory, processions, and offerings. However, all contact with sacred things is mediated by the designated, priestly master, who imposes his ministrations between the objects and the worshippers. Even in adoration, the sacra are protected by prohibitions.

Another set of objects is treated in terms of class, but, unlike the named sacra, these are *luli* only in relation to designated persons. An individual refers to a prohibited foodstuff as "my *lulin*" and denotes the act of abstention by the verbal form *luil*, "to observe prohibitions, to abstain from, to avoid." Here the object itself has no absolute character, for it is forbidden to some but not to others. Absence or lack of prohibitions is signified by the adjective *sau*, which may be glossed as "unrestricted" or "unbound."[12] Mambai sometimes classify persons into such categories as *sis ate lulin/sis ate saun*, those for whom liver is and is not prohibited.[13]

The verbal form *luil* is also used to describe the temporary abstentions that are ritually observed by particular individuals. During white ritual, designated elders must first abstain from eating the "old" crops of the previous year. Then, in the interval between planting and fruition, they avoid the "new," growing plants and refer to these as *luli*. Black ritual entails a harsher set of abstentions observed by close male and female kin of the dead. These persons are forbidden to bathe, shave, cut their hair, or engage in sexual activity. They are described as "black," "ugly," "old," "dry," and "dead."

To these three contexts are linked disparate but overlapping attitudes. Named, personalized sacra are honored and revered. Certain of these sacra are regarded as dangerous, and contact with them is regulated by particularly strict interdicts. The attitude toward prohibited classes is quite different. Their members evoke aversion, but not awe. For instance, an individual who abstains from liver regards it with an almost physical disgust and may voice a horror of the effect that ingestion would have. A permanent but mild "respect" comes closest to describing the attitude toward such things.

In the case of the temporary ritual prohibitions observed by individuals, one may still speak of "respect," but its qualities and intent are different again. In white ritual, the human actor intervenes between "old" and "new" crops. Abstention becomes something like a wish, evinced in an act of avoidance, which represents the desired separation of two groups of plants. By shunning the old as *luli*, the actor demonstrates his concern for the new; his attitude toward that which is prohibited (i.e., *luli*) is essentially neutral. The mortuary observances present yet another situation. Here, the actors who abstain (*luil*) are said to become *luli* themselves in relation to other persons, and their physical deprivation is accompanied by social seclusion. These persons evoke both awe and avoidance, attitudes which here are inseparable, since it is removal from ordinary social interactions that puts people into contact with the other world.

From these several usages, some general conclusions may be drawn. *Luli* does not signify an essence, but a relationship. An object that is called *luli* possesses no inherent quality or intrinsic force. Nothing is *luli* in and of itself but may become so by virtue of its separation from something else. In all its contexts, *luli* signifies a *relation of distance*, a boundary between things, created out of gestures of avoidance. This structural relation subsumes a set of disparate attitudes which range from mild respect to awe.

We have already seen that *lisa*, the cult or cult observances of a group, also connotes boundaries and separation. *Lisa* are associated with the "ban" that first "separates women and men" into the opposed categories of wife-givers and wife-takers. From the perspective of any one group of persons who observe a particular set of restrictions, their *lisa* is a boundary that encloses or encircles them, and so marks them off from other groups.[14]

While the Mother's house within a ritual center belongs to a designated group, it also stands for the ritual center as a whole, and the center stands for the community as a whole. Ritually, the Mother's house belongs to all humankind, since all women and all men are her children. Thus we arrive through the Mother's house at an idea of a universal cult that overrides social divisions and embraces all humanity, a cult that acts as a protective boundary to encircle a family of children and their Mother.

Opposed to this universal cult house is the "sacred" house of the Father, which in its relationship to humankind provides a paradigmatic instance of the distance connoted by *luli*. For the Father's house is dramatically set apart, separated from human beings, who regard it with awe and avoid it on all but the most solemn ritual occasions. Symbolically, women and men live inside their cult house with their Mother, and they look from afar upon the sacred house of their Father. These differentially drawn boundaries express the relative proximity of Mother Earth to her children, and the relative remoteness of Father Heaven.

The differing relations of the two deities to their children contribute to a tension that is inherent in the cosmos. Narrative representations of the cosmos trace its intrinsic imbalance back to a founding event: the death of Mother Earth and the reaction of Father Heaven, who recoils from the "stench and bitterness" of death and retreats into the gleaming purity of his White House. The death of Mother Earth negates her original sexual union with Father Heaven. Mambai are quite explicit on this point, explaining that "Our Father no longer desired Our Mother." Through death, the complementary balance of male and female is transformed into an antagonistic separation of opposites, and the cosmos lapses into an antisexual condition of radical disjunction.

This antagonism between the deities is materially expressed by the separation of their houses. In the houses, as in the mythic scheme, male and female appear as mutually threatening, contagious principles that must be kept apart. The stressed cause of their hostility is death. All contact between the White House and the dead is strictly forbidden. Corpses may not be brought inside it, and access is prohibited to persons who are involved in a death ceremony. Moreover, any objects that are used "to *keo* the black" must be stored inside the

Black House, which is also referred to as the "Death House" or "Death Ritual House" (*fad-maeta*).[15]

The opposition of the white and black houses is not, however, isomorphic with the division of rituals into the same two categories. Between white and black rituals there is a complementarity of contrary relations, but the radical antagonism between the two houses is based on a logic of contradictory relations. The White House and the Black House are opposed in terms of absence to presence, and the precise mode of opposition is central to the meaning of their relationship.

Heaven's house is frequently characterized as "white and clean" (*buti nor mo*), but other common attributes take a negative form. Heaven's abode

| Ba tad maet nor broen | Knows not death or decay |
| Ba tad houn nor felun. | Knows not stench or bitterness. |

If it is also called "fragrant" and "sweet," I can only say that I never heard such statements made of it. Although this might indicate little more than a gap in my ethnography, I suspect that the Mambai mean precisely what they say—or do not say. If Heaven's house knows neither stench nor bitterness, the message seems to be that it has no odor and no taste. It is defined by its absence of qualities, and even its symbolic "cleanliness" is not a positive, but a negative attribute. The house is not made clean through any act of purification. It is clean by default, automatically excluding any form of filth.

What is excluded from the White House is not only the filth of death and decay, but also the rhythms of ordinary social life. The most striking fact about the White House is its remoteness from daily activities. Mambai approach it only on solemn ritual occasions to offer homage and make obeisance. Indeed, unless an importunate ethnographer should request a special tour, they will not enter the White House until the priests convene them. Their comportment within its walls is marked by solemnity and restraint. Movements are formal and dignified, voices are low and respectful, and the atmosphere is one of awe and reverence.

Access itself is no freer. A set of special restrictions mark off the Father's house from the world. Before entering, one must divest oneself of all objects considered displeasing to Father Heaven. Foremost among these are tobacco and kerosene lighters. Kerosene, or "earth oil" as it is called in Mambai, is a product of the lower world and explicitly banned for that reason. With tobacco, it may be that a substance which is consumed and demolished is antithetical to the undying male. In some cases women are categorically excluded from the White House. Where entry is permitted, women are strictly relegated to the northern section of the house and may not touch the central hearth, which is ordinarily the female domain.

Interdictions are primarily designed to protect the White House against contagion. Nonetheless, danger flows two ways, and if the dying threaten the undying, so may the latter contaminate the living. The notion of reciprocal influence is implicit in the sanctions attendant on breaches of interdict. All such breaches are said to render the violator sterile. The risk is greatest for women and for young people, who will die without issue. Within the pattern that is emerging, it is clear that the White House is antithetical to all forms of movement and change. Itself threatened by death, it poses a reciprocal threat to the stirrings of life.

With its mythically and ritually stressed antagonism to death, the White House could be interpreted as the house of eternal life, but it is more suggestively represented as the house of the undying, or as the house of stagnant life. Heaven lives forever in his own house, but in this solitary condition, he too remains sterile. White and immortal, "knowing neither death nor decay," he exists outside of biological time, an immutable male principle that represents the stasis and sterility of perpetual order. Heaven, the active, open male who mobilizes space, fixes and freezes time.

Mother Earth, who stabilizes space, unleashes time. Her mythic death introduces into the world a temporality conceived of as a perpetual alternation of white and black, of life and death, of fertility and decay. In time she represents a dynamic principle of cyclic change, and her house ritually passes through these cycles. The Black House, which is the special place for the dead, is also the place of birth, nurturance, life, the sheltering "house of women and men/of pigs and dogs." And it is the place of procreation, where complementary balance is momentarily restored, and where the immortal male is reunited with the mortal female.

Social conduct in the Black House is altogether different than in the White House. The house built to receive a corpse is the house where everyday life unfolds. Although the Black House has its heightened, ritual moments, these are not characterized by the solemnity and formality evinced in the White House. Moreover, the house of the Mother also sways to the rhythms of domestic routines. Any ritual performance is punctuated by periods of waiting, and in these intervals people gather at the Black House to pass the time. There the women of the house cook great vats of rice and corn to feed the many visi-

146

tors. Throughout the day, visitors drift in to talk, eat, and relax. At night, the Black House is often filled to overflowing with sleeping people.

Through the two houses a dual divinity reveals itself to humanity. The house of the Father is remote, restricted, avoided, and it evokes expressions of respect and awe. Within the Mother's house, women and men move more freely. Their conduct bespeaks an easy, casual intimacy that Mambai attribute to the relation of Mother Earth to her children. But this very closeness is what divides Mother Earth from Father Heaven. For the forms of life that the divine couple together produce and sustain will eventually "follow the Mother" and return to her in a death abhorrent to Father Heaven. Life, by its very mortal nature, provokes anew the state of separation.

The totality of representations and practices associated with the houses project cosmology onto ritual space. The opposed houses embody the tension inherent in a cosmos in which male and female principles may alternately threaten and repel or attract and complement each other.

4. The Complementarity of the Cosmic Powers

The separation of the Black House from the White House signifies an antagonism of opposites and corresponds to the cosmogonic event of the Mother's death. The Black House also constitutes the closed space of the interior in opposition to the open air. In this scheme the Mother's abode is the reference point of complementary activities that unfold on a horizontal axis. Father Heaven represents the male principle of motion. His province is the outside world, but he returns periodically to the fixed and stable house of the female.

The opposition between inside and outside signifies the complementarity of opposites which is manifested in the sexual division of labor. As the lord of the outside, Heaven keeps his distance from human beings, but his remoteness in space is the condition for cooperation with the housebound goddess. Mambai speak of Father Heaven as wandering somewhere out of sight, "on the outside and edge" of space, an invisible presence who guides human affairs. His role is conceived of in two homologous aspects. In one perspective, he is the jural regulator whose function is to observe and punish transgressions against the moral order of the cosmos. In the other perspective, his regulatory function appears as his distinctive contribution to the promotion of life. The roaming deity withdraws into the outer realms of space in order to oversee the material needs of his children. He watches over them throughout the day, measuring their appetites, and at night he returns to his consort's house, where together they produce the life-giving rains.

Mambai speak soberly of the hardships and privations that Heaven endures on the outside. "Whipped by the wind/scorched by the sun," he suffers after his own fashion in the performance of his duty. Although the trials he undergoes elicit concern among human beings, they are not constitutive of any sense of intimacy. In all his manifestations Heaven is represented as a stern and dangerous figure. Myths tell of his sudden interventions that may cause his offspring to flee in terror. Ritually, a degree of distance is required in confronting Father Heaven, and special precautions are taken before invoking him. Articles of ceremonial attire iconic of the male deity are identified as shields that deflect his deadly glare and heat. Sacred shade trees serve a similar symbolic function. The great banyans "thrust back the heat/sweep back the burning" and protect the ritual center from celestial fire. The tips of the banyans are ritually tendered to Father Heaven, so that he may interpose their branches between his own person and his earthbound children.

The children wear no shields against the Mother, nor does any object intervene between her body and theirs. She clutches the youngest and weakest to her breast and folds her cloak around them to keep them safe. In both ritual and ordinary speech Mambai stress the warm and shady atmosphere of the Black House. With its temperate, culturally regulated climate, the maternal house provides shelter from celestial brightness and heat, which are deadly to growing things.

Mother Earth also suffers, not from the hardships of the outside, but from the ordeals of birth and nurturance. Mambai describe her trials in graphic terms. She is eternally confined to the house, where she wearily passes the time in counting the roof spars and the bundles of thatch grass. She is blackened by soot and ash from her cooking fire and fouled by the urine and excrement of her squealing infants.

The complementarity of spatial realms corresponds to the temporal alternation of the seasons. Father Heaven governs the dry season (*leolaia*, from *leola*, "heaven, sun"), the time of activity and plenty, when "the hearth is wide" to receive the harvested crops. The house opens itself to the world in the dry season, and women and men wander freely across the barren land. This symbolically open state alternates with the wet season governed by Mother Earth, a time of confinement, restricted motion, and scarcity. The wet season is when "the hearth is narrow," while the new crops are still growing in the gardens.

Irregularities in the alternation of the seasons are read as indexes of cosmic imbalance. Should either one of the cosmic powers manifest itself in its pure state over an extended period, it becomes a destructive force. Each destroys according to its own nature. Heaven, lord of the dry, can withhold the rains and extend his own rule, until his children wither and die beneath his untempered heat. Earth, lady of the wet, is responsible for an opposed form of excess. She may prolong the rains until they "tear open" the soil, turning it into mud, which Mambai name "rotten earth." Between the two extremes of the burned and the rotten, seasonal alternation represents a temporal balance of opposites.

A principle of recursivity operates in the symbolism of the seasons, with the result that complementary oppositions are replicated at different levels. The wet season is globally defined as female in opposition to the male dry season, but this classification is relative, and the wet season also includes both female and male, inside and outside. What characterizes the wet season is the relative predominance of the female, expressed in the image of the male who returns to the inside. Complementarity in its strongest form entails the sexual union of female and male, from which the rains of the wet season are created. That union is not taken to be a natural occurrence. If the deities are left to themselves, Mambai say, their desires fade. They retreat into their separate realms, where they grow listless and fall asleep. This possibility poses the problem to which white ritual responds.

The gods need human beings in order to realize their own sexual natures. Human beings, who depend on the gods for life, are also the instruments of the life that they receive. At this juncture we must return to the notion of "ritual noise" that is signified by *keo*, for the din of drum and gong is directly related to the latent asexuality of the Mambai cosmos. The stated purpose of percussive noise in white ritual performances is to startle the gods out of their slumber, and so to set creation in motion anew. People lift their voices in speech and song, and they beat upon their drums and gongs:

Oid knur au in ni ulun	To wake my Mother's head
Oid he au aman ni oen	To tug my Father's foot
Kikan oid mrue	So that the ears may be clear
Matan oid ada	So that the eyes may be bright
Au inan oid teik-li ni au aman	So that my Mother may lie down with my Father
Au aman oid teik-li ni au inan	So that my Father may lie down with my Mother

Bita oid bubu	So that the mat may swell
Saka oid ri	So that the bed may ooze
Oid mor loi	So that they may give birth again
Oid ko loi	So that they may bring forth again
Susu oid boko	So that the breast may hang heavy
Fa oid rema.	So that the lap may be flat.

In white ritual the primary offering of percussive sound is supplemented with animal sacrifices that are dedicated to Heaven and Earth as recompense for their labors. But there is a saying that the priests mutter in their chants, a somber variation of the white/black formula:

Hulu ba rat	When the hairy ones are not enough
Nor mrea fe naur	Join them with the hairless ones
Mrea ba natou	When the hairless ones are not sufficient
Nor hulu fe naur.	Supplement them with the hairy ones.

Mambai say that a sadness comes over them when they hear these words, for the "hairy ones" are the beasts sacrificed in white rituals, but the hairy ones are not enough. And the "hairless ones" who will make up the difference are the corpses of women and men, the final black gift of flesh that is presented to the Mother.

Her reward is greater, Mambai say, than that tendered to Heaven, for "it is Our Mother who suffers most." To her goes a dank, dark feast, from which Heaven averts his eyes, a last prestation which

Du man saun-lun	Sinks down into refuse
Du man rai-fafon	Sinks down into dust
Du man mudan	Sinks down into darkness
Du man metan.	Sinks down into blackness.

In a grim inversion of maternity, Mother Earth draws her cloak around the dead to devour them.

No one disputes her claim. The priests simply endeavor to regulate her appetites by sating her temporarily with offerings of animal flesh. White ritual oratory is threaded with their supplications. They beseech her to "draw the hems of the cloak closely/press the lips tightly." They ask her "not to go on and on swallowing women and men." They beg her to await the old ones who "sit on the buttocks/ press down with the hands," those who are bowed down by age into her own dying posture. Confronted by the Mother in her dark, ravening aspect, the children momentarily recoil like their Father. And the priests repeatedly mark them off with instructions that by now should need no further explanation:

Hina luli	Women are sacred
Maena luli	Men are sacred
Haiha luli	Pigs are sacred
Ausa luli	Dogs are sacred
Luli man au inan luli	Sacred as my Mother is sacred
Kero man au aman kero.	Forbidden as my Father is forbidden.

The cosmological purpose of white ritual is to bring about the sexual reunion of opposites. Black ritual finds Heaven and Earth in a state of radical disjunction that can only be terminated by properly disposing of the dead. Hence the ultimate success of white ritual is always already dependent on the complementary rites of death.

For the groups that perform these various rites, social and cosmological obligations are condensed, and the tensions inherent in the cosmos resonate with felt tensions in social life. At the social level, order is also based on ritually enacted relationships of complementarity. In their rituals Mambai play out the collective premises or institutionalized fictions of existence: that one's own life derives from others; that gifts of life create mutual obligations; and that interdependent social groups must unite to fulfill obligations to the cosmos.

PART TWO

Rituals of White and Black

EIGHT

White Ritual: The Path of Rain

1. Scope of the Analysis

The category of white ritual includes three types of performance: (1) an annual cycle of agricultural rituals that unfolds over the course of the wet season; (2) rituals "of rice," held at harvest time; (3) rituals "of the house," held for the rebuilding or repair of cult houses.[1] With the exception of rice ritual, all white performances are public events which take place in designated origin villages. They are collectively organized by house groups and participation is based on house affiliation. Rice rituals are comparatively private affairs, set in the rice fields of individual households. Participation is optional and is based on residence.[2]

My presentation is limited to performances included in the annual cycle, which unfolds at two levels of organization. At the lower level, clusters of agnatically related houses perform silent *beha* rites. The higher level of the cycle unfolds in the ritual centers of communities, and all performances are accompanied by drum and gong. It is this level of the ritual system that I address.

The annual cycle is composed of three stages, each one coordinated with a specific event. The first stage marks the transition from the dry season to the wet season. The second stage celebrates the first appearance of "green" corn and the ripening of "pigeon peas and beans." The celebration of the corn harvest marks the onset of the dry season and closes the cycle. A major concern throughout the cycle is to regulate the rains that govern agricultural growth. The symbolic purpose of the first stage is "to *keo* rain." It takes place only in the ritual centers and is represented as a prerogative of the community authorities. Abbreviated versions of the next two stages are performed at the local level by house groups which are subsequently included within the centralizing communal cult.

I deal primarily with the first two stages of the cycle, as I never attended the closing harvest celebration. The inaugural rites are called Aif-Lulin, "Prohibition of Fire" or "Prohibited Fire." I attended one performance of this event in Raimaus. It is a relatively simple ritual, to which only a few people are invited. The second stage of the cycle is called Er-Soia, "Drawing of Water." Representatives of the entire community converge upon the ritual centers for this event and enact status relations. I attended two performances of this event, the first in Raimaus and the second in Hohul. For the purpose of this presentation, all descriptive material relates to performances staged in Raimaus.

2. Seasonal Alternation in Ritual Symbolism

In the sixth and last native month of the dry season (usually coinciding with October), the elders of Raimaus begin "to observe the moon." As the lunar cycle approaches its end, members of the ritual center assemble in Raimaus to open the ceremonial cycle at the moment when the "moon dies." The dark of the moon signals two concurrent natural events: the end of the dry season and the emergence of new plant life underground. The first half of the inaugural performance consists of rites of transition that are intended

Oid ket usa nor leola	To separate rain and sun
Oid ket heua nor aika.	To separate new and old.

Seasonal alternation, which is associated with Heaven and Earth, is also represented as a change that takes place inside the Black House. Two pairs of mythical women personify the seasons. They are identified as the mistresses of the house's two hearth fires. The eastern fire, presided over by Soi Loko and Soi Lelo, governs the dry season of activity and abundance, when "the hearth is wide," and the house opens itself to the outside world. The wet season begins when Soi Loko and Soi Lelo yield to their sisters, Nam Loko and Nam Oro, who preside over the western hearth fire. These two govern a period of scarcity and confinement, symbolized by a "narrow hearth" and a closed house.

The white cycle unfolds over the course of a female season that is paradigmatically associated with birth and nurturance. Ritually, all births occur during the wet season, but only cultivated plants experience the ideal order as a literal truth. For human beings, the connection of birth with the rains must remain figurative, as it is up to them to regulate the alternation of the seasons. If all women were actually to give birth in the wet season, these concurrent births would result in concurrent deaths. And then, Mau Bere once remarked, "who would *keo* Our Mother and Our Father?" In order to meet their ritual obligations, women and men must stagger their reproduction, "some in the dry, some in the wet," Mau Bere explained.

However, Mambai enact the ideal structure of the year in their ritual practices. All life symbolically begins in the wet season, when scattered house members reassemble at their origin place to commemorate their dependence on the source. After the final rites have ushered in the dry season, the origin place is abandoned once more. Its members go out from the house and scatter themselves throughout the outer realm of space. A ceremonial hush ensues. The drum and gong of white *keo* remain silent throughout the active regime of the dry season, to sound once more in celebration of the new life that arrives with the rains.

Then the "new" plants must be separated from their "old" precursors, and the wet season must be separated from the dry season. Human beings help to bring about these separations, and then they call upon the deities to nourish their new children. These two tasks define two stages of the total ritual performance. First is a period of transition, when prohibitions are observed in order to bring about the desired separations. Then comes the period of reunion, when invocations and offerings are made to bring the two deities together.

3. Rites of Transition

The name "Prohibited Fire," which designates the entire performance, derives from the opening rites. These are held late at night, in an atmosphere of secrecy and seclusion that contrasts with the public character of the rites that follow.[3] Whereas young people participate in the rites of reunion, old people are solely responsible for the rites of transition.[4]

The rites themselves are relatively simple. On the night of the "dark moon," four men gather in the Mother's house, Nunu Fun.[5] They include the custodians of the two cult houses; the eldest female member of Nunu Fun may join them if she wishes. "New" yams, sweet potatoes, and taro are placed upon the sacred stones of the two hearths. "Old" foods of any kind are expressly forbidden (*luli*). After the offerings have been made, the remaining tubers are divided among six small baskets, two for each of the three Raimaus houses. The elders visit each house in turn, beginning in Nunu Fun, crossing to Fad Fusun, the White House, and ending in Mau Nunun, the youngest house "of rule and ban." At each house they boil tubers and mash them together to form a porridge called *klaia*. Then they boil a cock. When the food is prepared, they shave bits of porridge and meat over the eastern hearth and the western hearth in turn. Both hearths are then extinguished. The performers "eat in darkness."[6] That is all—a silent meal of chicken and unripe tubers; and outside, a moonless night.

The rites of transition are based on a set of negative observances that are intended to separate the dry from the wet and the crops of the old year from those of the new year. The performance as a whole is *luli*, forbidden to the young. The acts of extinguishing the hearth fire and of abstaining from the old year's crops are described in the same idiom; the elders are said to *luil* fire and old foods. Should they fail in these observances, tempests will result.

Mambai isolate the extinguishing of the hearth fire as the central element in the rites. The same act is performed when a woman gives birth. Both observances have mythological significance, and it is often remarked that Mother Earth first brought forth her progeny in the Night. Cooking fire is associated with the separation of Night and Day, for the smoke from the Mother's fire makes Heaven's eye fly from its socket to become the globe of the sun. Hence the extinguishing of the hearth fire at the time of plant and human births suggests a recreation of origins. Mambai say of both acts: "We follow Our Mother," or "We follow the earth."

As I understand the logic of these rites, transition is brought about by cancelling distinctions. Extinguishing the fires that mediate between night and day, and between earth and sky, is the sign and instrument of a return to a primordial, undifferentiated state. In the moment that precedes transition, the dry must return to the wet, the old year to the new year. By rekindling the hearth fires, distinctions are restored. The new plants now replace the old ones, as the rainy season replaces the dry.

But with transition navigated and the rains installed, the ritual tasks are not completed. Additional rites are required to regulate the rainfall. These are the rites of reunion that establish the proper balance between Heaven and Earth:

Ausa liu ana sois	The dog has already whelped its pup
Mauna hoh telo sois.	The hen has already hatched its egg.
Au ina, tul-li ni ramun	My Mother, bear down on the root
Au ama, fail tu ni dikin	My Father, take hold of the bud
Dikin oid bou-leol	For the bud to brush the sky
Ramun oid ses-rai.	For the root to cleave to the earth.

4. Rites of Reunion: The Setting

On the following day, performance assumes a public character. Mambai identify the next rite with one of postpartum called "to rinse the eyes," in which close paternal and maternal relatives gather for a ceremonial cleansing of the newborn infant. The formal intent of the rite is "to roll the eyes/to rinse the dead blood" (*oid lil mata/oid frau lar maten*), in other words, to bring the infant to a higher level of awareness by removing the blood of birth that clouds its eyes.

In the homologous rite of the agricultural cycle the "child" is identified as "all the foods, for it is as if they were all brought forth." The formal intent of performance is "to beseech rain that they may nurse well and grow big." The rite is attended by men, women, and children of the ritual center, their domestic servants the Dat Raia, and their messengers the Alferes and Kafitan, who represent the community.

The rite begins at the altar place and involves a procession around the village, with stops before the sacred rocks and trees. Similar rites recur throughout the white cycle and cannot be presented without reference to their spatial setting. Hence I will begin by describing the organization of ritual space in Raimaus (see figure 5).

Origin villages are formally oriented along an east-west axis. Ritually, entrance and exit are through the eastern "door," which is known as the "head of the origin village" (*ri-ulun*). The western door or "tail" (*ri-ion*) is used in exorcising spirits.

The altar (*boska*) marks the conceptual center of ritual space. It is a round, tiered structure built of stone and earth. A circular wall of "interlaced rocks" encloses a flattened mound of "piled earth." The altar, like the house, is oriented along a south-north axis. The "door" (little more than a cleft in the rocks) is located on the north.[7] The center of the altar itself is marked by a high cairn of rocks that Mambai call the *haut lau*, "rock height." In Raimaus, the cairn extends to the southern rim of the altar, so that, seen from above, the entire edifice looks like a semicircle of earth and a small full circle of rock.

At the center of the cairn, a ring of tall, slender bark plants (*buka*) encircle a huge hollow rock. To the west of the rock is the altar post shrine, the *ai tosa*, which is often called *mau maena*, "male fellow." Approximately five feet in height and two feet in circumference, the post branches out into three prongs, described as "teeth" in ritual language.[8] Two of these prongs fork to the east and west and are unadorned. The third rises upward and is carved into a globe at the top. Flat offering stones, the "placing stones," surround

159

the base of the post. On the southeastern edge of the cairn are the *titir*, the great masculine drum, and the *koa*, the masculine gong.

The north-south axis divides the earthen area of the altar into "white" and "black" sections. The "white" eastern ground is used for dances and presentations in white ritual. The "black" ground to the

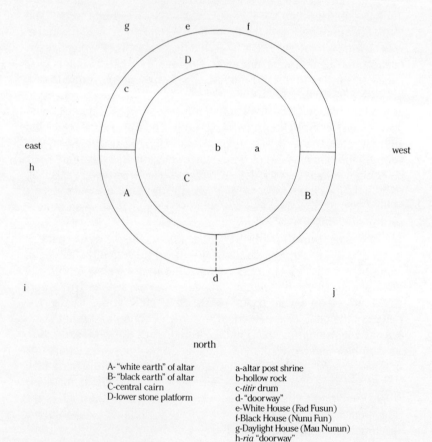

A-"white earth" of altar
B-"black earth" of altar
C-central cairn
D-lower stone platform

a-altar post shrine
b-hollow rock
c-*titir* drum
d-"doorway"
e-White House (Fad Fusun)
f-Black House (Nunu Fun)
g-Daylight House (Mau Nunun)
h-*ria* "doorway"
i-banyan Tai Talo
j-rocks Ber Koli and
   Maun Koli

Figure 5: Plan of Raimaus

west is the graveyard (*rate*). No white performance may impinge on this space.[9]

The houses border the altar. In Raimaus, the three major houses, Nunu Fun (the Black House), Fad Fusun (the White House), and Mau Nunun (the Daylight House) run from west to east along the southern rim of the altar. The south of the altar fronts upon a house in all origin villages, but the precise configuration of houses varies according to their number and to the size of the altar.

As the conceptual center of space, the altar is symbolically linked to the surrounding temples and to the sacred trees which mark the periphery of the village. The connection is established through the altar post, which "tilts up" to the house post shrine (*keora*) and to the banyan trees. Sacred rocks "tilt up" to the tree.

In Raimaus these linkages have cosmogonic significance. For the banyan is Tai Talo, the eldest shade tree, tree "of women and men." A massive tangle of roots and branches, its sheer physical presence dominates the village. The tree is located at the eastern periphery of the village, but its twisting, outspread limbs reach to the edge of the altar and cast a long shadow over the "white" earth. Multiple meanings are condensed in Tai Talo. The banyan is opposed to the sacred rocks and mediates between them and the altar post.[10] By itself, it evokes the union of its myriad branches, grown upward and outward to the heavens, and its gnarled, thick roots, which disappear into the earth. In their chants, the priests often allude to the ritual process as a whole by declaring:

Au fe se fu	I look down only at the trunk
Au ktar se lau.	I look up only at the tip.

No less imposing are the sacred rocks of Raimaus. Parallel to Tai Talo, northwest of the altar, a large, oval rock sits upon a raised platform of interlaced stones. Beneath it, wedged into a tiny crevice, is another rock which in size and shape resembles a large egg. These are named Ber Koli and Maun Koli. They are identified with two mythical brothers who "blow the seas dry." And at the very center of the altar place is the great "hollow rock," a gaping stone crater partially concealed by the curtain of plants. Here, altar rites begin and end; here, the priests lay the final offerings, unwatched and unattended, whispering silent words into the "mouth" of the rock. If this rock has a name, I never learned it. Mambai themselves refer to it as the "hollow rock" or "rock that is hollow." Sometimes they describe it as an "urn, mother and father of all urns." And in solemn moments, such as when I first entered Raimaus to attend the very performance I am describing, or when we had delved deep into the walk of the earth, then my guides would whisper to me: "That is the earth navel."[11]

5. The Altar Rite

All rites held within the village are performed either outside on the altar or inside one of the houses. I refer to the former as altar rites and to the latter as house rites. Both follow a set form.

Altar rites are composed of two segments, distinguished according to the content of the offerings. In the first segment, "areca and betel descend," and the offerings are bits of crumbled areca and shredded betel leaves. At the conclusion of the oblations, a chicken or a beast is sacrificed to be used in the second segment of the rite. After the sacrifice has been cooked (which may not be until the following day), "winnowing baskets and serving baskets descend" and are filled with offerings of cooked meat and rice. The rite concludes with a communal meal. The internal patterning of each segment is based on a circuit from the altar to the rock and tree and back to the altar.

Mambai associate the two segments of an altar rite with the conventional forms of hospitality. To receive a guest, one first offers a chew of areca and betel. Then while the visitor rests and refreshes himself, the hosts prepare a meal. Ritual offerings are said to follow the same pattern.

The key guests received at the altar are the divinities, and they are welcomed as one welcomes a human visitor, with a chew and then with a meal. Yet there is this one difference: the divinities are never seen, and no one can be sure that the visit has taken place. The entire stage is set for the reception of Heaven and Earth. Every word, object, and gesture alludes in some way to the "descent of Heaven/ascent of Earth." Upon this desired event Mambai lavish such an array of representations that the entire rite appears as an embroidery upon this one theme, a multimedia enactment of a cosmic reunion. If I seem to be stressing the obvious by remarking on the invisibility of the divine guests, I do so because Mambai themselves are so insistent on this point. In interpreting their own ritual life, they move back and forth between the precision of its symbolism and the haunting uncertainty at its core. Over and over, Mambai act out the same drama in the "descending and arising" places of Heaven and Earth, without any assurance that the central actors have come to perform their roles. Nor do Mambai expect any such assurance, for theirs, to follow their own imagery, is a cult of "orphans and lost ones."

The rite I am about to examine is rich in semantic meanings, and Mambai speak in exegetical contexts as if the ritual representations corresponded to an actual event. But in their more general (and often unelicited) comments upon ritual performance, Mambai would lay great stress upon a gap between symbolic forms and their referents. A profound "perhaps" enters into evaluations of the efficacy of ritual acts. Doubt would be too strong a word, but Mambai simply do not *know*. "We place rocks and fill baskets," people would say, "we offer areca and betel, meat and rice. We call on Our Mother and Our Father to receive these things. But if they come or do not come, receive or do not receive, this we cannot know."

Performance itself speaks in a declarative mode, through vivid enactments of desired events. Yet seen in a larger context of ideas, ritual utterances are set in a conditional mode. Human beings petition, phrasing their requests in the set, immutable forms passed down by the ancestors, who received them in turn from the deities themselves. The efficacy of symbolic action is held to rest upon the continuity between an original archetype and an inherited tradition:

Au inan ba dedi selun id	My mother did not pass on some different thing
Au aman ba fahe knair id	My father did not hand down some altered thing
Au tuir ni oe haita	I follow in the footprint
Au dad ni kneora	I track the grass track
Au hoda ba tad	I know not the night
Au ada ba tad	I know not the day
Au keo foro-leo	I *keo* over all the days that are past
Au noir sai-ad.	I preserve the tradition for all the days that are to come.

So the priests say in their chants, casting their actions in moulds fashioned in the past. Ritual forms are the tangible link with original time, and with the lost parents whose bodies are unseen, whose names are unknown. Ritual gives representation to a wish. The public pretense of performance is that the wish is realized within the ritual frame, and that the deities are reunited with their children. Perhaps events unfold in this way.

With these remarks as background, let us examine the performance on the altar. I shall describe the proceedings in some detail, for they recur repeatedly throughout the white ceremonial cycle.

Early in the morning, the participants begin to assemble at the altar place to perform their several duties. Work is interspersed with talk, and the initial preparations may take several hours. Curious, expectant children weave in and out. Occasionally, an adult will brusquely shoo them away, and they retreat a few paces to perch along the altar rim.

The women set to work first. Their place is on the edge of the central cairn, at the southern rim of the altar.[12] Two women, the female elders of the leading houses Nunu Fun and Mau Nunun, spread a mat upon the rocks and set down two rectangular baskets.[13] These are called *mam-hatin*, "chew place." They are used in all formal presentations of areca and betel. The materials are stored inside the basket; to make an offering, nuts and leaves are counted out according to the number of guests and placed in the lid of the basket. The baskets used in white ritual are regarded as *luli* and are kept within the Mother's temple. They are classified as female or male, according to the length of their "legs." The male basket has "long legs in order to walk," and the female basket has "short legs in order to sit in the house."

From the baskets the two women take sticks strung with dried areca nuts and sheaves of betel leaves. They arrange these by first placing the nuts in the basket lids and then rolling the betel leaves (*dul maula*) into cones. The cones are inserted between the lids and bodies of the baskets, so as to stand upright. In formal speech the arrangement of betel leaves is a metonym for the baskets, which are referred to as *dulun nor sorun*, "rolled up and standing erect."

Mambai invariantly identify the white *mam-hatin* as the "sitting places of Heaven and Earth," his place being the male basket and hers the female basket. The distribution of betel leaves follows a system of numerical symbolism by which all ritual offerings are calculated.

The primary terms in this system are three, four, seven, and eight, and multiplications within this set such as seven times four, seven times three, eight times four, eight times three. In such multiplications, what concerns Mambai is not the total (which they rarely state), but the relation between the symbolic values of the base and the multiplier. The odd numbers, three and seven, are classified as "hot" (*banan*) and the even numbers, four and eight, as "cool" (*suman*). Hot and cool are associated with maleness and femaleness, above and below.[14]

The female basket receives eight times three leaves, "for Earth to ascend"; the male basket receives seven times four leaves "for

Heaven to descend." My informants interpreted these computations as a technique of tempering and balancing opposed principles which are dangerous in their pure state. Father Heaven is hot like the base number seven. The multiplier four is cool and has a cooling effect on the base, so that seven times four is classified as cool. Mother Earth and eight are cool, and multiplication by three achieves the reverse effect, so that the operation eight times three generates heat. The baskets thus take on the inverse constitutions of their divine owners, and this helps establish a balance of opposites.[15]

Although women prepare the baskets, it is men who will eventually carry them and make the offerings. The female prerogative is to set the "sitting places" in order, and Mambai are particularly adamant on this point. No man would dream of interfering with the female tasks, nor of advising the women as to how they should be performed. In daily life, a woman's domain is the house. If guests arrive, they are received on the veranda, while the women of the house prepare betel and areca for them. In ritual, Mambai say, it is the same. Women spread the mat and prepare the *mam-hatin* for the reception of the divine guests.

But these female activities are susceptible to another interpretation. If Mother Earth is to be the recipient of the "female" basket, Mambai also speak of her as the mistress of the woman's work. When the women bring out the mat and baskets, Mau Balen said, "it is as if Our Mother opens the mat to roll betel." In ritual, as in myth, the divine female appears first upon the scene. Mambai women, quietly filling baskets, give expression to a central theme of religious life: the proximity of Mother Earth, mistress of the house, eternally awaiting the male wanderer.

While the women engage in their work, the center of the cairn is given over to a parallel male activity. Assisted by Dat Raia, the priests bring a collection of sacred objects from the White House. First, they lay a sheaf of spears inside the crater of the hollow rock. Then they turn to the preparation of the altar post.

The post, the "male fellow," is described as "Our Father's descending place and arising place."[16] Ritually, it represents the final lap of his long journey from the upperworld. He is said to settle upon its central prong and gaze down at Mother Earth, who awaits him at the base of the post. The post is also interpreted as an icon of Heaven's person. A sword hung upon the eastern prong represents the sword that Heaven slings across his right side. A cloth wound over the western prong represents the cloth he drapes across his left shoulder. The spears propped against the post column represent the spear that he balances on his back. In yet another interpretation, the same spears are said to represent the *esa*, a pole associated with Heaven, who vaults between the earth and the sky.[17]

Interpretation of the altar post wavers between index (Heaven's path) and icon (Heaven's person), but the subsequent garbing of male performers is interpreted solely in idioms of contiguity. One priest and two male assistants will offer their bodies to Father Heaven as stepping-stones. For this, they array themselves in special attire intended to protect them from Heaven's dangerous heat. On their heads they wear the *maun-lai*, the headdresses of "cock's tailfeathers." Worn upon the "tip" of the human body, pointing upward to the sky and fashioned from the cock, sentinel of the rooftop, *maun-lai* have strong heavenly associations. They are used only in white ritual and have no counterpart in mortuary. *Tada*, the drooping anklets of goat hair, have black ritual counterparts. In myth, *tada* are created by Mother Earth for her mortuary feast, but those worn in white ritual cannot be used for black purposes. Mambai say that Father Heaven settles upon the headdress, slides down over the metal disks (*fila*) which the performers hang across their chests, and leaps onto the foot-ornaments, gradually closing the gap between himself and Mother Earth. While the men dress themselves by the altar post, the final preparations are made. The women set out more areca and betel in "four white bowls and four black bowls." The white bowls are for the Malaia, the "children of the sea," and the black are for the Timorese "children of the interior," all of whom are formally invited to the ceremony. Small round baskets called *taka* are also filled with betel and areca, destined for the spirits of the outside and inside who come in the deities' wake. Beginning with the male and female baskets, a Dat Raia bears all the offerings to the foot of the altar post.

Now everyone takes his or her place. Women, young people, and children, together with the Alferes and Kafitan, perch along the edge of the cairn. Four women (including the two female elders) hold small drums (*bakaduda*) or gongs (*dadir*) in their laps. The elder men of the village, assisted by three Dat Raia, cluster between the hollow rock and the altar post, forming a ring around the priest who will perform the chants.[18] The latter pours palm liquor into a tin cup, drinks, and passes it to those near him. As he begins to speak, the men around him draw closer. Some accompany him softly, intoning the alternate parallel lines of ritual speech.

The opening speech is in a form known as *foder*. *Foder* is said to have "neither trunk nor tip," and so it "jumps here, jumps there." The end of a recitation is not determined by content, but by the number of sets.

As the priest trails off, indicating the close of a set, the women on the edge play their drums and gongs, until the priest raises his voice again. Sets of *foder* are calculated in sevens, the number of totality. Where *foder* is followed by other speech forms, the seventh set is the signal for transition. In the Aif-Lulin rites the chant segment consists of fourteen sets of *foder*.[19]

At the end of the fourteenth set, the men at the altar place rise. Two young men approach the *titir*, the masculine drum. Accompanied by a third man on the large masculine gong, they pound out an altered rhythm named *keula*, "wind." As they play, the robed and ornamented priest turns his back to the altar post. His two assistants, who are also in full ceremonial attire, seize the spears and stand side by side behind the priest. A Dat Raia lifts the two offering baskets and moves them slowly up and down, silently computing seven times four and eight times three. Led by the Dat Raia who carries the baskets, the men walk stiffly down from the cairn to the eastern earthen area, accompanied by the din of the great drum and gong. The four women join them there, and the male rhythms give way to those of the small drums and gongs, as the women play and dance.

Mambai interpret the sequence of words, percussion, and acts as a means of communicating with the divinities, and in particular, with the remote male. The initial sounds of speech, drum, and gong open a channel of contact. Performers emphasize the difficulty of establishing contact with Father Heaven, who is said to be startled and alerted by the great clamor. The temporal unfolding of audial display represents a progressive narrowing of distance. As the chant proceeds, Heaven arises, dresses, saddles his horse, and sets out. The moment when the chant gives way to the thundering din of the *titir* signals his arrival, for he himself "walks with the wind." The percussive pronouncement is interwoven with the visual signs of his advent at the altar post, where the spears are lifted and presented to the priest's shoulders. Thus Heaven is carried slowly and majestically to join the women and their unseen mistress. Once reunited the deities take their respective seats in the baskets.

Then the procession forms, led by the Dat Raia holding aloft the baskets. Behind him follow the priest, the two spear-bearers, and last of all, the four women. They leave the altar by the northern "door," and proceed to the sacred rocks, Ber Koli and Maun Koli. Again, the Dat Raia shakes his baskets up and down to present the deities to the village sacra. The priest lays a breast disk upon the rock and lights a candle over it. He "shreds" (*koi*) tiny bits of areca and betel from a separate bowl and places these upon the disk. A second Dat Raia hands him a cock. He shakes it up and down, seven times four and eight times three, and slowly strangles it to death. Then they descend from the rock and march to Tai Talo, the banyan, to perform the same actions. The procession returns to the altar place, where the Dat Raia sets the baskets down before the hollow rock. The priest lays a breast disk upon its rim and makes the final offerings. This concludes the rite.

During the afternoon, the women cook pots of rice inside the Black House. Dat Raia boil the sacrificed fowls and "new" tubers. When the food is ready, the "winnowing baskets and covered baskets descend" from the Mother's house. The women scoop out handfuls of rice to cover the bottoms of the baskets. They pass them to a "sitting priest," who distributes pieces of the sacrificial meat among the winnowing baskets, the covered baskets, the white bowls, and the black bowls. When all these containers have been "stuffed" with rice and meat, Dat Raia set them in front of the altar post, surrounding the two *mam-hatin*. The rest of the rite follows the same sequence as the preceding segment. Now, however, the offerings are tiny bits of meat and spoonfuls of rice. When these oblations are completed, the rite concludes with a communal meal. The elder men, again ensconced between the rock and the altar post, eat first. Their portion is the head, neck, and jaw. Once they have begun to eat, women fill bowls with rice, and the sitting priest adds bits of meat and tubers. Everyone down to the smallest child receives his or her portion, and all participants eat together at the altar place.

6. Intent and Representation

Similar two-part rites recur in all white performances. Formal statements of intent identify the specific purpose of each such rite. In the Aif-Lulin ceremony, the altar rite is held "to beseech rain" or, more obliquely, "to open the lid of the vessel." When discussing his ritual function, a priest may speak as if the phrase "opening a vessel" were a descriptive account of his actions. One priest once spoke to me in such matter-of-fact, demonstrative idioms that I began to think the "vessels" he had referred to were materially present, and that I had somehow failed to observe this sequence of the rite. Mau Balen and Mau Bere hastened to correct that impression. "It is words which open," they said, "it is only with words."[20]

The rite, however, is not composed solely of words. Performance is a multimedia display. Objects, acts, speech, and music are all attributed referential meanings that are connected in exegetical commentaries.

Performance as a whole is conventionally interpreted as a formalized sequence of greeting behavior. One level of native exegesis consists of pinning every stage in the temporal unfolding of the performance to a corresponding movement of the deities, and I have interlaced my descriptive account with these commentaries. In this, I essentially replicate the process of my field investigations, for I first understood the rite as a dramatic representation of the arrival and reception of the deities. Later, I learned of multiple connotations implicit in the sequential development of the rite. In its entirety, performance is not only a "mural" unfolding in time, but also a complex "palimpsest," a layered structure of parallel representations. Superimposed upon the scene of the reception of the divinities is a cosmic conjunction which liberates the rite from the confines of time and space and sets the poignant "perhaps" that I spoke of earlier in a larger context.

The initial sequence of chant and percussion is positionally defined as a loud invocation, intended to awaken the deities, but the words that are actually spoken do not narrate the arrival of Heaven and Earth. The journey format that characterizes mythology and other forms of ritual oratory is not used in addressing the deities.[21] *Foder* is composed of fragments of myths, lists of names, references to the social order, and invocations. There is, however, a narrated event obliquely recounted in this discourse.

Two recurrent refrains weave through ritual speech. The one is an invocation, expressed in manifestly sexual idioms:

Au ama teula du ma	My Three Fathers, descend here
Du ni inkai fata	Descend upon my Four Mothers
Tita oid bubu	For the wetness to swell
Raia oid ri.	For the earth to ooze.

Or, as in this variation:

Au ama teula du ma	My Three Fathers, descend here
Kde ni inkai fata	Sit upon my Four Mothers
It inan lohe ni malan	Our Mother opens her cloth
It inan lohe ni saunetan	Our Mother opens her garment
Teiki ulun mreo	Lays down the head in the proper position

Fod oen kmesa.   Stretches out the legs in the correct position.

Such utterances alternate with others of the following type:

Loh Buti	Loh Buti
Loh Meta	Loh Meta
Er-inun	Water of the nose
Ma-mahun	Moisture of the jaws
Uf Mau uf ma	Mist Fellow [come] mist here
Tah Mau tah ma	Fog Fellow [come] fog here
Oid ma hdeol ni Tai Talo	To come swing from Tai Talo
Oid ma ke ni Maun Koli	To come straddle Maun Koli
Hdeol ni nor-hukun	Swing from the drooping-leaved one
Fali ni tete-reman	Grasp hold of the flat-backed one
Oid lo	To shower
Oid kair	To scatter
Ruik Bebili	Drench Bebili
Mahu Behaila	Becloud Behaila
Tita oid bubu	For the wetness to swell
Raia oid ri.	For the earth to ooze.

A single sequence of events is signified by these two refrains. In ritual speech Mambai use various discursive means to evoke the idea of the production of rain.

To discuss whiteness in the context of ritual performance is to discuss what Mambai refer to as the "path of rain." The generalized prosperity invoked in white ritual is made possible by rain, which emerges as the underlying objective of all white ritual action. "Everything needs rain," Mau Balen used to tell me, "and when they speak [in ritual], though they beseech all sorts of things, yet they beseech one thing alone, which is rain." And then he would look away and murmur: "The rain does not come from heaven, Menina. It arises in the earth." But when I eagerly plied him with questions, he silenced me, saying that these were sacred matters, though we might speak of them in time.

In white ritual, one speaks of little else. Whether it is a matter of promoting plant and human fertility, or of consecrating a new house, the priests call over and over upon the "white wetness" of the "white lower earth." There, at its source, it is not called "rain" (*usa*), but "milk" (*susun*). Whatever lives and grows must sink its "roots" into the lower world to nurse. Grass and tree, peas and beans, potato and cassava, banana and yam, white rice and red rice, white corn and yellow corn, snake and lizard, wild bird and tame bird, mouse and *flura* bird, shrimp and eel, shark and crocodile, goat and pig, horse and buffalo, dog and cock, woman and man—the list goes on and on to include all the denizens of the earth, the water, and the air. All their "roots cleave to the earth" to nurse and grow tall, "so that the bud may brush the sky." And each year brings new births, and the milk must be replenished.

Sacred springs located outside of the village link the upperworld, the underworld, and the sea. These still pools of water are said to be connected to the sea by terrestrial channels. The white waters of the underground seep into the springs and pass outward to the sea. Loh Buti and Loh Meta are the sacred eels who guard the portals of the springs and distribute milk to all the creatures of water and sea. All these "wild things/water innards" open their mouths and exhale through their noses. The milk wafts up with their breath, "arises in the water of the nose, arises in the moisture of the jaw." Once it has congealed in the air, it is called Mist Fellow and Fog Fellow. These are the moist thick airs of the early morning that float over the grass, bamboos, trees and "straddle" Maun Koli, the "flat-topped" rock of Raimaus. Maun Koli, the "balance and scales," weighs out the mists and tosses the day's measure of moisture up into the air, where it is caught by the branches of Tai Talo and "swings from the drooping-leaved one." The banyan flings the mists upward once more to "strad-dle *maun-ura* bird and *kakeora* bird," two small, high-flying birds that are said to "play in the clouds." By midday, the birds arrive at Us Luli, mountain of "Sacred Rain," and the mists have now thickened into clouds. The birds tender the clouds to the four guardians of Us Luli, Us Keul/Sa Kok and Mau Toh/Rai Hul, who pour them into the eight sacred "vessels and urns." Soon "the urn froths over/the vessel smokes," as the churning clouds split apart and release their moisture. Then the rains "drench Bebili," and the clouds recongeal to follow the rains and waft over Behaila.

The preceding paragraph is a summary account of the events that are elliptically recounted in ritual speeches. The segment I quoted is part of a longer sequence:

Loh Buti	Loh Buti
Loh Meta	Loh Meta
Saun-huin	Wild things
Er-lalan	Water innards
Neo ro	Fool one another

171

Dobo ro	Play with one another
Fe duak nor soruk	It is [they] who are lined up and erect
Mrusu nor dlai	Unsteady and shaken
Her loda rua	In the two wildernesses
Her loda teula	In the three wildernesses
Oid sai ni er-inun	To arise in the water of the nose
Oid sai ni ma-mahun	To arise in the [moisture of the jaws][22]
Ble doen nor salin	Awake in the still pool and streaming water
Ble liman nor flan	Awake in the arm and canal[23]
Uf Mau oid blei hei	For Mist Fellow to awake already
Tah Mau oid blei hei	For Fog Fellow to awake already
Sai ni Ur Mau	Rise up onto White Eucalyptus Fellow
Sai ni Foi Mau	Rise up onto Black Eucalyptus Fellow
Sai ni Kur Sa	Rise up onto Grass Brother
Sai ni Lei Sa	Rise up onto Reed Brother
Sai ni Betu Sa	Rise up onto Bamboo Brother
Sai ni Or Sa	Rise up onto Bamboo Sister[24]
Hdelu ni Tai Talo	Swing from Tai Talo
Ke ni Maun Koli	Straddle Maun Koli
Hdelu ni nora be huku	Swing from the one with the drooping leaves
Ke ni tete be rema	Straddle the one with the broad back
Hdelu ni maun-ura	Swing from *maun-ura* bird
Ke ni kakeora	Straddle *kakeora* bird
Sai la ni Faut Mau nor Mau Ohar	Rise up to Faut Mau and Mau Ohar
La ni Kait Bere nor Ber Lau	Go into Kait Bere and Ber Lau
No Buti nor Sa Lau	No Buti and Sa Lau
Bes Bere nor Lel Bau	Bes Bere and Lel Bau[25]
La ni Us Keul nor Sa Kok	Go to Us Keul and Sa Kok
La ni Mau Toh nor Rai Hul	Go to Mau Toh and Rai Hul[26]
Usin oid hdeinu	For the vessel to froth
Bian oid masu	For the urn to smoke
Ruik Bebili ma hei	Come drench Bebili already
Mahu Behaila ma hei.	Come becloud Behaila already.

This is a way of speaking especially congenial to ritual contexts. Transformations of substance are expressed through a barrage of metaphors: mists and fog are the exhalations of sacred eels; atmospheric eddies are a game of catch involving rocks, trees, birds;

rain clouds are frothing, smoking vessels. Like much of ritual discourse, such utterances are regarded as opaque messages which can be interpreted, that is, translated into other messages, for instance, into the sexual union of the deities.

In the chants, the ascent of the rains begins with the eels and ends in the sacred vessels of Us Luli, which the priests "open" with their words. Heaven and Earth are not directly implicated in the chain of transmission. However, juxtaposed to the ornate images of the path of rain, one finds the simpler invocations:

Au ama teula du ma	My Three Fathers, descend here
Du ni inkai fata . . .	Descend to my Four Mothers . . .

In exegetical commentaries, Mambai associate the cosmic path of rain with a paradigm of divine sexuality that we have encountered before. The terrestrial female yields up her milk; the celestial male returns it as semen; the female reconverts this substance into milk. Milk is the rising moisture; semen is the falling rain; new milk is the rain that seeps down into the soil. The pattern expressed in the theory of procreation reappears in the pattern of cosmic creation.

When they wish (or perhaps I should say, when they are goaded), Mambai treat physiological and cosmic processes as isomorphic, equating rain with semen, or "white blood," and rainfall with insemination. I would stress, however, that they neither willingly nor readily draw such equivalences. Ordinarily, they retain only part of the sexual vocabulary, designating both rain and the underground waters as "milk." The seeming incongruity of a male heaven pouring down maternal milk mystified me for long months, until I learned to see rain and semen alike as "milk to be," "milk in becoming," "milk that was," the volatile substance of the male contribution to life.

Mambai tend to veer away from overtly sexual interpretations of cosmic processes. "This matter is *luli*," as Mau Balen used to say when I plied him with questions about the rains, "it is what we do not say." Ritual speech overlays the sexual imagery with another set of metaphors. Glimmering through the palimpsest, divine sexuality preserves the mysterious character that imbues cosmological origins, yearly renewal, and human procreation.

Heaven and Earth do lie down together. To imagine anything less concrete in a cosmos formed out of the emissions of birth would be thoroughly wrong-headed. It is the human role in all of this which demands clarification, and I return again to that profound "perhaps" of Mambai commentary, the haunting uncertainty that underlies the stylized ritual representations. Perhaps Heaven and Earth respond to the sounds of *keo*; perhaps they sit side by side in the greeting baskets to "peer at the mat" laden with offerings; perhaps they will lie down together in the Black House. Mambai pile up symbolic representations of the desired reunion, only to fall back on the mournful lament:

Au inan du her raia sois	My Mother has descended to the earth
Au aman sai her leola sois.	My Father has arisen to the sky.
Au ba eot	I do not see
Au ba tad.	I do not know.

Year in and year out, the orphans gather to *keo* at the "descending and arising places" of Heaven and Earth. But "if they hear or do not hear, come or do not come, this we cannot know, we cannot see."

What can be seen are a series of indexes: mists, fog, clouds, rain. And within a performance, participants see the "silent and motionless" guardians of the village, the rocks and trees that stand "fixed and steady" between below and above. "I watch over only a rock/I look after only a tree," say the priests. In the presence of rock and tree, the priests turn their backs to the onlookers and make the offerings. The rite moves from oratory to oblation, from public to private. Its purpose is stated anew in each flick of the priest's knife, each shred of meat that he presents to rock and tree.

The making of offerings is referred to as *koia*, "opening, shredding."[27] Oblatory techniques are regarded as central components of priestly knowledge, and I cannot say how widely such knowledge is distributed among laymen.[28] Although other participants are not prohibited from observing the offerings, few people do so, saying that it is the "old ones" who understand these things. What is public knowledge is that the sacred rocks and trees receive the offerings in the name of the deities. But the precise messages that the priests transmit with their tiny piles of shredded meat and spoonfuls of rice are esoteric knowledge.

Offerings are calculated according to the numerical code. The number four is associated with falling, with trunks and roots, with coolness, and with the Mother. Three is associated with rising, with branches and tips, with heat, and with the Father. Manipulating three, four, seven, and eight, the priest makes his circuit from the altar and back. At the rocks Ber Koli and Maun Koli, four "steadies" the "four legs" of the bottom rock, anchoring the rocks in the earth. Three follows "like a key to open the rain" and then to "lift" the rain up to the drooping leaves of Tai Talo. The procession enacts this sequence, passing from the rock to the banyan tree. There, the priest steadies the great roots and "anchors them in white water" with fours. Additional fours cool the water and cover them with "black earth." Three lifts up all that is "hot and burning" and lodges such things above the great shade tree Tai Talo. The final threes "lift up" the center branches of the tree, which receive the rains from Ber Koli and Maun Koli, pass them on upward, and open a channel to the altar post, where the falling rain is "received."

Again the procession enacts the symbolic sequence, passing from the banyan back to the altar, where offerings are made at the altar post. The post iconically represents a system of relations. Poised between Heaven and Earth, it is described as the feasting ground for all living things. The "children of the interior/children of the sea" come and "swing" from its outer branches. And all the creatures of the world gather around the "placing rocks" at its base, to feast upon the offerings. Here, all offerings are in sevens, the number of totality: four is to "anchor the trunk," three is to "secure the tip," and so to balance all creatures between Heaven and Earth.

Last of all, the priest approaches the hollow rock, where all offerings are to the Mother and the Father. Four goes to the Four Mothers "to cover Our Mother." Three goes to the Three Fathers "to cover Our Father." A "remainder of one" goes to Mother Earth herself, that she may gather together the roots of all her children and hold them fast in her hand.

Although the precise techniques for making offerings are specialized knowledge, the themes associated with these techniques pervade public speech and action. The overall purpose of the ritual is to establish a balance of opposites, by tempering forces that are dangerous in their pure state. The ideal order that is projected onto the offerings is publicly expressed through the multiple media of performance, poetic oratory, and percussive music, manipulation of objects and representational actions.

Yet the presentation of offerings to rock and tree occupies a privileged position and stands for the entirety of a performance. More precisely, the division of shares in the offerings symbolizes the relationship between silent and speaking mouths, on which Mambai ritual life is based. Priests are the agents of this division. The task that Mambai use to evoke the ritual function is the consecration of all offerings to the sacred rocks and trees, who then release the remainder for human consumption.

Hoit man hauta	Spoon food to the rock
Hoit hail ma	Spoon food back here
Fa man aia	Hand food to the tree
Fa hail ma.	Hand food back here.

The food that people eat in ritual celebrations is symbolically given back to them by their silent elder kin, as recompense for the honors shown them by the speaking mouths. The idea of an exchange, connoted by the sequencing of offerings, in turn conveys other meanings. Throughout a performance rocks and trees are the tangible mediators between above and below, tokens of the desired reunion of the deities. At this level of interpretation, what is handed back to women and men is the fertility of the new year.

6. The Rites of the House

The performance as a whole composes a circuit from the house to the altar and its surroundings and then back to the house. Initially sacred objects are brought out from the houses and displayed upon the altar, where contacts are negotiated. In the final rites, called "Ascend to the House," the sacred objects are returned to their resting places and displayed before the *keora*. Located at the middle of the southern wall of a house, these post shrines are symbolically connected to the outside altar post and they "receive" the rains beseeched on the outside. When the collocations are in order, participants are summoned to the Black House and to the White House in turn, for what may be described as rites of incorporation. Each house rite consists of chants, offerings to the house and its sacra, and a communal meal that marks the close of the performance. From this point on, the elders who observed the initial prohibitions must avoid (*luil*) the "new" crops.

The total spatiotemporal patterning of performance expresses a set of similarities and differences between persons and plants. Human beings pass through a cycle of cool and hot states, marked in private rites of passage. A newborn infant is classified as "cool." It must be ritually heated inside the house, through a series of warm baths that last for seven months. At the end of the baths, the child is pronounced warm, but it is still vulnerable to the extreme heat of Father Heaven. Thus nursing children are symbolically confined to the "warm and shading" house and do not venture outside until their personal heat has increased. Personal heat reaches its zenith in the reproductive years, after which it is said to decline gradually. Old age closes the cycle, and elderly people are described as "cool," like newborn infants.

Cultivated plants go through the same cycle, but their life processes unfold outside of the house. Tubers complete their growth underground, nestled against Mother Earth, but corn, beans, and peas (the crops addressed throughout the ritual cycle) emerge from the earth while still immature and confront Father Heaven. "When they come to life, they see the sun immediately," Mambai say. Extreme heat is equally dangerous to human children and young plants. The former are sheltered inside the house, whereas the latter depend on the clouds that follow the rain and block out the midday sun.

The rites of the wet season are intended to obviate the two opposed forms of excess, the burnt and the rotten. Rain and clouds, at once the products of cosmic balance and the mediators between earth and sky, avert the danger of a dry, withered, barren world. But if the rains are not regulated, the wet turns to the rotten, and the time of birth becomes a time of death.

These dangers are negotiated through the performance as a whole. The central protagonists, the elder representatives of Raimaus, play a critical if undramatic role. They first avoid the old plants of the old year and identify themselves with the new ones in the moment of transition. For in that moment when oppositions are suspended, the two ends of the cycle meet, and old people are equivalent to newborn plants. After the transition has been effected, the identification is broken. The elders avoid the new plants, thereby reestablishing distance between old and young. Two intents are attributed to these avoidances. Positively, the elders observe prohibitions "in order to embrace Our Mother/in order to enclasp Our Father," that is, to bring about the reunion that obviates the one extreme of dryness. Negatively, the effect of the prohibitions is to ward off storms and tempests and so to obviate the other extreme of the wet.

Through acts of avoidance the elders sacralize new life. Their conduct represents the conduct desired of the deities, with whom both life and death ultimately rest. Here, at the symbolic center, the elder representatives of the community act to set creation in motion. And here, as the white cycle unfolds, the community will reunite to offer such forms of assistance as the "old mothers and old fathers" require.

NINE
♦
White Ritual:
The Meeting at the Spring

We seem at times to glimpse behind a word another
sense, deeper and half hidden, and to hear faintly the
entry of another meaning, in and with which others
begin to sound, and all accompany the original
meaning of the word like the sympathetic chimes of
a bell.
—Friedrich Waismann, *"Language Strata"*

1. Communication in Ritual

Ritual performances are complex displays, involving oratory, percussive music, song, dance, collocations, sacrificial offerings, food distribution, and feasting. I have described in some detail how these
various elements are combined in the unfolding of a single performance. What I have sought to convey is the semantic density of ritual
action. Messages coded in different media may refer to one another,
and any one message may be interpreted in multiple ways.

Without claiming that hermeneutic competence is equally distributed, I want to reiterate once more the shared assumption that
Mambai bring to ritual events. They approach these events as meaningful experiences that are susceptible to interpretation—or better,
that require interpretation. Communication in ritual contexts is regarded as deliberately opaque and indirect. It is distinguished from
another, more transparent and direct way of conveying sacred knowledge that is purposively avoided. This other form of communication
is equated with narrative discourse and proceeds ideally "from trunk
to tip," relating events in their precise temporal order of occurrence.
The highly patterned sequential order of ritual events is understood
to be modeled on primordial processes, but the narrative truths are
not thought to be immediately apparent. "Those who know," Mambai
say, "will understand." What such culturally privileged hermeneutes
grasp composes the "trunk" of ritual practices. Others engage in the
same practices, yet they "know only the tip." Rites both conceal and
reveal their underlying meaning, depending on what a particular in-
terpreter brings to the hermeneutic situation.

Rock and tree might tell the trunk story of ritual life. But the

178

elderly guardians of the cosmos have fallen silent, and many people seem to take comfort in the taciturnity of their most valued sacra. In poetic language it is said:

Hin nirin ma, ro eot se hauta	When the many women come, they see only the rock
Maen nirin ma, ro tad se aia.	When the many men come, they know only the tree.

The assertion has a double reference. Seeing only rock and tree, women and men may remain ignorant. On the other hand, if they know how to interpret these icons, they will understand everything; and then, of course, they would know to keep silent.

I, however, cannot take this latter tack. In this chapter I adopt procedures that are at odds with the techniques of Mambai ritual communication, but in accordance, I believe, with the interpretive strategies of my guides. I intend to "come straight, go straight," shifting the focus from the vehicles of ritual communication to an underlying system of meanings.

2. Social Morphology of the Water-Drawing Ritual

Initiating the white ceremonial cycle is the responsibility and prerogative of designated ritual centers and is one index of their hierarchical status. As the cycle unfolds, that status is dramatically enacted in rites that involve the community as a whole. This chapter is addressed to the second stage in the annual cycle, the celebration that Mambai call Er-Soia, "Drawing of Water," or Soi Era, "To Draw Water."

The annual water-drawing celebration encompasses a series of performances that begin at the local level and climax in the ritual centers. There is also a tradition that the ritual centers of different communities stage their respective celebrations in a fixed order, but this seems to be more an ideal than a practice. Within a community, however, the temporal sequencing of performances signifies the relative statuses of the performers. My presentation relates to the community centered around Hohul and Raimaus.

A number of house groups claim descent from houses in Hohul or Raimaus and are ranked as junior "tips." These tip houses maintain sacred springs near their own cult houses, in an area which counts as "garden and palm" in relation to the centers. A spring is shared by a cluster of agnatically related houses. Each house keeps its own sacred gourd, which is dipped in the communal spring at the local water-drawing celebration. These rites are classified as *beha* and they are relatively "silent." "In *beha* rites," people say, "there is only talk. Drum and gong do not sound. There is no solo dancing and no circle dancing." In opposition to these "silent" local performances, the percussive noise of *keo* ceremonies is an indexical symbol of the seniority of ritual centers.

Houses ranked as junior tips to Hohul or Raimaus are expected to participate in the annual performances held in the centers. Strictly speaking, the relationship of a center to peripheral tip houses is classified as *kaka nor ali*, "elder and younger people." On ritual occasions, however, Mambai use symbolic categories that emphasize the dependence of juniors on their seniors. Junior participants represent Hohul or Raimaus as their "old mother/old father," and they are reciprocally represented as "children of garden and palm" (*ankaua nama nor naua*), "children of areca and betel" (*ankaua bua nor maula*), or "young people of the forest" (*losa ai-lalan*). They are symbolically identified with the products of the outside, which they are required to bring to the rites of the "parent" house. This identity is also stressed in narrative traditions, where the founders of junior houses are defined as men who left Hohul or Raimaus to plant gardens, raise livestock, and gather wild produce "on the outside."

The categories *kaka* and *ali* are used to differentiate among different ritual centers. Raimaus stands as "eldest man" to Hohul and to a third origin village named Haut Oen.[1] Relative statuses are reflected in the temporal sequencing of performances. As the eldest, Raimaus initiates all stages of the white cycle. Hohul follows Raimaus, and each stage is closed in Haut Oen.

The narrative charter for the sequencing of ritual performances is the story of Nun Loko and Mau Loko, to which I have alluded in chapter 6. In the full story, Nun Loko of Nunu Fun in Raimaus performs the water-drawing rites in his younger brother's absence. Enraged by this affront, Mau Loko runs away to Hohul, taking all the sacred objects that he can carry, and founds the house Haih Nua. In the next generation, four of his sons, Nun Bere, Mau Leiki, Koil Bere, and Lak Bau, leave Hohul, bearing away the breast disk Ber Batu and a slip from the column of Haih Nua. They settle in Haut Oen where they name their house Lak Batu, after the breast disk. Later, their kin in Hohul appoint them to guard the sacred spear named Tat Mea, which was originally removed from Raimaus by Mau Loko.

Tat Mea must attend ceremonies held in all three origin villages, Raimaus, Hohul, and Haut Oen. Transportation of the spear is a perilous undertaking, conducted only in the dead of night. Before they set out, the bearers are supposed to blow a resounding blast on a horn, as a warning to passersby. Whoever hears the horn knows that Tat Mea is on the road and should keep to the house, lest he or she encounter the stealthy entourage. Chance meetings with Tat Mea are said to bring immediate death.

We have met Tat Mea before, though not his actual person, which is bundled in cloths and kept inside the White House throughout each ritual performance. But his designated representatives are the spears that are placed against the postshrine in all altar rites and presented to rock and tree when offerings are made. The body of Tat Mea may not be displayed. And when Mambai spoke to me of the sacred spear, they recounted his "path" in urgent whispers. That path begins in the Night. Tat Mea is the name given to the *esa*, a pole that Heaven is said to have fashioned out of his own spine, so that he might vault between the upperworld and the underworld.

The ritually stressed relationship among Raimaus, Hohul, and Haut Oen is symbolically constituted by a sacred spear that mythological tradition links directly to Father Heaven. That link is dramatized in altar rites, in which representatives of Tat Mea serve as a means of contacting the male deity. Men from Haut Oen attend performances in Hohul and Raimaus "in order to bear Tat Mea" in the altar rites. They are visible throughout white performances, standing upright and erect, with stern, impassive faces, arrayed in ceremonial attire that marks their association with the god.

I have already called attention to the cosmological notions of order that are refracted through sacred spears, swords, and breast disks. These objects are often invoked as the source of ritual obligations among agnatically related houses. Few sacra are so potent or prestigious as Tat Mea, but the basic idea is the same. It receives condensed expression in the dutiful men of Haut Oen, who annually return Tat Mea to its original sources, to be presented to the deity. Ties among men derive from Father Heaven, and it is to honor Father Heaven that they are ritually reconstituted. Through white ritual performances, with their emphasis on the *kaka nor ali* relationship, the idea that order emanates from the male god is translated into social reality.

Whereas the ritual status of Haut Oen is defined solely by relations to Hohul and Raimaus, these latter are also centers of a wider community. When Hohul and Raimaus hold their rituals, various types of relationships are mobilized. Mambai say that "some people come [in honor of] elder and younger ties and some people come [in honor of] rock and tree. Those said to come in the second capacity include Dat Raia and the groups contained within the *reinu antiku* of the ritual centers.

As the custodians of the soil, Dat Raia must arrive first to set the grounds in order. Then when the great drum actually sounds, the two chieftains of the outside, the Alferes and the Kafitan, convoke the origin villages under their jurisdiction. They call upon each village in a fixed order, but once the villages are assembled, they are collectively designated "children of plains and peaks" (*ankaua rema nor lau*) or "white eucalyptus and black eucalyptus" (*ai ura nor ai foia*), after the trees that grow on the lowlands and the mountain slopes.

Those affiliated with a center by common agnatic descent and those who belong to the reinu participate in different ways. The "children of garden and palm" receive no official summons. In practice, they are informally alerted by members of the ritual centers, but Mambai say that they simply hear the noise of the great drum, which indeed reaches down into the valleys. At this signal, "those who fear rock and tree" are said to go scurrying off to the center, with a chicken, a few sprigs of areca, a sheaf of betel leaves, and a sack of raw rice. On arrival, they will quietly and unobtrusively tender these gifts to elder women of their trunk houses. All such gifts will be consumed in the course of the ceremony. In contrast, the "children of plains and peaks" are formally summoned by their chiefs, according to a fixed order of status that is later replicated in the order of seating at communal meals. They make formal prestations to the male elders of the ritual center, and at the rites of house building they are responsible for presenting a prestation known as "chicken of the Koronel/ egg of the Liurai," which is associated with the old tribute gifts. This prestation consists of a live goat, two chickens, a pig, and two baskets of rice. It is offered with great pomp and formality, in a highly stylized enactment of the community's ideal hierarchical structure.

In summary, the participants at the water-drawing celebration are divisible into five categories:

1. The first includes "people of long ago" (*atub-akin*), "old ones" (*mai mai*), or "house masters/village masters" (*fad-ubun/ri-ubun*). To this category belong the members of the ritual centers, who stand as hosts to all other participants. People of the centers are also identified as "those who light candles" when they visit the White House.

2. The category of "elder and younger people" includes representatives from closely related origin villages, who must bring ritually important sacred objects to the centers. Persons in this category carry the sacred spears that are displayed in altar rites. They may be lin-

guistically assimilated to the category of the hosts, and they receive the host's share in ceremonial meals.

3. "New people," "children of garden and palm," "children of areca and betel," or "young people of the forest" may also be categorized as *kaka nor ali*. These are the members of junior houses who contribute food that is used in the course of the performance. Their defining role as participants is to perform the circle dance, and Mambai sometimes say of those classified as "young people" that "they make the rites beautiful."

4. Dat Raia are the domestic servants. They bring no material gifts but discharge formally specified services in all rites. They look after the grounds, carry the offering baskets in processions, and cook all sacrificial meat.

5. "Children of plains and peaks" or "white eucalyptus and black eucalyptus" are the members of the reinu, who are led by the Alferes and the Kafitan. These persons may join in the circle dance as individuals, but their collective responsibility is to make formal prestations that express their dependent status.

Conspicuously absent from the program is any mention of marital alliance. Although many of the participants are in fact from affinally related houses, marital ties are regarded as irrelevant to white ritual. "That of the white," Mambai say, "does not touch upon women and men. It touches upon rock and tree." Many people single out the communal meals held on the altar as a distinctive feature of white ritual. In contrast to black rituals, where food distribution marks alliance statuses and "people sit separately to eat goat or pork," the emphasis in white ritual meals is on communality. "In the white," Mambai say, "we all sit together and we eat the same food."[2]

In point of fact, white ritual participants eat different portions of the same animal sacrifices, and the portions they receive mark their relative statuses. Distribution of sacrificial animals is based on a semiology of the body, by which particular body parts signify social categories.

White ritual is in no way egalitarian. It does not cancel social distinctions and merge participants into an undifferentiated whole but rather represents a hierarchical whole by a part. The "old ones" of the centers are the part that stands for the encompassing whole. Performances celebrate and recreate an idea of unity in division that in turn evokes the idea of unity before division, on which hierarchy is based. When unity is enacted in ritual centers, two images of the past are brought together. On the one hand, ritual centers are the trunks of agnatically related houses, the ultimate sources of men and sacra. On the other hand, they are also the sources of titles and regalia of office, now vested in active chiefs. Both categories of recipients return to the center to commemorate the past. They bring their received possessions with them, "to show respect for rock and tree." They do not, however, turn over those possessions to the original owners but rather bear them throughout the performance. In ritual contexts participants mark their present divisions in the act that unites them.

The language of social divisions foregrounds one particular metaphor of hierarchy. Although participants are connected to a center in various ways, they may all be represented as "children" who come back into the house after a sojourn on the outside and pay their respects to the "old mother/old father." Through the use of this metaphor, certain social distinctions are symbolically muted—not the hierarchical distinction between superiors and dependents, but the distinctions between different categories of dependents. The dominant metaphor for the community as a whole is the house, and a basic polarity of old and young distributes all its members into the two complementary but unequal categories of life-givers and life-receivers.

I began this study with Mambai representations of ritual as an activity that originates in the cosmogonic Night and so antecedes contemporary institutional divisions. As ritual forms are handed down by original predecessors to their descendants, the forms are, as it were, saddled with a social organization of considerable complexity. Mambai are in no way unaware of the status relations at stake in ritual performances. Yet symbolic categories work to remind participants of the "original" purpose of their ritual practices. Recurrent metaphors of parenthood and age make ritually enacted status relations reflect the hierarchical structure of the cosmos, a structure which encompasses social divisions and gives them meaning to Mambai. In the cosmological model of ritual cooperation, all the younger, speaking children of the land must render service to their silent elder kin. At this level, the eldest member of the human community, the Ritual Lord who participates in the cosmos and represents it to other human beings, is himself a child among other children, united to *keo* the ultimate sources of life.

3. The Living and the Dead

My problem in describing the water-drawing celebration is one of selection and focus. The rich symbolism of the rites that make up a performance would sustain a much more extended treatment than I intend to provide. My purpose is to use the rites to elucidate an ideology of reciprocity that underlies the white cycle as a whole. These ideas lead necessarily to the black rituals of death. Had we begun with the death rites, the same connection would have emerged, for the complementarity of white and black is fundamental. The Mambai themselves assert the holistic character of their ritual system in formal statements of interdependence, and they evoke the whole in each part.

The water drawing takes place at a time identified with the "sun meeting/moon meeting" (*leol-botun/hul-botun*). This meeting marks the stage in agricultural growth when "everything forms flesh." The corn is still green, but the early-flowering cultigens have come to fruition, and an alternate name for the entire ceremony is "to scatter pigeon peas and beans" (*sbar tuira nor kasa*). Restrictions on eating "new" plants are lifted in this stage of the cycle.

Lunar imagery associated with the first two stages of the white cycle suggests an equation of botanic growth with the lunar cycle. Since plants are born at the dark of the moon, it would seem that they grow in conjunction with the waxing moon. However, even if this association is valid, it does not appear to be culturally stressed. What Mambai articulate is a relation between plant fertility and the sea.[3] The symbolic "meeting" of sun and moon marks the moment for another meeting. At the sacred springs where the central rites unfold, the living reencounter the shades of the dead, who return from the sea.

This reunion is foretold in black ritual during a rite called "to exorcise the tree trunk" (*deder ai fun*). At the same time, the dead are enjoined to accept the "bad breast/bad horn" (*susu klaun/diu klaun*), a metonym for the water buffalo that are sacrificed to the dead. The dead are told to bear away these "bad" gifts and await "another year" (*tonan selu*). At the time of the "sun meeting/moon meeting," the dead are to rejoin the living at the spring and make a return gift referred to as the "good breast/good horn" (*susu koden/diu koden*).

These two symbolic transactions express a theme of considerable importance: the living and the dead are linked in a relationship of reciprocal gift-giving which spans the two classes of ritual action. In black ritual, the living dedicate costly sacrifices to the dead. In white ritual, the dead return to bring luck, prosperity, and fertility.

The black dead who receive mortuary gifts are referred to as *maeta*, from *maet*, "to die," or *maet-smakan*, which I translate as "spirits of the dead." Until the dead depart for the sea (discussed in the next chapter), they retain their individual, ancestral identities and may be addressed by their personal names. The journey to the sea radically transforms their relationship to the living by depriving them of their distinctive personalities. "We do not know you anymore/you do not know us anymore" runs the final mortuary oration.

The returning, gift-bearing dead compose a generalized collectivity of ancestral beings. They are addressed as "ancient ones and recent ones" (*munan nor fnorin*) or "ancestors and grandparents" (*bei nor tata*), and they must be referred to as *mahiura* rather than as *maeta*. I shall translate the term *mahiura* as "shades" and I reserve the term "spirits" for their black ritual manifestations. Essentially, the translations are intended to preserve the native lexical distinction between returning, gift-bearing, generalized dead and departing, gift-receiving, individualized dead. Fortunately, the term "shade" is consistent with Mambai metaphors, since, like the sacred shade tree and the "warm and shading" house, the shades of the dead promote human life.

4. The Land and the Sea: Cosmology of the Meeting

The pattern of the water drawing is based on a circuit from inside to outside and back again. The origin village constitutes the inside in opposition to sacred shrines located beyond the village boundary. A sequence of house and altar rites opens the performance. These are intended to invoke Heaven and Earth, who must authorize the exit from the village. Upon conclusion of the altar rite, men, women, and children march out of the village to the accompaniment of female drums and gongs. Their destination is the "tree and spring" (*ai-fu nor er-mata*), paired shrines located a short distance from the village. The one is a named tree with a ring of stones piled around its base. Near by it is the sacred spring, a still pool of water, level with the ground and encircled by a flat ring of stones.[4]

The spatial patterning of performance marks a tension in the relationship between the living and the shades of the dead. Although these two groups must meet, a degree of distance is maintained. On no account may the shades enter the village itself. They are invoked from the altar place, but they are not invited to enter the inner realm of space. They are instructed to awaken and rendezvous with the living on the outside, at the tree and the spring.

The living and the dead are opposed as beings of the dry land (*rai klian*) and beings of the sea (*taisa*). This is the maximal expression of the opposition between inside and outside, for the sea represents the ultimate perimeter of the world. Sacred springs are a logical meeting place for the living and the dead. These still, landlocked pools of water are said to flow into the sea and thus mediate between the two extremes of ordered space. Ritually, however, the spring is not a term in an abstract logic but a concrete channel of contact, an efficacious locus for an encounter between the two radically opposed camps.

These same springs have another level of significance that derives from the mythological relationship of sea to land. Opposed in space as outside to inside, sea and land are also opposed on an axis that unfolds in time, and Mambai place great emphasis on the temporal order of their appearance. That "water and sea" precede "dry land" is a ubiquitous theme in ritual oratory. Chanters repeatedly evoke images of a primordial deluge, after which dry land emerges and gradually grows "wide and broad" (*mlua nor beka*). In any one performance, one is likely to hear many times over such lines as these:

Era benu	The waters overflow
Taisa lau	The sea is at its highest
Raia ba mlua	The land is not wide
Ba beka	It is not broad
Maun Koli koli	Maun Koli [becomes]
Tai Talo talo	Tai Talo [becomes][5]
Era oid ba benu	So that the waters no longer overflow
Taisa oid ba lau	So that the sea is no longer at its highest
Raia mlua sois	The land is wide already
Beka sois.	It is broad already.

In ritual speech these images are not organized into a coherent, narrative account of creation. What is publicly recited is a temporal sequence in which the sea comes first, and the dry land follows. Mambai repeatedly and urgently confided to me that this sequence is part of a story, the walk of the earth. As elements of a narrative, geographical distinctions relate to procreative processes. Myth-tellers identified the primordial waters with the fluids that a woman discharges immediately prior to giving birth. In this case, the woman is Mother Earth. Later, her firstborn child, the dry land, grows "wide and broad," pressed outward by her own reluctant corpse, and the waters slowly recede. From a cosmogonic perspective, the dead who depart for the sea return to the primordial waters of birth. And the springs, where they rejoin the living, represent the terrestrial remnants of these waters, said to be sweetened by the Mother's presence.

The cosmogonic meaning of the spring, its "trunk meaning," is not necessary to an interpretation of the rites. Ritually, what is stressed about spring water are its life-giving, transformative properties rather than its mythic origins. Toward the end of the performance, water drawn from the spring is used to annoint the ritual participants, and there is an implicit parallelism between the images of the dead, who are "changed" by emersion in the sea, and of the living, who are also "changed" by lustrations with spring water.

Yet the connections to original creation are there to be made. Ritual representations of the sacred spring form another palimpsest of layered meanings, and the very potency accorded to the spring in ritual hints at its cosmic origin. I see the connection between the ritual icon and its mythological meaning as an implicit possibility or promise. The spring has the same semantic resonance as certain familiar words which are imbued with what Waismann calls a "deep and sonorous ring" of multiple meanings. The spring is not unique in its chiming, sonorous quality. Tai Talo, the hollow rock, the altar post shrine, these too resonate with mythological meanings that are obliquely expressed in performance, but pervade the larger ritual context in which such icons appear.

5. Greeting and Farewell

The rites for receiving the shades at the spring are similar in pattern to the rites for the reception of the deities. Collocation, chant, presentation, sacrifice, oblation, percussion, dance, and feast are the invariant elements of ritualized receptions. However, the spring setting is different from that of altar or house rites, and the entire atmosphere has a distinctive character.

When the living gather at the spring, the atmosphere of performance blends grief and gaiety. These attitudes are formally distributed along lines of old and young. While the elders of the ritual center hover around the spring to greet the shades with tearful lamentations, visiting young people withdraw a short distance to perform the *tea*, a circle dance accompanied by collective singing. The lilting, often humorous and provocative refrains of the *tea* mingle and harmonize with the more solemn tones of priestly oratory.

The spring itself composes the center of ritual space. As in an altar rite, the center is occupied by the male elders, who squat in a ring around the still pool of water. Older women sit quietly in the background, surrounded by their baskets of areca and betel, patiently awaiting the conclusion of the masculine address.

Much of the oratory is in a form called *taiflakon*, a mode of discourse used in addressing the dead. The content of the oration, as well as its slow, heavy rhythms, imbue the scene with a sad, mournful quality. It is not uncommon for a chanter to weep as he speaks, his broken phrases rising over the sobs of those around him.[6]

In *taiflakon*, the shades are greeted, invited to sit upon the mat that has been spread for them and to gaze upon the feast that is being prepared. They are addressed as a collectivity of ancestors whose names have been forgotten, but whose coming evokes tears and sorrow:

Munan nor fnorin	Ancient ones and recent ones
Hoir au bein	Since [the time of] my ancestor
Hoir au tatan	Since [the time of] my grandfather
Usa heli	The rain [endures]
Lelo heli.	The sun [endures].
Let bout nea	Cross to meet here
Sam suit nea	Step to join here
Nafai du bout nea	Today descend to meet here
Nafai sam suit nea	Today step to join here
Du mret der man huit-raka	All of you descend and gaze upon the spread-out yams
La ni huit-koan	Go on the hollow yam
La ni nau-butin	Go on the white wine
Kde ni bit-lohen	Sit on the open grass mat
Kde ni bor-nafin	Sit on the spread pandanus mat
Oid kikan ma se	Bring your ears here to present
Oid matan ma ha.	Bring your eyes here to show.
Etan au ba eot	I see not your bodies
Kalan au ba tad	I know not your names
Luan ma tita	Tears flow from the eyes
Inun ma sali.	Mucus streams from the nose.

Taiflakon gives way to another speech form called *slor*, in which the chanter narrates the mythical history of the particular spring. He takes up the tale at the moment when one of the ancestors first shouldered his house column, and continues until the ancestor erects his house and "digs a hole/opens a stream" (*doi doin/sai salin*), the ritual language formula for the construction of a spring.

The same speech form is also used to invoke and to exorcise spirits, and to consecrate a new cult house. *Slor* always involves the recitation of a "path" (*dan*)—whether the path taken by the spirits or by the ancestors with their house pillars. Mambai seem to attribute an instrumental function to this particular way of speaking, and they characterize *slor* as a technique of enacting the path in question. The formal intent of the *slor* at the spring is to reunify the waters. By reciting the origin path of a spring, the priest recreates its first foundation and restores the spring to its original fullness. This task completed, the priest goes on to recite the path taken by the shades with their gifts. When he has conducted the shades to the threshold of the spring, he verbally "opens the door of the interior" (the southern co-ordinate of the spring), in order to "receive from the sea" all the wealth brought by the shades.

The offerings made at the spring reiterate these themes. The symbolic intent is to encircle and purify the waters, and to open the "door" of the spring to the shades. The priest then scoops up a handful of water (*dleus era*) which represents an offering made by the shades, as a token of their promised gifts. Finally, the priest "draws water" with a sacred gourd (*tauha*). He makes "cool" offerings counted in fours and eights, intended to drag down all that is "bitter and sour" (*felu nor bar*) to the base of the gourd; "hot" threes raise what is "tasty and pleasant" (*meki nor mali*) to the top of the gourd. The water itself is referred to as oil and the milk of a young coconut.

After the water drawing, four women of the ritual center play upon drum and gong. As they play they dance in a circle around the spring. The shades are said to accompany them, delighting in the sound of drum and gong. Then the shades escort their hosts to the tree shrine, where a meal of rice and chicken is served. The shades depart at the conclusion of the meal, and the performers return to the village.

The parting is not final. The shades are said to linger nearby until all the springs connected with the village have been visited in turn. Mambai point to the rains as an index of their presence, for the shades "walk with tempests and wind" (*lolai nor us meta nor lu mau*). Storms are expected to continue until their final departure, and at the two performances that I witnessed, these expectations were not disappointed. On both occasions, the rain fell almost without a break from our foray to the first spring until our final reentry into the village.

Before the living may formally return to the village, a decisive separation must take place. This is effected at another tree shrine, situated immediately outside of the village. Here, at the threshold between outside and inside, the priest once again addresses the shades with tearful *taiflakon*, mournfully bidding them farewell. The path of the gifts is again recited in *slor*, and the shades are sent away on their return journey to the sea. The living reenter the village alone, where they stop to pay homage to rock and tree, and then ascend to the altar place.

6. Altar and House Rites

The ceremony reaches a climax at a communal feast served on the altar place. In this rite the "old ones" enact their life-giving role. They provide food for all their assembled guests, and they also lay out offerings dedicated to every manner of being recognized in Mambai cosmology, nonhuman as well as human.

Status relations among those physically present at the feast are expressed in the obligatory seating arrangement. The male elders of the ritual center sit in the place reserved for them, on the raised cairn between the rock and the altar post shrine. Before they take their places, a Dat Raia sets out banana leaves on the "white" eastern part of the earthen area below the cairn. He arranges the leaves into an arc that represents the mythical table at which the "children of the four quarters" were once seated. In ritual performance this place is occupied by the members of the kingdom, the "children of plains and peaks," who sit north to south, in an order that reflects their respective ranks. Above them, but on the outside of the elders, the "young people of the forest" squat along the rim of the altar, together with women and children of the center. Public speech at this occasion emphasizes the idea that all participants partake of the feast together:

Mu mret sois	All eat already
Eun mret sois	All drink already
Hoit man hauta la	Spoon out to rock there
Hoit hail ma	Spoon back here
Fa man aia la	Hand out to tree there
Fa hail ma	Hand back here
Man an-reman	To the Plains Children
Man an-laun	To the Peaks Children
Man ai ura	To the White Eucalyptus
Man ai foia	To the Black Eucalyptus
Man an-hoha	To the children of the interior
Man an-taisa.	To the children of the sea.[7]

191

The order in which participants are served also expresses status distinctions. First of all are the eldest of all participants, the sacred rocks and trees. After offerings have been consecrated to them, their guardians, the elder representatives of the ritual center, take as their portion the "cool" parts of the sacrifice, the head, the jaw, the neck, and the loins. The remainder of the sacrifice is distributed among the visitors and the women, young people, and children of the center. In one metaphor for the eating order, the elders are the "old mother/old father" who eat first to soften the food for their young charges, as a parent may chew tough morsels before feeding them to an infant.

The performance concludes with a series of house rites that begin in the White House. Only the male "masters of the village" enter this house, to light candles and prostrate themselves before Father Heaven's sacred table. In contrast, the rite held in Mother Earth's temple is open to representatives of all the visiting groups.

All the sacred objects of each house are set out in a great collocation in front of the post shrine, to witness the proceedings and receive their share of the feast. The priest sprinkles water from the sacred gourd, scattering it to the four corners of the house. The lustration is intended "to mould women and men/to mould pigs and dogs" (*oid lum hina nor maena/oid lum haiha nor ausa*).

In their exegetical commentaries, informants drew an analogy between the ritual lustration and the bathing of an infant. They explained that in this rite, all women and men are "as little children." The spring water is also poetically likened to the lubricating oils extracted from the nut of the candlewood tree (*muira*), and to the milk of a young, green coconut. The act of "moulding" people with this substance is said to have a cleansing, cosmetic, and fertilizing effect. Young people are made white and beautiful, so that they may become enamored of one another, make love, and bring forth offspring:

It ti luk buti	Let us wash white
It ti riu mo	Let us bathe clean
Inun oid lete	For the nose to be curved
Fau oid sabe	For the cheeks to be plump
Hina oid luru hail maena	For women to be pleasing to men
Maena oid luru hail hina	For men to be pleasing to women
Hina oid loko hail maena	For women to desire men
Maena oid loko hail hina	For men to desire women
Oid teiki ulun mreo	To lay down their heads in the proper position
Oid fod oen kmesa	To stretch out their legs in the correct position

Bita oid bubu	For the mat to swell
Saka oid ri	For the bed to ooze
Oid mor loi	To give birth again
Oid ko loi	To bring forth again
Hina oid sai selu	For women to emerge changed
Maena oid sai selu.	For men to emerge changed.

7. White Reciprocity

A ceremony directed to the growth and ripening of cultivated plants thus concludes with images of human beauty and fertility. At one level, the coincidence of human and botanic well-being simply extends the person/plant analogy introduced in the Prohibition of Fire. To Mambai, however, the metaphoric association of persons and plants is more than a decorative figure. The full meaning of the metaphor derives from the cosmology of exchange. A highly abbreviated discussion of the water-drawing performance has left the organization of exchange relations implicit in the notion of a gift given to the living by the shades of the dead.

What, after all, is the "gift" of the shades? The chants tell of buffalo, goats, breast disks, and money, of pigs and cloths, which are the traditional prestation items exchanged between affinally linked groups. Moreover, the shades are said to be presenting countergifts for the "bad breast/bad horn" that their wife-takers sacrificed at a previous mortuary ritual. Thus the transaction at the spring is symbolically dependent upon marital exchange relations.

Mambai say that the shades do not bring the actual "bodies" (*etan*) of the gift items invoked. What they give is a promise of fertility and prosperity. They "turn their faces" (*klil ahen*) toward the living, and their blessing makes the crops thrive. The abundant harvest brings wealth, which is used to purchase pigs. Eventually, these pigs go to "meet a buffalo," that is, to contract a marital alliance with a wife-taking affine. Then Mambai say: "My mother and father have turned around," for the "bad" buffalo sacrificed in a long-past mortuary has been replaced with the promise of a "good" new one. Hence the dead, in their two roles as receivers and givers of gifts, symbolically mediate the exchanges transacted by allied groups.

But the shades also play another role in the life of house groups, and in the life of the cosmos as a whole. We have in fact already observed them at their labors, which unfold over the course of the white cycle. Ritually, the meeting of the living with the dead at the spring is represented as a physical encounter between two opposed camps. In much the same way, the reception of Heaven and Earth is dramatically enacted in the rites of cosmic reunion. Both these ritual encounters, however, are themselves oblique microcosms of macrocosmic events.

Let us inquire further into the meaning of the gift-bearing shades who come from the sea and who "walk with the rains." We have met them before, in the oratory and the offerings of the earlier rites performed "to invoke the rains." In a Mambai theory of the afterlife, to which I will return in the next chapter, the dead who depart overseas are transformed into various forms of marine life. Loh Buti and Loh Meta, the sacred eels who guard the entries of the springs, are the leaders of this marine host. As mediators between the land and the sea and between below and above, their role is to negotiate a cosmic exchange.

Those who "sleep inside of the water/sleep inside of the sea" have no hands, Mambai often point out, but they use their "breath" (*snukan*) "to care for those of the surface of the earth." We know already the nature of their service. They exhale the moisture of the earth that rises up to the sky and returns as nourishing rain. The rain penetrates the soil and gives life to growing plants, which in turn are the sustenance of women and men. But cultivated plants provide more than physical sustenance. The rising "breath" of the shades comes back with the rains, is transmitted to the plants, and passed on to the people who eventually consume the plants. Thus the shades rejoin the living through the medium of cultivated plants. This metapsychotic cycle is obliquely signified in the invocation of the shades at the spring.

Ma bout ni doen nor salin	Come meet at the still pool and streaming water
Liman nor flan	The arm and canal
Ni ai fu nor er mata	At the tree base and spring
Du ni Loh Buti	Descend to Loh Buti
Du ni Loh Meta	Descend to Loh Meta
Uf Mau uf ma	Mist Fellow mists here
Tah Mau tah ma	Fog Fellow fogs here
Oid du ni sel-butin nor sel-kmein	To descend into the white corn and yellow corn
Oid du ni kas-butin nor bal-oen	To descend into the white bean and yam
Oid du ni Bi Lebu nor Mail Kei	To descend into the gardens of Bi Lebu and Mail Kei

Isin oid maklili	For flesh to turn about
Eran oid takali	For water to turn around
Hina oid sai selu	For women to emerge changed
Maena oid sai selu.	For men to emerge changed.

The ritual representation of gift-giving shades includes among its significations a cycle of death and rebirth, whereby the ancestors return to perpetuate their own descent lines. The continuity of human life is only achieved through the ritually secured productivity of the soil, for human sexuality is explicitly associated with the abundant harvest. Ritually, the water drawing concludes with images of the well-being of both persons and plants, and Mambai expand on the connection. When women and men are hungry, they are said to become sexually listless. "They do not desire one another unless their stomachs are full." Everything takes place exactly as at the cosmic level, where sexual contacts are not the product of "natural" appetites, but rather require the ritually effected reversal of an innate lethargy that draws male and female apart.

In the social realm continuity also depends on such reversals, for the sexual act is the means by which the ancestors return to life. Embodied in cultivated plants which stimulate desire, the essence of an ancestral shade is transmitted to women through sexual intercourse, and the child that is born will have a "face like an ancestor" (*ahen man tata*). Then, Mambai say:

Isi maklili sois	Flesh has turned about
Era takali sois.	Water has turned around.

Mambai do not forget that the continuity of human life is premised on human consumption of plants. Human beings can only nurse from Mother Earth's breast by devouring the produce of the soil, and so, in the end, "they eat their elder kin" (*ro mu ni kakan*). What is most characteristic of Mambai thought is a tendency to conceive of these interactions with the plant world as reciprocal obligations that unfold over the course of a total system of ritual activities.

In white ritual the speaking mouths fulfill their obligations to the cosmos by setting creation in motion. The entire silent world depends on them for this service, and the new plants, which cannot live without rain, are among the prime beneficiaries. They are not, however, the ultimate beneficiaries. In a consistent idiom of reciprocity, Mambai explain that the plants that have been nurtured through ritual intervention must now give themselves to their human benefactors in the form of food. As Mau Bere once put it: "We spoon and hand food out to them, but now we call on them to spoon and hand [themselves] to us." Restrictions on consumption are lifted at the water drawing, and the new cultigens are no longer *luli*. A metaphoric relation between persons and plants evolves into a metonymic one, where cultivated plants exist within human society and promote the well-being of women and men. In short, the new crops become the return gift for ritual services, a gift associated with milk, beauty, sexual appetite, fertility, and with the very continuity of an ancestral line over time.

The exchange relation between persons and plants is connected to the relation between the living and the dead. When the water-drawing ceremony begins, there is also an imbalance in the latter relation, which originates outside the performance. The shades are bound to the living by a prior obligation, incurred through their acceptance of death gifts. Whether the return gift they make is represented as the blessing that they bestow on the crops, as the rains that they regulate, or as their own essence transmitted to the plants, what the shades of the dead bring is a gift of life.

Though the ceremony closes with imagery of fertility and renewal, Mambai know that they have only reached a temporary halting place and that new obligations lurk just ahead. Ideas introduced in the water drawing come to the foreground in the final performance in the white cycle, held to celebrate the corn harvest. Dried by the sun and ritually interred in the sacred storage vats, harvested corn provides a strong iconic representation of "dead" cultigens, and it is described as "old," "dry," "ugly," "ruined," like a dead person. Indeed, though the harvest rites are part of the white cycle, Mambai identify them as a mortuary ceremony for cultivated plants. In white ritual, women and men make what restitution they can. The spirits of the dead plants are sent away along a cosmic path of regeneration. They are verbally conducted southward to Nama Rau, the mountain of origins, where chant paths end abruptly. At this point a chanter will softly murmur:

Hulun tui	The hair snaps
Maran hdor	The fruit falls
Hetun taudali ma	The flower comes fluttering
Huan baskari ma.	The seed comes scattering.

And then he switches quickly to a recitation of the return path taken by the new seed that tumbles down from the mountain.

The white, however, is not enough. Such is the Mambai evaluation of one half of their ritual life. Always the promotion of life leads to death and depletion. The plants age and die. The harvest ceremony presages the termination of the rainy season. Then Father Heaven withdraws from his consort to roam at will across the land. He leaves her almost drained, her milk depleted by the constant demands of her hungry children.

When Mambai discuss ritual obligations, they harp upon the sufferings and tribulations of the divinities, openly emphasizing the ordeals of Mother Earth. She must, they say, be repaid for the milk that she has provided. And though her children help her to renew her milk each year, by offering the clamor of *keo* and material gifts of animal flesh, they know that they can never eradicate the debt by these means alone. The imbalance in their relationship to the cosmos is implied in the total organization of ritual life.

Buti ba rat	When white is not enough
Nor meta fe tlut.	It is increased with black.

The insufficiency of white ritual is sometimes reformulated as an insufficiency of "hairy" animal sacrifices. In the end, the "hairless" sacrificer must become the sacrifice, the giver must become the gift, the feaster must become the food. For human death is but another prestation, a gift of black, decayed flesh that is "as food already." Thus the association between persons and plants evolves from a metaphor into a metonym, and at length into an identity. Persons, "planted" (*taen*, "to plant, to bury") in the earth, become the food of Mother Earth and in this way they repay the plants which died so that they might live.

This ritually regulated cycle of life, death, and renewal resonates with a founding mythological event. As people and plants move through the stages of the cycle, progressing from a state of whiteness to the blackness of death and decay, they replicate the primordial experience of Mother Earth, who first vitalized the soil with her own decaying flesh. In narrative discourse Mambai project the cycle onto the deity's existential condition, and represent her as "half white and half black, half clean and half dirty, half alive and half dead." Ritual discourse is more oblique. White rites are suffused with verbal allusions to a vessel that is foul and putrescent on the outside, but sweet and pure on the inside, a black container that holds white contents. The vessel is a metaphor for the cosmic sphere of the below. Mambai represent the underworld as a two-tiered realm, composed of a black surface layer and the pure white lower depths.

Mother Earth's temporal alternations are the narrative model for the cosmological scheme, but no one tells the story of the lower world in public ritual contexts. There is, however, a story to be told. It is implicit in the verbal conjunction of cosmic imagery with an anthropomorphic representation of the structure of the below. At key moments in white ritual speech, the priests recite an enigmatic invocation:

Iru butin	White chest
Rai buti suan	White lower earth
Iru metan	Black chest
Rai meta teten.	Black upper earth.

Let us return to the primary stated purpose of the white ritual cycle, which is to assure abundant rainfall. The means to this end is the sexual union of male and female. From the point of view of the system, rain is unclassifiable, participating in both the male upperworld and the female underworld. The Mambai solution to a taxonomic problem produced by their own symbolic schemes is implicit in the theory of conception, where semen appears as both the source and the product of maternal milk. Semen, rain, and milk are symbols of the type that Bourdieu isolates, "so overdetermined as to be indeterminate even from the point of view of the schemes which determine [them]" (1977, 141).

The overdetermined indeterminacy of rain provides a representation of the white ritual task. Defined in terms of its cosmological content, that task is to promote the rains that replenish the "white lower chest" of Mother Earth. The complementary task of replenishing the "black upper chest" is deferred until the dry season, when the black rituals of death are performed.

Mambai play out their cosmology in performing these oppositionally defined ritual tasks, and in the process they reproduce a meaningful opposition between types of social relationships. The community that unites to replenish the "white chest" is represented as an encompassing house. Viewed from within, the house is divided into life-giving parents and their dependent children. These groups cooperate to secure a cosmic balance of male and female that is also reflected in the house itself. But white ritual alone would lead inevitably to imbalance, in the cosmos and in the house. No matter how much milk Father Heaven and Mother Earth jointly produce, it is consumed by their multitudinous children; Mother Earth grows weary from her labors, and Father Heaven turns away from her. And although a house group may reconstitute itself each year, it is part of a wider social universe and depends on others for its reproductive vitality.

The community that unites to replenish the "black chest" is bound together by marital ties. In the face of death, marital allies must simultaneously discharge their obligations to the cosmos and to one another. The cosmological obligations are simpler, for there is only one woman who craves both the white and the black. But in Mambai society there are always two women: she who brings life into a house, and she who takes life away.

TEN

Black Ritual: The Journeys of the Dead

1. The Afterlife in Mambai Theory and Performance

Mambai do not regard death as a single event, but as a protracted process. Like many other Indonesian peoples, Mambai attribute different stages to the afterlife. Dying initiates a series of passages which take the dead farther and farther away from the living.

In beginning with white ritual, I presented a relationship of maximal distance and its dissolution in the metapsychosis. Before the dead can attain the status of nameless, returning shades, they must undergo a transitional period of indeterminate length, during which they retain their individual identities. According to the commonest conception, they pass the interim on the top of Nama Rau, in the ultimate house of origins. In another conception, they take up residence in the cult houses of the groups to which they belong. Still another version locates them on the mountain, but in invisible spirit houses associated with their own groups.

All changes in the condition of the dead are effected through the system of black rituals. This category of ritual action comprises funerary rites (*taen maeta*, "to bury, to plant the dead"), postburial rites (*maeta ni hun*, "the lifting of the dead"), and a spectacular, climactic celebration called a *maeta*, from *maet*, "to die." Mambai refer to this last stage in the sequence as "to dispatch the dead" (*toil maeta*). It is the only stage that is accompanied by drum and gong, and it is also distinguished as "to *keo* the dead," or simply *maet-keon*. Each stage of the mortuary process requires the cooperation of maritally allied groups. The comparatively simple gift exchanges at the funeral initiate a series of transactions that culminate, years later, at the rites of final dispatch.[1]

When an individual dies, the corpse is returned to the cult house of his or her group, which, in the case of a married woman, is her husband's house.[2] Members of the dead person's family call upon their wife-givers and wife-takers to gather at the cult house with pigs and goats for a funeral feast. While the participants await the proper moment for burial, the corpse is interned inside the house. Its head is pointed toward the south and its feet toward the north. It must lie in this position until its foul stench indicates that decomposition is underway. In the ideal, a corpse is exposed for seven days and seven nights, the duration of the interval between Mother Earth's death and the decay of her flesh. The actual period for human corpses is considerably shorter and varies in particular cases. What is constant is the idea of waiting for the tangible signs of decay. "Seven days, that we cannot endure," Mau Bere said to me, "but we endure it as long as we can, and we wait until the corpse begins to stink." When the corpse is finally buried, it is described as "refuse and dust."

The burial rites also involve the spirit (*smakan*) of the dead. A spirit sets out on a journey that it may have to make several times over. According to the priests, it travels southward to Nama Rau. No one views this departure as decisive, and my impression was that many people are not sure exactly where a spirit goes on its first foray. It is ritually required to withdraw from the immediate environs of the living, to give its surviving relatives time to prepare for a post-burial celebration.

Approximately seven months after burial, the same cast reassembles for the "lifting of the dead."[3] The wife-givers contribute pigs for the feast, and they dedicate cloths to the dead. Wife-takers make the costlier payments of goats, metal disks, and money. Native rubrics identify all prestations with particular obligations to the dead. Both women and men must be repaid for their "fatigue and prostration." In the case of a woman, stress is placed on her ordeals inside the house, nursing and tending her children. A man is repaid for his labor outside in the fields. All prestations are collectively received by men of the deceased's house, who may add livestock of their own, if necessary. These agnates slaughter the gift animals, and redistribute the meat among the participants. They regale their wife-givers with goat and their wife-takers with pig, reserving select portions of each kind of animal for themselves and their families.

All livestock offered at this stage are consecrated to the dead and consumed in the ceremony. The spirits of the sacrifices are represented as the personal wealth of the deceased, which it carries away with it on its journey. Sacrificial gifts presuppose a reciprocal relationship between the living and the dead. In accepting the sacrifices, the dead pledge not to return to the realm of the living in the form of wild pigs and deer, the animals that characteristically ravage the gardens.

Should a water buffalo be sacrificed at this stage of the ritual process, its horns are detached and added to those left over from previous black rites. All these horns are hung from a pole that is typically located on the western part of the altar place. With its burden of upturned buffalo horns, the pole is a material sign of an ongoing involvement between the living, who have made preliminary offerings, and the dead, who still linger in this world.

Throughout this period, the relationship is characterized by formal amity and mild antagonism. The dead are supposed to "look after the house pillar/watch over the roof" (*deiki fad-oen/bale huhun*) of their own houses. As named, individuated ancestral spirits, they accept offerings and protect their living kin from harm. However, they can also cause illness, which they are particularly prone to do if they feel dissatisfied with the gifts that they have received. Chronic illnesses (especially in children) are diagnosed as afflictions of the dead and may lead to a decision to hold either another *hun* or a larger dispatch ceremony.

Overall, Mambai do not evince violent fear or horror of the dead.[4] Some people claim to have encountered roaming spirits late at night in the forest, and there is a considerable stock of folklore addressed to such encounters. Usually, the dead can be recognized by the white color of the betel-juice that they spit. One does well to withdraw quickly at this sign, for a spirit well-disposed to the living would not have left its abode in the first place. As do illnesses, such apparitions may precipitate ritual action.[5]

In general, however, Mambai emphasize the positive aspects of their relationship with the dead and they speak of an ongoing emotional bond. "We still feel for them," people say, using the verb *hanoin*, which Mambai gloss with the Portuguese *ter pena*, "to pity, to feel compassion." The ideal relationship between the living and the dead is one of balanced opposition. If the dead should venture into the realm of the living, their very presence is construed as an index of their displeasure. More important, it is a sign that the living have failed in their obligations, for though the dead may be stern and demanding, they are neither wantonly destructive nor unjust. In death, as in life, Mambai actions are guided by a principle of reciprocity.

This relationship is radically altered by the performance known as "to dispatch the dead," "to *keo* the dead," or simply as *maeta*, "ceremony for the dead, mortuary ceremony." When such a performance is carried to its final conclusion, the buffalo horns from long-past sacrifices are laid upon the "ship of the dead" and dispatched (*toil*) to the sea. There the dead take on "different ears/different faces" (*kika selun/ahe selun*). "We do not know you anymore/you do not know us anymore," goes the final chant. The horn-hung post is dismantled, and as the material token of their presence vanishes, so too does the memory of the dead fade. "Then we no longer feel for them," Mambai say.

Typically, the last rites are held only many years after death. The dead linger in this world indefinitely, awaiting a *maet-keon*. There is no strictly formulated doctrinal justification for this interim. Ideas of the afterlife determine neither a specific date nor a minimum interval for a *maeta*.[6] On the contrary, the theory of the afterlife is consistent with varying interpretations of ideal ritual procedure.

From one point of view, the paramount obligation is to send the dead away to the sea with all possible haste, minimizing the intermediary period. Such a strategy is culturally acceptable in theory, since there is no prescriptive belief in the necessity for an intermediary period. It is generally acknowledged that if an individual possessed the inclination, as well as the material means, he could complete the mortuary rites promptly after burial. Mau Bere presented this strategy to me as his own preferred course of action. "Mine," he said, "is to bury and dispatch immediately, so that they may walk at once to the sea." While he sadly conceded that practical difficulties might well intervene, his stated ideal was to reduce the delay to a minimum.[7]

Mau Bere's opinion reflects both his own personality and the special ritual status of his origin village, Hohul. Throughout our long acquaintanceship, he himself displayed an intense concern for cosmological processes and a profound appreciation of their significance. To him, death and death ritual are sacred obligations to the cosmos, and he was more unbending on this point than many others. Widely acknowledged as one of "those who know," Mau Bere commanded a general respect not often accorded to one so young. His own pride and confidence in his "words inside the stomach" were manifested in all his actions.

He is, moreover, a leading member of a ritual center, where death necessitates special precautions. Mortuary posts hung with buffalo horns are not displayed in either Hohul or Raimaus, as is the practice in lesser villages. The avoidance was explained to me in terms of white and black. As the communal sources of life and fertility, Hohul and Raimaus are categorized as white. The mortuary post is a paradigm of the class of black things, and such an icon is held to be incompatible with intensive white ritual activity. Hence people of Hohul and Raimaus conceal their buffalo horns. They cast them up into the branches of trees outside of the village and retrieve them only when it is time to *keo* the dead.

Personal disposition and ritual status both contributed to Mau Bere's interest in a speedy dispatch of the dead. By his own admission, he himself was unable to realize his ideal strategy, nor is the ideal widely espoused. Elimination of the interval between burial and the final rites is not a goal toward which Mambai characteristically strive.

When Mambai comment on the inevitable delay before a *maeta* can be held, they uniformly isolate socioeconomic constraints. A full-scale *maet-keon* is a collective endeavor, for no one man could support the cost of such an enterprise by himself. The primary material constraint that Mambai single out are pigs, which feast-holders must present to their wife-takers in great quantity. Secondarily, they point (and with considerable bitterness) to a tax that the colonial administration levies on all water buffalo sacrificed at a mortuary ceremony. Payment of this tax devolves upon the feast-holders. Consequently, while the dead linger in this world, the living must cooperate with one another in order to defray the costs of a *matea*.

Commonly, a core of close agnates band together and begin to plan a collective *maeta*. Months and often years intervene between the initial deliberations and the final ritual outcome. Throughout this interval, those who have resolved to hold a *maeta* attempt to increase their stock of pigs.

Any funeral opens a new and heightened stage in alliance relations. Death, with its protracted rites, renews the sense of being mutually obliged to others—to one's agnates, on whose cooperation the fate of the dead depends, and to one's wife-givers and wife-takers, whose participation is also required at all stages in the ritual process. In the charged lag between the initiation and the conclusion of a series of black performances, there is ample opportunity to work on social relations, and room to implement various strategies.

Even a full-scale *maet-keon* may not end the interval, for Mambai will sometimes mount such a spectacle, only to omit the climactic rite in which the dead are sent to the sea. In such cases, they say that they "dispatch the dead, but do not dispatch the buffalo horn." The horns of all beasts sacrificed in the *maeta* are then set aside, and the dead are told to await "another day and another year" to make their journey to the sea. From the perspective of the dead, all that has changed is their personal wealth, increased by the elaborate death gifts made at a *maet-keon*. Mambai say that a person is free to hold as many *keo* ceremonies as he can afford, postponing the final separation indefinitely.

The social benefits of holding multiple *maeta* cannot be ignored.

Mambai themselves are well aware of the enhanced status that accrues to mortuary feast-holders. Moreover, although such persons will stress their ordeals and tribulations, the general opinion is that a skillful negotiator can "win," that is, draw a profit not only in status, but also in material gifts of "live buffalo" which supplement the sacrifices. Indeed, I suspect that one motive for omitting the final rite of dispatch is that it requires special buffalo sacrifices that might leave the wife-takers unable to provide the additional prestations of livestock.

Nonetheless, it would be a mistake to reduce ritual strategies solely to pragmatic considerations. The possibility of multiple *maeta* is embedded in the theory of reciprocity between the living and the dead. Even an unfinished *maeta* is a potent and efficacious gesture of respect to the dead, for in materially enhancing their condition upon the mountain, it strengthens their obligations to the living.[8]

Individual attitudes toward deceased relatives may also play a part in ritual strategies. Mambai conventionally retain strong emotional attachments to the recent dead. They "feel for them," as they say. Love, compassion, loss, sorrow, these sentiments enter into particular relationships and may provoke an individual's decision to prolong a spirit's sojourn in this world. Mau Bere might subordinate personal loss to cosmological convictions, but not everyone is so stern.

A small incident that occurred at the end of a long *maeta* impressed me greatly at the time. They had begun to prepare the "ship" of the dead and were about to load it with its cargo of buffalo horns. One of the feast-holders, Mau Rem, silently drew a horn from the pile and set it aside, a signal that the spirit to whom it had been consecrated was not to make the final voyage. A buzz of conversation ensued. It was ascertained that the horn belonged to Kai Seu, Mau Rem's wife, who had died only a year ago. Mau Rem approached me later to explain his decision. He said that Kai Seu's death was so recent, and he did not wish to lose her so soon. She was to stay behind and "look after the pillar/watch over the roof" of the house.[9]

By playing with time, shortening or extending the interval between death and final passage, individuals may pursue a variety of material, social, religious, and emotional interests. But what needs appreciation is that the idea of a lapse of time is implied in the total system of white and black rituals. With its symbolism of returning shades who bring luck and well-being, white ritual connects a past and a future *maeta* through the intervention of human fertility. The shades of distant, departed ancestors set in motion the accumulation of wealth that will at length make possible a new *maeta*. For without

205

the shades, fertility falters, and there are no new offspring; without offspring, there can be no new marriages; without marriages, one cannot accumulate pigs; and without pigs, there can be no new *maeta*, and no shades to return and reopen the cycle. Here the total character of exchange comes into sharp focus. Any *maeta* represents the convergence of multiple, interconnected exchange obligations that necessarily unfold over the course of a lengthy ritual process. From this perspective, the time that must pass before a *maeta* is not symbolically determined by a theory of the afterlife, but rather by the perpetual interplay between rituals of white and black.

In fact, when Mambai hold a *maeta* they go to great lengths to obliterate the interval between death and its last rites. Everything takes place in a *maeta* as if death had only just occurred and the ritual process were just beginning. The founding pretense of performance is that the *maeta* itself is really a lavish, noisy funeral feast. The significance of this highly stylized conceit is implicit in conduct toward the corpse at the actual funeral.

The appropriate attitudes toward the corpse are strictly prescribed. The period of the corpse's internment in the Black House is represented and, I assume, experienced as an occasion when individuals consciously submit to collective constraints. The conventional procedure for disposal of a corpse entails that people must "suffer the stench of the dead." Not only must they prolong internment until putrescence has begun, but they must suppress the sense of discomfort that they are expected to feel. Precisely the same etiquette is prescribed in a Hohul rite for the rebuilding of a cult house. At a certain point in the ceremony, a water buffalo is sacrificed, "to beat the earth" that receives the house columns. One half of the sacrifice must lie upon the altar for the full seven days and seven nights. Ritual participants are required to dance around the stinking carcass all week long, without showing any outward sign of distress. At the end of the week, by which time the foul odor has permeated the entire village, the rotten flesh is consumed with the utmost respect and formality.

Ritual conduct toward these manifestations of decay is based on an openly acknowledged tension between spontaneous reactions and culturally correct responses. The attitudes enjoined by tradition are understood to be in conflict with a "natural" feeling of aversion, with the result that ritual participants experience a culturally induced ambivalence toward decay. They must subordinate their instinctual impulses to a collectively defined duty, in a sense sacrificing their personal sensibilities to a higher cause. To "suffer the stench of the dead" is itself a prestation, a way of showing respect through self-restraint and submission to tradition.

Ambivalence toward decay is also expressed in a less agonistic mode, in the jokes that Mambai make about their own ritual practices. An informal tradition of humor revolves around the generally unpleasant odors associated with ritual events. Death ceremonies are notorious in this regard. "These rites stink!" Mambai will jocularly exclaim once they are outside of the ritual frame, and it is not only corpses that are held responsible. In death ceremonies scores of animals are slaughtered, and the meat often goes unconsumed for days, attracting insects and vermin who join in the celebration. Verbal wits are prone to elaborate on the themes of stench and filth, using them as metonyms for the whole of ritual life. Although certain ritual acts have aesthetic import, beauty is not the culturally salient feature of performance to participants.

The ambivalence that finds expression in humor is also manifested in anxiety about ritual practices. Even verbal allusions to the sacrificial buffalo rotting upon the Hohul altar arouse attitudes of fear and awe. Long before I ever visited Hohul, I had heard hushed accounts from outsiders of the "rotten meat" consumed in that village. And when I eventually attended the Hohul house rites with Mau Balen of Raimaus, a man versed in the sacred meanings of decay, he too professed to feel "unhappy" about the situation. He kept away from the village as much as he could during the week that the buffalo was exposed.

The human corpse, the rotting buffalo sacrifice, and the bad odor of performances are variations on a single cultural theme of decay, a theme that patterns dispositions toward ritual practices. Even in the midst of joyous white celebrations of life, there is something dark and grim in the atmosphere. What was latent in the white cycle is made manifest at a *maeta*, and the ambivalence that participants feel toward their own practices is most likely to receive expression, now in idioms of stoic endurance, now in jest, now in confessions of anxiety and displeasure. The attributes that Mambai themselves obsessively predicate of their ritual life are blackness, filth, and stench. Onto the various icons of decay they project a distinctive form of potency. The decaying corpse and animal sacrifice, the black Ritual Lord who sits amid refuse and filth, the foul-smelling Black House of women and men that funnels offal down to the beasts beneath it—these are tokens of a single divine type, the putrescent, vitalizing body of Mother Earth.

Mambai participate through their ritual practices in the primordial nature of the female source of life. They enact their inability to escape the conditions of their own origins, but the symbolic return to the primordial is not a regression. Ritual is a technique of simultaneously accepting necessity and actively, creatively, controlling it.

There is a danger of reducing ritual action to a naive "primitive" belief in the "magical" restorative powers of decayed matter. But the final rites for the dead eloquently contradict any such view. At a *maeta*, the actual corpses of the dead have been buried long ago, and Mother Earth has long since feasted on their flesh. There is no recourse to the material remains of the dead. Instead, death and burial are symbolically reenacted, and shortly afterward, the spirits of the dead are sent away to the sea. Mau Bere's ideal strategy of burial followed immediately by dispatch is symbolically realized in ritual performance.[10]

It is through creating an image of death as an immediate, present reality that symbolism of decay can logically dominate the final mortuary rites. This is precisely what happens in a *maeta*. The vitalizing potency of decay and the perishable nature of vitality are powerfully represented in ritual action. A *maeta* remains as firmly anchored in the care of the "black earth" as is the actual burial of a corpse. In this way, the performance sheds the boisterous, even ridiculous character that the performers themselves sometimes attribute to it and emerges as a vivid, forceful expression of the price of life.

2. Social Morphology of Performance

Of all black performances, a *maeta* activates by far the widest network of social relations, and this holds for the dead as well as for the living. At the center of any *maeta* is a core of male agnates. These are usually genealogical brothers who unite to honor their deceased parents, and sometimes also their paternal grandparents. But once such a core has announced their intentions, other men of their house will join with them "in order to dispatch jointly" (*oid toil fut*). These men add their own deceased but undispatched kin to the collectivity of the dead. By the time of performance, literally scores of spirits are implicated in a single *maeta*.[11] The total number may increase as the performance unfolds and still other men spontaneously decide to take advantage of the opportunity by dispatching their dead.

The three categories of participants at a *maeta* are elder and younger people, wife-givers, and wife-takers. The first category comprises the immediate sponsors, people of their house, and people of houses linked to theirs either by common descent or by a shared marital alliance. All those who are dispatching dead relatives at the ceremony are categorized as *maet-ubun*, "masters of the mortuary ceremony," and are usually of the same house as the sponsors. They are also called *saun-ubun*, a label for the class of blood-sucking insects.[12] Men from *kak-ali* houses may sometimes dispatch their own dead at the ceremony, but their official function is "to help and support the *maet-ubun*." They are expected to offer material assistance to the sponsors, and they perform designated roles in the rites.

In one *maeta* that I attended, the sponsors themselves were of different houses, but they shared a marital connection. Their fathers had married two genealogical sisters, so that the sons had the same mother's brother. This link creates a close, cooperative relationship among men, and such persons would ordinarily attend one another's *maeta* "to help and support." In this particular case, one of the parties had no brothers of his own, and so he took the somewhat unusual step of actually co-sponsoring a *maeta* with his matrilateral parallel cousins (see figure 6). It was not, however, a harmonious arrangement. Throughout the performance a running quarrel went on as to which of them was the true *maet-ubun*, and which had come to "help and support."

The deceased parents of the sponsors represent the entire spirit host, and they alone are referred to by name in ritual oratory. These representatives of the dead are always a conjugal pair, a man and his wife. By this convention two sets of maritally incurred obligations are necessarily activated at a *maeta*. Through the dead man, or rather through his sisters and daughters, the sponsors are linked to their wife-takers. Through the deceased's wife, they are linked to their wife-givers. Moreover, a *maeta* requires the presence of representatives of the houses which stand as primordial marital allies to those of the *maet-ubun*, the "wife-givers of origin" and "paternal aunts of long ago."

Wife-givers and wife-takers receive formal invitations to a *maeta*. Refusal to accept such an invitation is tantamount to the denial of an alliance relationship. It is the supreme negation of reciprocity. To Mambai, persons who shirk their obligations to the dead are not "human beings." The continuity of alliances literally depends on the fulfillment of contracts made with those who are now dead.

All guests participate as representatives of their houses. Thus attendance at any *maeta* composes an intricate social map of alliances contracted over time.[13] Exchange transactions are expressed in terms of alliance relations among groups, and the circulation of gifts follows the maritally transmitted flow of "female and male

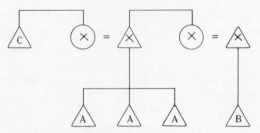

Figure 6: Maritally allied sponsors of death ceremony

X = Focal dead ancestors

A
  } = Cosponsors
B

C = Common wife-giver

Note: Cooperation between A and B is not unusual. If the A men had held a *maeta* alone, B would almost certainly have come and assisted them with the arrangements, very likely contributing pigs. What was somewhat irregular was that they should actually sponsor together. The tie between them is articulated in terms of the shared affinal link. "They share a *nai*," Mambai say.

blood." Symbolically male goods move from the wife-taking groups to host groups, and onward to the hosts' own wife-givers, while female gifts circulate in the reverse direction. These transactions are negotiated over the course of the performance. The formal intent of all prestations is "to pay for the fatigue and prostration of the dead."

The prestations made by the visiting wife-takers are by far the most elaborate. During a series of intense, often acrimonious confrontations with their wife-givers, they agree to make specific payments, calculated in breast-disks, goats, and money. As the performance draws to a close, the wife-takers must provide water buffalo, to be sacrificed in the names of individual spirits. They must also pledge additional gifts of "live water buffalo" before the performance ends. In return, they receive pigs, which are sacrificed by the hosts in great quantities and consumed during the performance. For the visiting wife-givers, the affair is less onerous. They may, if they wish, contribute pigs for the great feast. Alternately, they discharge their obligations through gifts of cooked rice, liquor, and cloths. In return, they receive a portion of all water buffalo that are sacrificed during a performance. When Mambai talk about attending a *maeta*, they lay particular emphasis on animal sacrifice, and the entire occasion is often described as an opportunity "to eat meat."

The formal pattern of prestations is simple, but the actual transactions are extraordinarily complex. Over the course of the *maeta*, all the hosts confront a number of different wife-giving and wife-taking groups, linked to them by particular marriages or as their houses' primordial alliance partners. Tempo and verbal dexterity are considered essential in these negotiations. The express goal of the hosts is to "prod" or "quicken" their wife-takers, so that gifts are readily forthcoming, the performance moves along smoothly, and in the end, they themselves will withdraw from the proceedings with at least the pledge, if not the actual "body," of a live water buffalo.[14]

Socially and economically, the most important relations at a *maeta* are those between visiting wife-takers and their wife-giving hosts. The social focus of these alliances is the tie between a sister and a brother, or between a daughter and a son. Whereas specific transactions are negotiated by alliance partners and express their differential statuses as wife-givers and wife-takers, Mambai use the familial model to represent the total circulation of goods. In that model, wife-takers are symbolically identified with the sister/daughter, who returns to her origin place to honor her old mother/old father. The same gifts that in one perspective mark the present division of allied groups also evoke the idea of the whole prior to division.

Key women of the wife-taking groups transcend social divisions, for they have as much to do with the hosts as with their groups by marriage. The actual sisters and daughters of the focal dead man take charge of domestic activities at a *maeta*. They preside over the female work that goes on inside the cooking house, where they supervise other women who have married into their own natal house.

There is a double emphasis in a *maeta*. On the one hand, tremendous interest is directed to exchange obligations among the living, who are categorized as wife-givers and wife-takers. On the other hand, those relationships are symbolically constituted in reference to the dead, and the obligations between the living and the dead are foregrounded when participants use the daughter/son idiom for exchange. There are other indexes of a double perspective on the *maeta*. Mambai are well aware that any *maeta* is enmeshed in the politics of affinal alliance. A great part of the social action consists of prestation negotiations among affines, and various rites take the form of dramatic enactments of mythical alliances. But many verbal and visual images bear directly upon the relationship between children and their parents. Over the course of a performance, participants enact a powerful conception of the dead as parental nurturers who have sacrificed their own bodies in giving life to their children. This metaphor for alliance relationships evokes a cosmological model, and it refers the ritual proceedings back to a time before marital institutions existed.

When people are asked to identify the origin of mortuary ritual, two different mythical charters figure in their responses. One of these is classified as a narrative "of Night," while the other belongs to Day. The categories imply both complementarity and asymmetry. They presuppose two levels of understanding of a *maeta*, in relation to its ultimate, nocturnal origins, and in the context of the relatively recent institutional conditions under which human beings inherited an ancient task. These levels are not seen as mutually exclusive, but they are hierarchically ordered. By the premise that full knowledge derives from the past, an understanding based in ultimate origins encompasses the partial understanding based in more recent events.

3. The Sham Death and the True Death

These events took place in the Day. For reasons known only to himself, it is said, the ancestor hero Ki Sa once decided to feign death. Disguising his voice and person, he cried out to his sisters' husbands Loe Mau and Dad Mau and to his wife's parents Su Mali and Bloe Mali:

> Old Ki Sa has died and fled! Come, all of you,
> for us to perform his mortuary ceremony.

When his wife-takers and wife-givers had assembled, he "fooled and tricked them." He covered two mortars and two pestles with black cloths and presented them to his affines as his own corpse and the corpse of his wife Ba Loe. The archdeceiver then set forth in fine detail the form of the *maeta* rites. His servants hurried off to obtain the various ritual objects required for the performance, while his affines retired to fetch either buffalo, goats, and breast disks or pigs, rice, and cloths. When all the participants had reconvened in Ur Bou/Ai Datu, they performed the ceremony according to the instructions of the deceitful Ki Sa.

The narrative of Ki Sa's "sham death" (*maet hudi*, from *huid*, "to jump back and forth, to deceive") is long and complicated. It describes the preparation and performance of what is sometimes called the first *maeta*, and it provides an intricate narrative charter for the ritual proceedings. Mambai priests commonly identify ritual paraphernalia, characters, and actions by reference to their narrative counterparts. Entire segments of a *maeta* may be interpreted as dramatizations of the myth.

The myth of Ki Sa's "sham death" grounds the *maeta* firmly in the politics of affinal alliance. Much of the narrative revolves around the distribution of ritual roles and prestation obligations among Ki Sa's affines. Moreover, the plot associates interactions among affines with deceit, trickery, and stylized deception. In this the myth reflects a wider cultural etiquette for conduct toward affines. Pretense and cunning are the prescribed modes for confronting affines, and a *maeta* offers ample opportunity for this kind of gamesmanship. In ritual performance, and in the endless "backroom" bargaining sessions, the respective parties deliberately distort and misrepresent their situations and prestation expectations. In these contexts, saying that something is what everyone knows it is not is a verbal art that Mambai men practice with a showman's delight. Wife-takers formulaically invoke their poverty, while simultaneously affirming their good intentions toward the dead. Alternately, they inflate and extol the virtues of what are transparently simple gifts. Their wife-givers listen to all these protestations impassively, and then, assuming stylized attitudes of fortitude and patience, they speak pointedly of their own generosity, and of the immense sacrifices made by the long-suffering dead. Again and again they put it to their wife-takers that all this "fatigue and prostration" must be compensated.

From this perspective, the trickster hero Ki Sa is the paradigmatic affine, a cunning, eloquent, inscrutable, and supremely successful strategist. A *maeta* founded upon his mythical maneuvers is a celebration of the consummate social skill required to maintain alliance relations. The myth characterizes the *maeta* as an elaborate masquerade, an artful, sophisticated sham, designed to recreate and renew status relations. A performance is an ideal opportunity to deploy strategies of status negotiation.

I first learned of this narrative charter from the priest presiding over a *maeta* I was attending.[15] I quickly put together a substantial exegetical tradition based in the mythological narrative, and I was content for quite some time to map the myth onto the rites as they unfolded. However, several factors combined to undermine my complacency.

For one thing, a wealth of emergent ritual symbolism had no apparent basis in the myth. Much of ritual oratory and drama graphically evoke the decayed bodies of the dead, whereas in the "sham death," there is no actual corpse. Second, a central category of ritual actors seemed quite tangential to the narrative. Throughout performance, the sponsors and their spouses observe particularly stringent mourning prohibitions categorized as *luila*. These persons must abstain from bathing, haircutting, and sexual intercourse. They are intimately associated with the dead through both contiguity and similarity. Ritually, they act out several physical encounters with the dead, and they are said to escort the spirit host part way to the mountain. They are strongly identified with symbolism of blackness and dirt, evocative of death itself, and their sexual abstinence signifies a condition antithetical to life. They are, Mambai say, "as if dead."

Their relation to other participants resembles that of the dead to the living, for they are represented as the still, silent elders among the human protagonists, the "ancient and old ones" of the proceedings. They are supposed to pass their time in a silent vigil over a cold hearth, and they are expressly forbidden from taking an active part in the prestation negotiations. Their observances have a cooling effect on their surroundings. Mambai say that if the elders keep their vigil faithfully, angry words do not erupt into hot quarrels. These persons speak of their privations in idioms of personal sacrifice. They say that the dead suffered for them, and now they must repay the dead for their fatigue with their own ritually assumed abnegations. They identify themselves with the dead by withdrawing from ordinary social rhythms, strengthening a connection that is soon to be severed. The idea of a sham or feigned death informs a *maeta* in several ways. The *maeta* opens with an artful and highly stylized hoax, wherein it is asserted, quite contrary to reality, that the dead have only just died. This "death" is visually enacted in the rite called "the mortar descends." In this exuberant ceremonial charade, two sets of mortar and pestle are carried out from the cult house and laid upon the ground, where the chill of the air causes them to sicken. Amid doleful lamentations, the priest "casts banana stalks," the traditional form of divination that is used in curing rites. To the dismay of those around him, he learns that the disease will prove fatal. When the wife-takers of the "patients" make their first formal entry, they learn that the sick ones have "died already/fled already" (*maet sois/flair sois*). And so the *maeta* officially begins with a mock funeral feast.

It was Mau Balen who interpreted the rite in this way, supporting his interpretation with a wealth of oral poetry and exegetical comments. The same rite is also interpreted as a dramatization of the corresponding episode in Ki Sa's deception. Yet, as Mau Balen's related version suggests, there is a subtler form of deception at work in ritual: the pretense that a death which took place long ago is transpiring in the present. This idea, sustained throughout the performance, di-

214

verges from the mythological sham. The ritual ruse evokes a true death (for the dead have really died) and tampers only with time.

But it was not only the exegetical lacunae left by the myth of a sham death that led me to question its interpretive power. My dissatisfaction was reinforced by the oblique comments and grave expressions of various people who came and asked to hear what the priest had said to me. Mau Balen, my guide on that occasion, was the first.[16] And in the weeks to come, my interviews with that particular priest became the object of general concern and debate. Although I acquired very little concrete information during that period, much of my subsequent inquiry was to be guided by the thoughtful, measured responses of those who had come to question me.

> "It is like that," one old man said to me some days after the ceremony was over, "Grandfather Ki Sa did pretend to die as he says. But it was the woman who died first, Our Mother died first. The words that he told you, they touch upon the Day. He did not speak of the Night."

It was not at a mortuary, but only many months later, at the Hohul house-building rites, that the significance of the nocturnal death was entrusted to me in a coherent narrative. With the stinking buffalo carcass rotting outside on the altar, Mau Bere and Mau Balen first spoke of the solemn funeral cortege, and of the final putrescence of Mother Earth's reluctant corpse. Later, as we went to yet other mortuary performances, they were to speak of these events as the "true death" (*maet tus*), which anteceded and outweighed Ki Sa's sham. It was Mother Earth, they said, who first taught her children how to *keo* the dead.[17]

The two myths do not correspond to ritual action in the same way. While the "sham death" provides a detailed, if incomplete program for performance, the "true death" is not sequentially enacted.[18] The sacred myth informs and organizes a performance thematically. It is not used as a program for unfolding events, but as a way of incorporating different aspects of the rite into a paradigm. So Mambai seemed to say with their troubled, enigmatic allusions to the "woman who died first." Ki Sa may have bequeathed the theatrical, stylized strategies for daylight social interaction, but the idea of obligations to the dead relentlessly draw death ritual back to the Night, when death itself first originated.

Mother Earth's death resonates through performance, until black ritual assumes the same chiming, sonorous quality as the white, where symbolism of cosmic birth reverberates in representations of the rain. In a *maeta*, it is an idea of sacrifice and obligation, ruin and restitution, that one hears darkly chiming, never entirely drowned out by the din of human affairs.

The very structure of ritual metaphor evokes the deity. She is to all creatures as the dead are to their mourning children, the suffering, life-giving elder whose "fatigue" demands restitution. The parent/child idiom of prestation stresses this resemblance, and it is strengthened in ritual speech that identifies the dead with the deity's own imagery. They are addressed as the "urn that is rotten/vessel that is decayed" (*uis be broe/bia be dome*), nurturers ravaged by their past services; as "skin that is broken/bone that is split" (*lita be kdout/rui be fo*), "bowels that are burst/blood that is spilt" (*tei be ktoia/lara be hdaka*). Oratory alone builds up a composite image of the ruined, wasted bodies of the dead, who have spent their substance in giving life to others. Yet in the very act of departure, the dead are also portrayed as givers of new whiteness and life. The dead, like Mother Earth, are inextricably entangled in ideas of white and black. Nor is it an unmotivated substitution when Mambai alternately identify the purpose of black ritual as "to repay the fatigue of the dead" and "to repay the fatigue of the earth."

4. Performance
The Maeta *as Drama*

Even a relatively simple *maeta* practically defies summary. Of the three performances that I attended, one took just over a week, one lasted for well over a month, and the third dragged on over a three-month period. It is never a question of continuous ritual activity, for perhaps the most characteristic feature of a *maeta* is its intermittent unfolding. Interruptions and delays break up and protract performance. The rites proper may idle for days or weeks on end, while the hosts await tardy guests or scurry off in search of additional pigs. During such intervals, some of the guests scatter, only to regroup again when the black *titir* drum sounds. But others linger to participate in the daily solo dancing and the nightly singing, which contribute to the festival aspect of performance.

However, it is not simply the duration of the event that complicates exposition. The spectacular character of the endeavor, the pageantry and flamboyance, the piling up of plots and subplots all work against a concise summary. A *maeta* is high ritual drama and diverges markedly from white performances in its modal patterning.

White ritual is primarily oratorical, relying heavily on contrastive forms of speaking. While any white rite exploits both words and acts, the latter are highly stereotyped and are performed over and over, in rite after rite. Collocation, chanting, presentations, sacrifice, and feast are the stock elements of all white performances.

All the same elements occur in black ritual, but with a difference. Each individual rite vividly enacts a particular adventure of the living, the dead, or both. While priestly oratory also occupies a prominent position, black ritual tends toward ostension in its modal patterning.[19] I believe it is in acknowledgment of its spectacular nature that Mambai so often, and somewhat ruefully, refer to the *maeta* as their *komedi* (from Portuguese *comedia*).

I shall have to sacrifice much of the drama of a *maeta* in the interests of time and space. I discuss the overall patterning of performance and consider selected rites in some detail. My primary intent is to elucidate the ideas of reciprocity that take shape around representations of the body and the spirit.

Preparation for the Journey

The total drama divides into a number of acts. These are identified in idioms of rising and falling, ascents and descents. Up to and including the *maet tolin* or "dispatch of the dead," ritual action relates the elaborate, often hectic preparations required for the departure of the spirits. A long journey awaits the dead, who must set off toward the sloping, southern interior and climb to the summit of Nama Rau. Before they go, the living must provide them with their own gardens, livestock, and wealth, and with raw food to eat during their travels. The provisioning of the dead is effected in a series of ritual charades, performed on a cleared plot of ground outside the cult house.

While the living are so engaged, the dead linger inside the house, nestling in the roofbeams. Every night, a random group of participants gathers in the house to entertain the dead with the mortuary song-fest (*mlore*). Mambai describe the *mlore* singing as a vigil held to "watch over the dead" (*blei maeta*). The verb *blei* also has the intransitive sense "to be awake; to wake up," and the idea—much as in our own wake—seems to be of remaining awake to keep company with the dead and regale them with the strange, lilting melodies.

In anticipation of their approaching journey, the dead make a series of nocturnal forays, to reconnoiter the road and to convene with a bird host which will eventually escort them to the mountain. These expeditions are evoked in a series of rites, performed at night in the cult house. Each performance exploits a particular form of speech, all peculiar to black ritual and involving a high proportion of "meaningless" words, reversals of normal stress patterns, and unusual pronunciations of familiar terms. The end result is a distinctly weird, though far from meaningless, use of language. In part, the motivation for the linguistic distortions seems to be to create an image of the dead through audial channels.[20]

The rites of the daytime and the nighttime converge and end in the *maet tolin*. On the afternoon of the *toli*, sacrificial buffalo, referred to as "bad breast/bad horn," are verbally consecrated to the dead in the rite mentioned in the previous chapter. Amid allusions to white ritual, the dead are promised their gifts and are instructed to withdraw. The *toli*, held late at night inside the cult house, brings about this withdrawal.

Maet Tolin: The Dispatch of the Dead

Toli, from *toil*, "to dispatch, to send away, to dismiss," refers to the speech form itself, as well as to the act of banishing the dead. This particular way of speaking resembles other verbal exorcisms, in that words are spoken in a flat monotone, rather than chanted.

The *toli* as a whole forms a lengthy exhortation. It is composed out of a string of commands which the priest transmits to the dead. My impression was that the utterances themselves are regarded as efficacious, and that each verbal order corresponds to a spirit movement. If so, the perlocutionary consequences of the speech do not seem to make any particular impression on the audience. Despite the acknowledged solemnity of the occasion, the social atmosphere throughout the *toli* is distinctly casual. The cult house is crammed to overflowing with spectators, whose strident conversation often drowns out the priest's utterances.[21]

The *toli* unfolds in a fixed sequential order. The recitation proceeds from the immediate environs of the house to the highest peak of Nama Rau, conducting the dead along a prescribed path. They must visit a series of places—which is to say, these places must all be named in the correct order. As the speech moves southward into the sacred lands of the interior, the sequence of place names is charged with significance. At this point, any confusion or omission is a serious matter. In one *maet tolin*, old Leik Mau of Hohul angrily berated his son, Mau Lear, for neglecting to utter the name of a particular land. Leik Mau peremptorily took over the recitation, returning first to rectify the omission.

The *toli* begins with the dead sleeping soundly inside the house. They are ordered to awake and pack their belongings for the journey.

Amid exhortations to refrain from grief and fear, they are slowly conducted out of the house to where the consecrated buffalo await them.
The dead pass into and through the bodies of these animals. The
priest names each individual organ and body part in a metonymical
reconstruction of the prime sacrificial offering. Then the dead leave
the origin village and are taken on a winding tour of neighboring villages, to pay their respects to the sacred objects of those places.
Much of the *toli* is taken up with the recitation of the place names
along their route as they "turn around/turn about" (*maklili/takali*)
again and again.

As the dead travel southward, they encounter the several guardians of the sacred lands. Without the consent of these watchers, the
dead cannot gain admission, and they must display the gifts they
have received as a sign of their legitimacy. Finally, they ascend the
named peaks of Nama Rau and enter the origin house.[22] They are told
to "play" on the summit of the mountain, and not to stray into the
lands west of Nama Rau, where the wild spirits dwell. They are to wait
until the "roof gives way/column crumbles" (*huhun mrauf/oen kere*),
when they will begin their descent to the water and the sea.

To an outsider, the flatly enunciated discourse of the *toli* may
seem less gripping than the colorful and dramatic rites that precede
and follow it. This perception is not unrelated to that of the participants. Other rites mobilize an array of media and act simultaneously
through multiple sensory channels, whereas the *toli* is almost entirely oratorical. It is performed without musical accompaniment,
and without melodious delivery that might attract the ear of the listeners by its pleasing form. Emphasis in this discourse is on semantic
content, and that, by convention at least, is primarily the concern of
priestly specialists. In contrast to other ritual contexts, participants
give the impression of being psychically distanced from the proceedings of the *toli*.

Nevertheless, the role of speech in Mambai ritual is essential.
The subdued, stark verbal performance in the cult house is the part
that Mambai use to represent the whole of a *maeta*, and the entire
ceremony is oriented around it. All the preceding events are perceived as leading up to the *toli*, which is also the condition for all that
follows. The relative detachment exhibited by participants is not an
index of noninvolvement. It is, rather, a characteristically Mambai
gesture of respect for what they represent as the most sacred, the
quintessentially *luli* moments in a ritual event.

The *toli* consists primarily of a lengthy string of place names.
These are recited in a formally fixed sequence that warrants increas-

ing precision as it leads southward toward the mountain. In the process, the speaker creates a verbal replica of primordial events by uttering the names of the sacred lands of origins in the reverse order of their first formation. The *toli* for the dead is one of several oratorical performances that project cosmogony onto a temporally unfolding discourse. The *toli* for the plants, recited at the harvest ceremony, is another similarly muted but powerful use of speech. Both discourses create a verbal image of the mountain as the ultimate origin point, the source of new seed and the final destination of the dead before they pass overseas.

The verbal mapping of the sacred origin lands in the *toli* is set in the context of statements of the symbolic value of those lands. Throughout the recitation, directives to proceed from one place to another alternate with a series of suggestive, poetic exhortations. In an oblique idiom of reciprocity, the priest forges a connection between the departure of the dead and the fertility of the earth. The bad, ruined things that the dead are told to "bear away as your own" are juxtaposed to the good things that they are instructed to "leave behind." Strikingly, these symbolic "droppings" of the dead are identified in the formulaic idioms that suffuse white ritual. Thus the dead give

Hin mor koden	The good bearing of women
Maen mor koden	The good bearing of men
Haih mloe koden	The good breeding of pigs
Aus mloe koden	The good breeding of dogs
Nei nor nam-isin	Give with the flesh of the garden
Nei nor nau-eran.	Give with the water of the palm.

Furthermore, they give pure oil and coconut water, they give "white wetness/sweet earth that clings," they enrich and cleanse the land. The piling up of white imagery over the course of the discourse identifies the very departure of the dead with a gift of life.

Following the Dead

The *toli* marks the end of the first half of the *maeta*. The ascent is over, and two descents must follow. First, the "satchel descends" (*biota du*). In this rite satchels that once belonged to the dead are buried in the graveyard. Shortly after this mock burial service, the "ship" of the dead is prepared and launched on its journey to the sea. Together, these two events form a coherent and logical sequence, but the relation of the burial rite to the previous *toli* is another matter. The ritual treatment accorded to the satchels momentarily negates the events that precede it.

In the *toli*, the dead are sent away to the mountain, and on the following day is a festive celebration called "to follow the dead" (*tom maeta*). In the morning, the sponsors and their close female kin bid a formal farewell to the spirits of the dead.[23] After this performance, the promised mortuary buffalo are sacrificed at last, amid growing excitement. The rest of the day is given over to feasting and boisterous, exuberant dancing, all said to mirror a parallel celebration held by the dead on the mountain.

Attendance swells dramatically at this juncture, for anyone who hears the morning drum rolls is welcome to come and join in the festivities. Total strangers, "different people" (*atub selun*) or "wild people" (*atub huin*), are expected to pour into the village throughout the day. By late afternoon, throngs of men and women jostle one another upon the dancing ground, and the atmosphere is one of pandemonium.[24]

With the separation effected by the *toli*, a long transition ends for both the living and the dead. Yet on the day after the festive celebration, the entire performance seems to go into reverse. The next rite entails still another enactment of death.

The Burial of the Satchels

The day's ritual activities begin in the cult house, where the sponsors with their wives and sisters huddle around a heap of weather-worn satchels. Weeping and lamenting the while, they run their hands over the satchels, searching for "breath" (*snukan*), exactly as one does with a dying person. But the breath has gone, and the bags are shrouded and borne from the house amid tearful lamentations.

What follows is one of the most visually suggestive of mortuary rites.[25] The head, buttocks, and large intestine from a sacrificial buffalo are hung upon the mortuary post shrine. The priest hands to each of the male sponsors in turn a wand called a *kabora*. A bit of goatskin and the bone of a dog are attached to the end of the wand. Constantly displayed through the performance, the *kabora* is a symbolic enunciation of death, a visual translation of the verbal pronouncement:

Litan kdout sois	The skin has already snapped
Ruin fo sois.	The bone has already broken.

One by one, each of the sponsors raises this object in his right hand. Accompanied by a resounding roll on the great *titir* drum, he dances slowly up to the post shrine and plunges the *kabora* into the suspended intestine. When the last man has performed this act, the great drum, "*titir* of the black," falls silent. It will not sound again for the duration of the *maeta*.

Immediately afterward, the funeral procession begins. All the satchels are carried outside of the village to the graveyard of the hosts' house. After chanting and offerings of cooked food, the satchels are cast onto the ground and covered over with earth. At this, four women take up their drums and gongs and, for the first time in the performance, they beat out the percussive rhythms played in white ritual. As they play, they dance round and round the gravesite, exactly as they circle the sacred spring to welcome the shades. In black ritual, the same movements are performed to bid farewell to the "bodies of the dead" as they are lowered into the earth.

These two rites together give visual expression to verbal messages conveyed in the *toli*. The spoken commands to "leave behind the flesh of the garden" have their referents in the twin rites of stabbing and burial. For though poetic speech portrays the dead as givers of white life, symbolic action associates their gift with images of decay.

Mambai usually refer to the first ostensive rite as "to stab the intestine of meat" (*sa sis-tein*), where the word *tei* means both "intestine" and "excrement." The rite is performed, as I was repeatedly told, "for women and men to be numerous," and it is expressly regarded as a symbolic act of fertilization.

The connection was so self-evident to the performers that I suspect they were frankly puzzled by my persistent inquiries. After several people had told me what they knew, and I continued to press hypothetical interpretations upon them, they grew almost grudging and diffident. They wanted to speak of maggots and bees; when I remained visibly perplexed after they had done so, I suspect even a patient instructor like Mau Balen may have temporarily despaired of me.

The "stabbing" rite is linked in exegetical accounts to the mythological theme of maggots that grow from a corpse. All my informants gave the same response to my queries about the suspended intestine: "That corpse began to stink and maggots appeared." Then they told how these maggots (*ulaia*) turned into bees (*aina*). There were two male bees and two female bees, Lik Meta/Ber Meta and Kais Olo/Nai Olo, and they went to live among the roof beams of a dark house. After a while, they separated from one another and flew away. The intestine is hung upon the post to "call the bees back again." Kais Olo/Nai Olo and Lik Meta/Ber Meta come flying from the west and the east to enter their "house and origin village," the worm-ridden intestine of a buffalo. When the meat is stabbed, the bees fly away again and then the "dead descend to the earth."

Such was the gist of the interpretation I received from some half dozen people, priests and lay people alike. It is a complete, if condensed interpretation which sets out the elements of a metaphor. For me, however, additional information about bees was needed to unpack the metaphor.

Mambai ideas regarding bees add up to a highly stressed species, for these creatures are unusual in several respects. In its larvae form, the bee is said to nurse upon its mother's excrement—to feed on decay. As it grows, it forms an exterior casing of "bone." Enclosed within this inverted skeleton, the tiny creature becomes gradually dry (*kmeka*). Its bodily fluids seep into the "bone"—the wax later used to fashion candles.[26] Finally the bee "sheds" (*kolu*) its larvae form and flies away, dry and imputrescent. Even in death, the bee neither withers nor decays. While alive, it sucks only the "sweet-sweet" (*bea-bea*) nectar of flowers, shunning the decayed matter that nourishes so many of its insect brothers.[27]

The rite does not exactly require these native zoological views, for its point is made through the idea of a maggot-ridden corpse and the material icon of a worm-ridden intestine. In the ritual metaphor, the maggots and worms stand for the "body of the dead," which is soon to be buried, while the newly liberated bees would seem to symbolize the enduring spirits which fly away, freed from their own decomposing flesh. I would stress, however, that Mambai do not speak of bees as manifestations of spirit. The resemblance is figurative, and it is not a heavily elaborated metaphor. Mambai are not exceptionally concerned with the bee in its metamorphosed and immutable form. What intrigues them is rather the total dialectic of decay and imputrescence. If they have singled out the bee from other metamorphosing insects, it seems to be because the bee suggests an extreme duality, with its progression from excrement-eating larvae to undecaying, honey-sucking denizen of the skies.

The rites of stabbing and burial articulate one and the same idea: the necessary, fertilizing potency of decay. Mambai characterize both rites with the single remark that "white and black join together here," and the sudden introduction of "white" music announces the conjunction.[28] Mambai expound on this abrupt juncture of ritual categories in idioms of reciprocity. Fertility and whiteness are not magically manipulated, but are paid for and renewed with the currency of human flesh.

The two ostensive rites reflect backward to the poetic utterances of the *toli*, translating into material acts and icons what the speech conveys in more abstract verbal imagery. In the *toli*, departing spirits carry away their mortuary gifts and "leave behind" fertility and prosperity. The subsequent rites coalesce into an ostensive definition of these return gifts. For the dead leave nothing other than their black, putrescent corpses, and their counterprestation consists of "refuse and dust."

The *toli* skirts the black gift and looks ahead to the eventual white benefits, but the ostensive rites are less elliptical. In the symbolic descent of "corpse" to earth, Mother Earth is graphically presented with her own reward, and it is made clear that whatever whiteness ensues is in her hands. It is her death, resonating through the entire ceremony, that endows human decomposition with a life-giving significance. The oblique allusions of the *toli*, the fertilizing release of maggots, and the solemn burial of mock corpses give content to the sacred image of an underworld split into a white chest and a black chest.

To Mambai, it is always a matter of sacrifice and restitution. The spirits of the dead, who suffered for the living, take their gifts and leave behind their corpses. But Mother Earth suffered for the dead, as she suffers for all her children. One by one, they repay her by becoming "black earth" that substitutes for her own decayed flesh.

In ritual action the idea of "black earth" is conveyed by images of maggots, excrement, and worms. Verbal metaphors for the corpse identify it both as the Mother's coverlet and as her sustenance. In ritual oratory, the content of the final prestation is left tacit. The priests say only that new life will follow from death, that the gardens will give forth, that whiteness will swell, that women and men will flourish and thrive. When the satchels are laid into the earth, the death act is itself described as a birth. The "corpses" are not verbally consecrated to the devourer, but to the nurturer, who once more takes her children into her arms.

To Dispatch the Buffalo Horn: The Descent to the Sea

Some performances end with the satchels buried in the earth and the well-provisioned spirits securely ensconced upon the mountain, but others continue until the dead have been sent on their descent to the sea. This last journey is effected in a rite called "to dispatch the buffalo horn" (*toil arabau diun*).

The three performances that I attended all included the final rites of sea passage, and the sponsors had made their intention clear from the outset. However, the progression from intention to action depends in part upon the social dynamics of a particular performance. The rites of sea passage entail additional buffalo sacrifices, and wife-takers may protest that the *toli* gifts have exhausted their resources. Successful hosts are those who can avoid this situation and maintain the momentum of the *maeta*. Should the hosts find themselves unable to keep their affines engaged, they may decide to postpone the final rites until "another day/another year," when they will mount yet another *maeta*.

A skillfully executed performance has its own momentum, and one pledged buffalo tends to elicit other pledges. Wife-takers closely connected to the hosts are especially influenced by social pressures, for a man who refuses to "repay the fatigue" of his own wife's or mother's dead kin is the object of collective disapproval. But fear of being publicly shamed is not the sole motive for gift-giving. The performance also promotes a pride in giving, and people speak of the delight they take in meeting obligations. When a man sacrifices his own water buffalo, he says that his "liver swells" (*aten tu*), he feels proud and strong. Nor can one predict actual prestations from marital patterns alone, for often a man only distantly allied to the hosts will suddenly come forward with a buffalo, stirred by what I would call the effervescent atmosphere of the socioritual context.

Assuming that the sea passage is to take place, preparations begin shortly after the burial. Feast-holders reconvene with their wife-takers for new negotiations. The former must promise additional pigs to "meet" each individually pledged buffalo. Officially, the priest is solely responsible for ascertaining the date of the rite, but in practice, he acts in concert with the hosts and awaits their word.

On the appointed day, the priest oversees a drastic alteration of the ritual stage. The "set" constructed for the spirits' climb up the mountain is dismantled piece by piece. The post shrine and the stand for the mortuary drum are taken down and set aside, and a seating platform where guests are received is disassembled. In a literal act of bricolage, the parts of the platform are put to a new use. Two sections of the platform surface are bound together and secured between two poles to form a long bier. This object is referred to as the "ship of the dead."

The dismantling of the set signifies a change in the symbolic geography of performance. When they prepare the dead for the first journey to the mountain, the performers are said to move through the lands of ancestral myth. The initial set represents particular places visited by the heroes as they make ready for Ki Sa's death ceremony. The new set represents a place called Rema Tu/Rema Loba located near the base of Nama Rau.

While the ship is being constructed, baskets laden with buffalo horns are set upon the ground. Some of the horns are old and weathered from long years of exposure on the mortuary post; others are still encrusted with blood from the recent killings for the *toli*. Later in the afternoon, more buffalo are sacrificed, and their severed horns are added to the pile. These fresh sacrifices are intended to "tread down sharp and pointed things" (*sam hatin nor blerin*) that might hinder the ship's passage.

By nightfall, the ship has been laden with its cargo of horns, and everyone flocks to it at the priest's call. Before the journey may begin, the wife-takers must give gifts of breast disks and money, so as to make the vessel fast and seaworthy. A diligent priest will not perform the rite until men have "paid" for the pegs, ropes, and masts of the ship.

Like the *toli*, the final rite of dispatch is predominantly oratorical. While everyone clusters around him, the priest breaks into the melodious strains of *foder* chanting. After a long segment of *foder*, he switches abruptly to the flat, clipped discourse of *toli*. The performance concludes with a final segment of *foder*.

The first *foder* consists of a lengthy address to the dead on the mountain. Once again, they are ordered to dress themselves, to gather their belongings, to refrain from grief or fear. They are told that their "fatigue" has now been paid in full, and that horses are waiting to take them down to the ship. "I will stay in Rema Tu/sleep in Rema Loba," chants the priest, and then he recites the names of the dead and calls upon them to meet him there.

If any individual spirits are to remain on the mountain, whether because their kin so wish it, or because no buffalo was dedicated to them, then the priest recites their names. He explains that the wife-taking houses have indeed brought buffalo, but "the breasts are not sufficient—O/the horns are not enough—O." Such spirits escort their kin only so far as Rema Tu/Rema Loba, where they must bid them farewell and return to the mountain to "look after the column/watch over the roof." The rest of the dead are to "descend to see the water/ descend to see the sea."

With this remark, the priest switches to the *toli* discourse and recites the long path to the sea. The path leads westward around the mountain, through the "wild" lands beyond it, and on across the territory between Nama Rau and the Loes River, which flows north to the sea. Slowly, amid repeated exhortations against grief and fear, the dead make their way along a dangerous path, one with which we are already familiar. For theirs is the road taken by the mythical Malaia ancestor on his flight across the sea, and by the Mambai ancestors who went in quest of the lost flag. The dead follow this same path, "stepping in the footprints of the Malaia," as Mau Bere once told me. They arrive at last

Her Be Diku/Be Hali	In Be Diku/Be Hali
Her Be Sui/Be Tam	In Be Sui/Be Tam
Her er-lalan	In the inside of the water
Her tais-lalan.	In the inside of the sea.

There they are received by Loer Sa, ancestor of the Malaia, who awaits them with his heavy "rule and ban." At the end of the *toli*, Loer Sa

Kok la ni lutan	Shows the corral
Kok la ni taka	Shows the enclosure
Du la ni ika	Descend to fish
Du la ni meita	Descend to shellfish
Saun-huin	Wild things
Er-lalan	Water innards
Du la ni era	Descend to water
Du la ni taisa	Descend to sea
Kikan oid hui	For the ears to be wild
Ahen oid selu.	For the faces to be different.

Thus are the dead identified with the sea and its denizens. Their own transformation is indicated by the "wildness and difference" that overtakes them. The sea, they are told, is now their pasture land, and there they must remain, never more to afflict the living with disease, or with the tempests which they now control. They have been repaid in full, and now their relationship to the living must change. The priest repeats this point throughout the chant, restating it in the simple *foder* peroration:

Im ba ten aim	You do not recognize us
Aim ba ten im	We do not recognize you
Im ba tad aim	You do not know us
Aim ba tad im	We do not know you
Im selu—la tilu—selu—O!	You are different—go play—
	different—O!

227

As soon as the oration concludes, two men lift the bier onto their shoulders. They run a short distance outside of the village, with whoever wishes tearing along behind them. Without further ceremony, they fling the ship into the bush, scattering its cargo of horns, and return immediately to the village. The dead are gone. The *maeta* is over.

Once the dead have departed, all participants are supposed to "divide and separate" on the very next day. At every performance I attended, conversation on the day of the final rite was filled with references to our imminent parting. "Tomorrow morning, we shall leave one another," people would say over and over.

In actuality, however, a *maeta* has no such conclusive finale, nor do Mambai really expect one. Guests and hosts linger on, arguing over death gifts still outstanding. Many gifts are only pledged in performance, given in "name," but not in "body," and the details of their future presentation remain to be worked out. In the ideal, most prestation obligations are fulfilled within the frame of the ceremony, but Mambai themselves admit that this is never the case. "We pay, but we do not pay enough," people say, "and so we have to owe."[29] Obligations contracted at a *maeta* may drag on for years, fulfilled in bits and pieces with wealth obtained through subsequent marital and mortuary transactions. The perpetual character of these ritualized exchanges transacted in honor of the dead is one of the most striking features of Mambai social life. For the dead may depart, but the living remain, still inextricably entangled in their reciprocal obligations to one another.

5. Meanings in Ritual Life

My intent has been to provide a selective presentation of a spectacular ceremonial complex. Scores of rites have gone almost unmentioned and those discussed have been presented in skeletal form. One consequence of my presentational strategy is that I have not adequately conveyed the sociable dimensions of the event. To do so would require closer attention than I have paid not only to formal rites and prestation obligations, but also to the festive and gamelike components of a *maeta*.[30] While I cannot pretend to remedy the lack in noting their occurrence, it should be kept in mind that Mambai experience a *maeta* in part as a protracted party, and in part as a competition. People actively, if ambivalently, anticipate these ceremonies. A *maeta* is an opportunity to sing, to dance, to dress up in one's finest clothes, to drink palm liquor, and to feast upon meat and rice. For men, it is also a context for displaying one's rhetorical prowess in stylized confrontations with marital allies.

White ritual is comparatively subdued, both in its emphasis on oratory over ostension and in its overall atmosphere. Even though the white performances that I have described are those that unfold at the highest organizational level of Mambai society, they are less extravagant than the mortuary ceremony that a house group may stage. I can only assume on the basis of statements made to me that a *maeta* held in a ritual center would rival those that I observed, but I never had the opportunity to make the comparison.

Mambai themselves allude to an atmospheric contrast between white and black rituals, emphasizing the relative absence or presence of competitive elements. In black rituals, status interests are more pronounced to an observer, and are openly acknowledged by participants. Moreover, the cultural expectation that marital allies will bicker is regularly fulfilled at black ritual events. It is not without reason that Mambai often refer to a *maeta* as an occasion "for us to argue with one another over goats and pigs."

For my part, embroiled as I was in cosmogonic mysteries, committed to a quest after trunk meanings, I tended to experience the continual quarreling and showmanship as a distraction from more important concerns. Mau Bere and Mau Balen reinforced that disposition. Although they were as ready as the next man to plunge into the politics of affinal alliance when the occasion arose, they would often tell me that the matter "of goats and pigs" was "only the tip" of what I had come to see and hear. Meeting late at night with the two of them, or with officiating priests, it was all too easy retrospectively to experience the rites I had witnessed as something that belonged to an ancient, archetypal past.

I did not experience the rites as participants do, and this is not a phenomenological account. For all of the intimacy between Mau Balen, Mau Bere, and myself, I came no closer to sharing their experience than that of other, less hermeneutically sophisticated Mambai. Nevertheless, years later, it seems to me that the mode of inquiry that my guides prescribed is one that facilitates *comprehension* of Mambai ritual practices. As in chapter 1, I intend the word in two senses, to signify the acts of understanding and of including or comprising the salient attributes of an object.

If, under the guidance of Mau Balen and Mau Bere, I came to interpret ritual acts as reenactments of mythical archetypes, I learned in the process that Mambai uniformly understand their present situation in terms of the past. The catch is that the precise content of the past is variable, although not in the sense that functionalism promotes. It is not a matter of the imagined past varying according to the present arrangements that interested participants seek to legitimize. It is rather that the same arrangements, in this case the ritualized confrontations of maritally allied groups, may be understood at two levels, in relationship to the collective histories of the participant groups, or in relationship to encompassing cosmological processes.

What I have argued throughout this book is that when social groups unite to commemorate and renew the ties that bind them, not only do they identify the cosmos as the ultimate purpose of their activities, but they also replicate the structure of the cosmos in their interactions with one another. In a *maeta*, the symbols that most powerfully condense social and cosmological concerns are the body and the spirit, whose opposed fates organize the performance as a whole.[31] Gift exchanges transacted at death ceremonies are represented as prestations consecrated to the spirits of the dead, in recompense for the ruined, wasted bodies which they must leave behind. Social groups assume responsibility for these prestations by virtue of their own particular relationships to the dead. At the same time, the departure of the dead has consequences for the cosmos, and these are repeatedly conveyed through verbal statements and material icons. Ritual symbolism invests social obligations with a heightened significance that participants internalize in and through practices. The performative effect of participating in a *maeta* is a more or less clear impression that the well-being of the cosmos somehow hinges on the fulfillment of maritally incurred obligations to others.

Let us begin with what Mambai call the "tip" of ritual life and draw together the symbolic aspects of black exchange relationships. Maritally allied groups come together at a *maeta* to repay the dead for their "fatigue and prostration," thereby fulfilling pledges that were exchanged at the time of previous marriages. Alliance relationships have a temporal dimension. They are constituted by the giving and receiving of women and they endure over the unfolding years, until at length a moment arrives when they must be either renewed or dissolved. That moment is symbolically marked by the final departure of the spirits, and in the face of this event Mambai create vivid images of the ruined, wasted body, drained of its life and vitality. The triad of groups who enact the conception of perishable vitality are symbolically connected by consanguineal ties. In bringing together their own wife-givers and wife-takers, the hosts reconstitute a single line of shared substance, transmitted by women, a line of life that participates in the mortality of the body.

It is only at this ritualized moment of death and decay that social groups can discharge the obligations they incurred through old marriages. This in turn is the precondition for new marriages. For the groups who attend a *maeta*, the exchange of mortuary gifts is at once an obligation from the marital past and a gateway to the marital future. In a variety of overlapping senses, the *maeta* belongs to the category of threshold rites. The living as much as the dead have reached a critical point of transition, and the *maeta* is the sole means to continuity. It is a continuity of a certain type, premised on alternations between life and death, fertility and decay, marital payments and mortuary payments, the gift of a woman and the burial of a corpse.

If alliance takes on the fate of the body and passes through cycles of fullness and depletion, agnatic descent represents a kind of social immortality. The fate of the spirit is the death ritual's symbol of a masculine form of continuity premised on endless duration. The body perishes, but the spirit endures, escaping dissolution and passing on to new forms of existence in the afterlife. In a *maeta* the spirits of the dead move progressively farther away from the living, as they travel from the house, to the mountain, to the sea. Yet even as they depart, they are told to await "another day/another year" when they must "turn around again/turn about again" and return to meet with the living at the sacred spring.

Whereas the body is derived from matrilateral affiliations, spirit is transmitted along agnatic lines. Transmission is as much a social as a psychological process. An association of spirit (*smakan*) with breath (*snukan*) is indicated by the equation of loss of breath with dying, and by the ritual emphasis on the breath of the shades. But a person's spirit is also associated with his or her *kalan* or personal name. Mambai naming practices entail the recitation of the names of an infant's paternal ancestors. When the infant cries out upon hearing a particular name, its shriek is interpreted as an index of the ancestor who has "turned around again/turned about again." The ancestor's name is then bestowed upon the infant, and in this way the ancestor returns to his own house. In the lists of ancestral names that symbolize a house's unity over time, the same names recur in different generations. To Mambai, the recurrence of male names is a concrete sign of the perennial returns of the shades.

Ideas of spirit and naming practices are part of the ideology of agnation. During their sojourn on the mountain, spirits retain their own names and personal identities, so that at any one moment, a house comprises a group of living and dead agnates. When spirits pass on to the sea and become shades, their names and personalities are temporarily lost to the living. In white ritual, the ancestors are recovered and reincorporated into their houses as their own lineal descendants. The continuity of an agnatic line is like that of the house itself and is based on the perpetual return of the same in the different.

The condition of possibility of this continuity is a social division of ritual tasks. In black rituals, agnates require the assistance of their affines to send the spirits away to the sea. Mortuary gifts exchanged by marital allies are intended to recompense spirits for the ruin of their bodies, and these gifts create the shades who will later return to perpetuate their own descent lines. Literal or figurative house groups act in white rituals to promote their own fertility, but the apparent autonomy of these closed ritual communities is contravened at another level. House groups depend on marital alliances, not only for female reproductive vitality, but also, indirectly, for their unbroken continuity with the ancestral past. Descent works like Father Heaven to freeze time, while alliance follows Mother Earth and unleashes it. The message conveyed in the complementary rituals of white and black is that the very immortality of an agnatic line is only possible through the mortality of alliance relationships.

The ritually enacted symbolism of body and spirit condenses social and cosmological processes. Overdetermined associative paths connect body and spirit to the cosmological couple. Produced from maternal blood, subject to cycles of fullness and depletion, iconic of perishable marital ties, the body bears a strong resemblance to Mother Earth. The spirit, transmitted along agnatic lines, immune to alterations, iconic of enduring ties of descent, evokes Father Heaven, the undying, immutable male.

From the metaphors of body and spirit, we pass smoothly to the "trunk" of Mambai ritual practices, and to the idea of an exchange contract with Mother Earth, which resonates through the *maeta*. The body, hovering over the *maeta* as a grim reminder of marital contracts, belongs to the female deity, and it is the token of a primordial obligation to return to her in death. The links between the spirit and Father Heaven are less direct, as is appropriate to the ritual occasion. For the *maeta* is Mother Earth's festival, and Father Heaven avoids her throughout its duration.

At the cosmic level, as at the social level, death rituals mark a perilous threshold. From the perspective of the deities, the *maeta* is a transitional period when sexual opposites repel each other, and the cosmos relapses into its antierotic state. Before the drums and gongs of white *keo* may sound in celebration of new reunions, Mother Earth must receive her own unique gifts. Father Heaven's major interest in these proceedings is that they come swiftly to a conclusion, without polluting him in any way.

Had I described the *maeta* in greater detail, we would have met him at the sidelines, where he presides over all sacrifices. It is Father Heaven who "opens the ban" (*lohe badun*) in order to separate the dead from the living. In all his appearances, however, he stringently avoids direct contact with the dead. Their bodies, he shuns entirely, and to the spirits, he merely shows a path. Mother Earth embraces the lowered corpse, but the spirit climbs no higher than the mountain, and then descends anew to the sea.

Figurative associations between divinity and spirit are not absent, but they are not of the same kind or strength as those that link the body to Mother Earth. The corpse is an image of the deity, identified with her through shared qualities of blackness and decay. Representations of the spirit, whether verbal or visual, are only obliquely evocative of Father Heaven. It is almost as if the structure of the tropes themselves were iconic of the distinction between the proximity of the divine female to human beings and the distance that separates the divine male from his offspring.

A rather loose metaphoric association of spirit with the undecaying, high-flying, pollen-drinking bee suggests a further resemblance to the undying celestial male. However, Mambai do not seem to stress any relation within this spirit-bee-divinity set. The dominant ritual symbols of spirit are the horns of sacrificial water buffalo.

Whether hanging on the post or piled upon the ship of the dead, each buffalo horn represents a particular spirit. Moreover, the totality of hard, enduring horns—the remnants of long consumed sacrifices—is iconic of a house's immortality. In a *maeta*, buffalo horn substitutes for both bone and metal sacra as a representation of the hard, enduring, masculine order of a house.[32] Substance vanishes and is renewed, but agnatic ties endure even after death.

In other contexts, buffalo horn stands in an indexical relation to Father Heaven. As the upturned crown of a symbolically male animal, the horns literally point toward the sky. In particular ritual contexts, they operate as a channel for contact with Father Heaven. Hung upon the house post shrine, buffalo horns are referred to as "Our Father's descending place/arising place" and "Our Father's stairway." The shape of curved, pointed horns is also taken as an icon of Father Heaven's two arms, raised over his head in the gesture of prohibition that constitutes the original cosmic "ban."

The selection of buffalo horn as a sign of spirit indirectly evokes

Father Heaven through two associative trains. On the one hand, the common quality of hardness places horn in relation with both bone and metal, and these latter elements are metonymic of the divine male who shaped the skeleton of the earth and distributed sacred tokens among his sons. On the other hand, buffalo horn is ritually associated with Father Heaven by two paths, as an index of his presence and an icon of his potency. In the context of a *maeta*, however, the association of horn, spirit, and divinity is notably weak. The undying male is refracted through the imagery of enduring spirit, but any direct equivalence is avoided, and the symbolism of the afterlife works to differentiate human and divine modes of existence. The dead dwell upon the mountain, suspended between earth and sky, and then pass on to the outermost realm of the world. They make their home in the "water and sea," symbolically fixed between the dry land and the upperworld, associated with rising moisture and falling rain.

To Mambai, the sea is a distant, mysterious realm, governed by laws of its own. Many people never see it in their lifetimes, and most profess an ignorance concerning its nature. Like its new spirit denizens, the sea is apprehended as something "wild and different." In mythological tradition it is the source of a strange, new, and "heavy" law, embodied in the Portugese flag.

By its own origins, the sea participates in primordial chaos and formlessness. It is the archetype of undifferentiated states of being. As the primeval condition out of which a differentiated cosmos first emerged, the sea is opposed to the order and regularity of celestial maleness. Indeed, it seems to connote an antiorder that has the opposite properties of the untempered masculine principle. Whereas prolonged exposure to the heat of the upperworld is destructive, emersion in the sea is revitalizing and converts spirits into "wild" shades whose breath is strong enough to connect below with above.

The opposition between the outer sea and the upper heavens encodes a significant distinction between forms of immortality. The divine celestial male lives forever, immutable and static, utterly antithetical to the contradictory condition of death. Human immortality is achieved through cycles of death and rebirth. An agnatic line lives forever, but its perpetuity is premised on circuits of departure and return, not on the frozen continuity of the male god. Human beings share in the experiences of Mother Earth and become images of the goddess. Their resemblance to Father Heaven is necessarily indirect, for to participate directly in his nature is more than men can endure.

The metaphysical import of death is implicit in the spatial patterning of the afterlife. According to the creation myth, the sea appears first, the mountain follows, and the wide land comes last. This original narrative sequence, the sequence that Mambai offered as a model for my inquiries, is reversed in the journeys of the dead, who pass from the land to the mountain to the sea. The death process is the symmetric inverse of cosmic birth. The dead must go backward through birth, before they can "turn around again/turn about again" when the black gives way to the white.

Conclusion

Everything indicates that symbolic systems constitute a
reservoir of meaning whose metaphoric potential is yet
to be spoken.
—Paul Ricoeur, *Interpretation Theory: Discourse
and the Surplus of Meaning*

Interpretation is a work, and mine began years ago. The initial stages
unfolded on Timor under circumstances that I have tried to keep in
evidence while setting out my present understanding. But the tempta-
tion to subordinate a process to a product is as constant as it is
subtle, and it has been at work since I first visited the Mambai.

Finding, not making, was the idiom of my ethnographic research.
Mambai framed my activity as an arduous journey, a quest after referential meanings that were presented as anterior to the rites that
conveyed them. Founding events, primordial interactions, archetypal
incidents, such were the quarry that I was urged to pursue. It was always difficult, often impossible, to resist the force of Mambai metaphors of knowledge. Verbal pictures of meaning as a fixed and steady
trunk acquired extra strength from the unfamiliarity of my surroundings. Set down in the midst of a foreign culture's symbolic revels,
overwhelmed by the vitality of Mambai ritual life, I came to believe in
univocality and closure with ever increasing fervor. In the presence of
such a manifest surplus of meaning, one takes solace in the faith that
the whole will someday be made clear.

The ideal recedes indefinitely, until the illusory faith must be put
aside. I confess that I did not renounce my wish for closure in the
time that I spent with the Mambai. Then it seemed always in reach,
tomorrow or the next day, or the day after that; at the final rite of the
ceremony, or perhaps when some new ceremony began; at Raimaus
or Hohul, or on the top of the mountain, where Mau Bere once promised to take me. In those days, I waited expectantly, in anticipation of
a voice that would speak with authority and finality. Only after I had
returned, to fret for still more years over such treasures as I had received, did I slowly come to comprehend the story that I had to tell.

If this book has a value, it is not because it embodies the mean-

236

ing of Mambai ritual life. What I hope to have conveyed is some sense of ritual's meaningfulness, its tremendous hermeneutic potential. My analytical language is structuralist, heavily laced with semiotics. Sign and sign system, opposition and correspondence, homology and analogy, resemblance and contiguity, paradigm and syntagmatic sequence, such are the conceptual tools that I have utilized, adapting them to a project that addresses interpretive possibilities and strategies.

Inasmuch as I regard meaning as a work, I also assume that works vary, and in Mambai society there is an official assumption that the work of interpretation varies along social lines, according to the status of a person's house and origin village. "Assumption" is perhaps not the best word here. Let us say that there is a collective representation of differentially distributed knowledge, and that this representation is integral to an ideology of hierarchy. Precisely how the representation influences interpretive practices is difficult to say, as it is not uncommon for individuals publicly to disclaim understandings that they may privately regard themselves as possessing. It is nevertheless the case that some persons are socially encouraged to formulate their ritual experiences in discourse, while others are expressly discouraged from that endeavor. If we grant that speaking is a constitutive act, we must conclude that the power of interpretation is unequally distributed in Mambai communities, and that understanding of ritual is not homogeneous.

Cosmological conceptions among the Mambai are highly susceptible to verbalization. This is as much a matter of values as of practice. Discourse, and specifically narrative discourse, is regarded as a privileged mode of conveying sacred knowledge. To tell the full story of creation, from its trunk to its tip, is the uniquely authoritative way of translating archetypal realities that may also be translated into other symbolic forms. Non-narrative messages, whether sent through audial or visual channels, are deemed appropriate and felicitous in public ritual contexts, adequate to the immediate communicative situation. The encompassing trunk narrative, ideally transparent on the events it relates, is restricted by convention to private, interpersonal contexts. Mambai justify the restrictions in terms of respect, etiquette, and status, and at times they appeal to mystical sanctions against the public revelation of sacred truths. Oblique representation of the trunk of knowledge is judged proper and necessary in the presence of the assembled community, despite the openly acknowledged risk that "those who see only the tip" may fail to comprehend their own dependence upon ritual authority.

In certain representations of the ritual process, Mambai seem to assert that prior knowledge of primordial events intensifies a participant's appreciation of the symbolic reenactments of those events. Yet it is possible to reverse this proposition. An outsider might need to orient herself in relation to a coherent represented narrative, but for more active participants, much of a rite's performative efficacy may derive from its relatively opaque and enigmatic character. As a culturally marked communicational form, Mambai ritual is characterized by a high proportion of allusive words, acts, and objects, all susceptible to multiple interpretations; by elisions, ellipses, and manifest breaks in the unfolding of verbal performances; by the profusion of alternating and overlapping semiotic vehicles that are used to convey different aspects of the same idea; by the resonant presence of condensed multimedia signifiers that compensate for the absence of transcendental signifieds.

A rite, however, is neither a mere array nor a random succession of symbols. Whether physically juxtaposed in space or sequentially connected over time, ritual words, acts, and objects are defined by systematic internal relations which participants experience, at one level, as a form of constraint. In ritual contexts, people are not free. They are aware of themselves, to varying degrees, as repeating preconstituted sequences of action, following a fixed model or plan inherited from the past. The model itself is ideally timeless, unchanging, static, but there is an essential temporal dimension to its enactment and interpretation.

If Mambai recognize and value a higher order of narrative discourse, one that faithfully replicates a primordial order of events, it is also true that their ritual performances have a structural affinity with storytelling. Ritual and verbal narratives stand in a similar contrast relationship to ordinary time. The contrast can be formulated in terms of the narratological concept of "plot" as the act of projecting pattern onto succession, making events into a story (Ricoeur 1981). In these terms, ritual participants temporarily depart from the relatively unstructured, episodic time of everyday life, with its contingent succession of mundane events, and they experience the twofold structure of narrative time, in which events unfold in a coherent, followable, meaningful order. Ricoeur defines narrative time by the combination of two dimensions, distinguished as the episodic and the configurational, sequence and pattern, linearly connected parts and systematically ordered whole. The corollary of the temporally unfolding, patterned plot is the ability of participants to perform the "configurational act" of grouping together parts into a whole.[1]

Let us go back to the fundamental problem, which is the question of the performative efficacy of ritual. Durkheim's insight was that rites give heightened meaning to social life, but his model of the process of semanticization is ultimately unable to account for the social effects. Inasmuch as Durkheim placed semantic meaning "beneath the symbols," entirely outside of the awareness of participants, at a great remove from actor understandings of the world, it is difficult to see how rites could achieve the social end of attaching individuals to the group. The real problem is to account for the structure of ritually enacted conceptions of the world, and also for the interpretive process by which those conceptions are internalized and made compelling.

Pattern recognition is surely one aspect of that process, and contributes to the comforting comprehensibility of ritual events. But while patterns alone may be intellectually, aesthetically, and emotionally pleasing, it is their multivocality and relative incomprehensibility that unleashes creative energies and most powerfully enchants ritual performers. Any heightening or intensification of meaning depends as much on the indirectness, overdetermination, and ambiguity of interrelated ritual symbols as on the orderly, coherent configuration of those symbols. Indeed, I would argue that the vitality of a ritual system, its capacity to engage and mould the consciousness of participants, resides precisely in a tension between chaos and order, opacity and clarity, the riotous surplus of meaning with which ritual symbols are invested and their highly predictable, patterned presentation within sequentially unfolding plots.[2]

Rites invite overinterpretation in a manner reminiscent of dreams as well as art. Their reliance on condensations and displacements has obvious affinities with the process that Freud called the dreamwork (1953; orig. 1900). In the case of Mambai ritual, evading a censorship appears as a conscious concern, but inasmuch as the masking intent is largely conscious, it remains in the service of the communicative intent, which is not necessarily true of dreams. Collective symbolism has properties of its own, irreducible to the individual psychological processes that it may engage and transform, as Durkheim never tired of reminding us.[3] With its highly structured, hypercodified internal organization, its orderly and purposive unfolding, its richness of potentially shareable meanings, ritual is a paradigmatically cultural achievement. Rites are constructed to be understood, if always provisionally, by a community that shares certain interpretive conventions and reconstitutes itself in exercising the communal power of interpretation. Though that power may be unequally distributed, possessed to different degrees by the members of the group, it is itself a collective product, inherited from the past and internalized by individuals in social situations.

Working at different levels of the symbolic life, Freud and Durkheim have in common a utilitarian view of their respective objects. Function and not form is the primary concern of each theorist.[4] For Freud, the problem posed and resolved in dreaming is to represent a wish, and the processes of the dreamwork are the means to that end, a crafty solution to the demands imposed by the censoring agency. For Durkheim, the function of ritual is to represent the social order, and symbolic forms, while they may somehow enhance the consciousness of performers, are finally masks to be stripped away. Both theorists might have been alerted by their own metaphors to the playful aspects of their objects. But Freud places the craftiness, guile, and disguise involved in dreaming in the service of necessity and does not treat dreams as pleasurable in themselves, while Durkheim reserves for the analyst the pleasure of penetrating the outward veil of ritual symbolism.

For all his appreciation of ritual's power to convert the obligatory into the desirable, Durkheim never succeeds in elucidating how the conversion takes place. Perhaps it is because he sees the strengthening, vitalizing, pleasurable aspect of ritual as something done to participants, rather than something implicit in the acts they perform. More precisely, the Durkheimian ritual actor submits to social authority and receives in return a heightened consciousness of his membership in a collectivity, which he both loves and respects. What is missing from the model is an adequate account of pleasure actively taken in the ritual experience itself.

I have been suggesting that the pleasure is of two kinds, combined in various proportions in individual cases. The one kind, corresponding approximately to the Durkheimian notion of the internalization of external constraint, derives from the sense of faithful submission to the authority of a meaningful tradition and is facilitated by the relative comprehensibility of tightly plotted sequences of action. The other derives from the openness and indeterminancy of meaning in ritual, which unleashes the freeplay of creative interpretation. The surrender of the subject to fixed procedures heightens consciousness of external controls and fosters a reassuring sense of dependence on the group, at the same time as the susceptibility of those procedures to multiple and variable interpretations may promote a heightened and exhilarating sense of personal freedom.

Mauss was more sensitive than Durkheim to the element of pleasure in symbolic acts, and in particular to the affinity of ritual with art. Durkheim relegated the aesthetic dimension of ritual to a secondary status, as the product of a surplus energy which employs itself in "supplementary and superfluous works of luxury" (1965, 426). But Mauss treated aesthetic pleasure as a constitutive part of his "total phenomena." The Maussian protagonists in ritualized exchange transactions play out their ambivalent, socially patterned interests and desires. They revel in the luxurious display of sacred objects, in the feasting and festivities, in the music, song, and dance, as well as in their own stylized, resonant enactments of order and status, and in the very richness of meaning implicit in confronting the various "others" on whom they depend. For Mauss, the goal is "to catch the fleeting moment when the society and its members take emotional stock of themselves and their situation as regards others" (1967, 77–78). Rites are privileged phenomena in this endeavor, because they engage the whole person, the total being, "consciousness *en bloc*, and in its relations with the body" (1979, 13).

For collective sentiments objectified in ritual symbols to succeed in "invading" individual minds, it is surely the case that the symbols must appeal to the libidinal sphere and tap unconscious mental processes. Durkheim spoke too easily of the replacement of one form of consciousness by another, the suppression of individual psychology by collective states of mind. The Maussian conception of the relationship between individual and collective psychology is based on notions of complementarity and interplay. There is a complicity between public, conscious symbolic display and the private, unconscious activity of the mind. The energy required to construct a ritual has social sources, yet the efficacy of the constructed rite derives in part from the cultural transfiguration of latent psychosexual desires and fears. It is no reduction of the social to the individual to concede that unconscious wishes are reworked in ritual contexts and force their way through into consciousness in culturally acceptable, sublimated forms.[5]

It will no doubt have occurred to some readers that Mambai ritual could be rewritten in terms of the "battle of the giants," the struggle between the Freudian Eros and Thanatos, Desire and Death, the sexual impulse toward union and the primordial impulse to return to an earlier state.[6] This is a powerful myth. Projected onto Mambai cosmological thought, the psychoanalytic myth foregrounds a manifest cultural anxiety where Eros is concerned. In their collective self-representations, Mambai come to the aid of an embattled Eros, a cosmic Desire that is in danger of atrophy. Not to control or inhibit sexuality, but rather to arouse and release it is the stated purpose of white ritual action. If Mambai knew the terms, they would declare themselves, albeit with conditions, to be on the side of the repressed against the repressive.

The conditions are essential, and Eros must wait its time. The mythically articulated threat to erotic life emanates from the female, who in her black manifestation repels the sublime male. Their interaction determines the situation of humankind in relation to the gods. Death intervenes in cosmogonic narrative as a necessary supplement, an additional mark that constitutes the enabling condition for human life and growth, even as it signifies the rupture of a relationship to the male. By allying mortal human children with their suffering Mother, death separates them from their immortal Father. In the ritually enacted definition of the human condition, relative distance from the Father and relative proximity to the Mother are mutually determined. The fate of human beings is cautiously to emulate a remote god whom they may not impersonate, for they themselves belong, irrevocably, to the goddess.

As an anthropologist and not a psychoanalyst, what concerns me are the social realizations of these collective fantasies of male and female. Whatever energy the fantasies may draw from libidinal sources, they arise and are perpetuated in social conditions which they work to reproduce. From an anthropological perspective, what is most striking in Mambai cosmological conceptions is the extension of a theory of reciprocity to the very metaphysical conditions of existence. Death, in this theory, is not a penalty imposed by the gods as a punishment for some archetypal transgression. It is the ultimate price of life, the final countergift, the paramount obligation to the cosmos, and as such it is both the sign and the instrument of humankind's affinity with the female. Death is an inescapable sacrifice, made so that others may live, so that the cosmos may be renewed, and so that the community may be recreated in its ideal form, as a complementary balance of male and female. If Mambai are forbidden to imitate the Father in his purest, sublime manifestation, they are permitted, indeed obligated, to model themselves on the cosmic totality.

In this society we find no god-kings, no glorious instantiations of divine celestial maleness, no representations of an inexhaustible center where potency and power are permanently condensed. We find instead a hierarchical ideology of a distinctive nature that rests upon exchange relations of a certain type. Exchange in Mambai society is predicated on the irreversibility of prior prestations of life. Culturally meaningful, efficacious claims to status are expressed in an erotic idiom, but it is the frailness and fragility of Eros that is symbolically elaborated and provides the sanction for reciprocity. Suffering life-givers, abandoned houses, depleted centers, wasted bodies, such are the icons of status and authority in human society, and Mother Earth is their modeling type. Mambai social life is structured by obligations to multiple sources of life, fertility, prosperity, and all these sources share a salient feature: they are not inexhaustible, but must be periodically renewed.

On ritual occasions, anxiety over cosmic Eros is openly acknowledged and symbolically transcended. Rites grounded in the represented possibility of an antagonism of sexual opposites enact the triumph of desire. In white ritual, the wish for union is represented as fulfilled; in black ritual, the conditions of fulfillment are achieved. At either stage in the total ritual process, such balance as results is understood to be provisional, temporary, mutable, a transient moment in a perpetual cycle of life and death, desire and cessation, abundance and depletion, gift and countergift. As Mambai play out the rituals of white and black, they put their anxiety to a creative use. They convert the worrisome fragility of Eros into the foundation of a form of social life.

Another type of anxiety also informs Mambai discourse and exerted a pervasive influence over my fieldwork. It is an anxiety that has less to do with the represented content of the cosmos than with the human capacity to master and preserve a system of representations. Mambai define themselves collectively as the privileged readers of the cosmos, and when I was with them, I tended to take them at their word. They appeared to me, mediated by their self-presentations and by my own wishes, as the receivers and guardians of a sacred text. It was only in the ongoing work of interpretation that I came to see my Mambai friends as worried text-builders, obsessively insisting upon the wholeness of life, constructing that wholeness over and over again in their discourse.

Their obsession with the possibility of full knowledge now appears to me as an outward sign of a profound uneasiness. By their faith in a plenitude of meaning that people keep "inside the stomach," in a fixed and immobile trunk of words that anchors present discourse, in an original cosmic situation that eternally centers collective life, it is as if Mambai strive to deny or repress awareness of a historically conditioned existence that may be fragmented, unanchored, decentered.

To explore this perspective on the Mambai would require another study, one that comprehends their society in the context of historical processes. We may, however, gain some idea of this other project by returning briefly to materials already presented. I have in mind the incorporation of colonial rule into Mambai culture, as embodied in the magnificent origin myth that was entrusted to me by my friends from Hohul and Raimaus. I presented that mythological model of order as a triumph of Mambai culture over history, a narrative testimony to the power of structure over event. And by extending symbolic categories into a new context, Mambai indeed gave meaning to their colonial experience. But if one takes account of the history of that experience, it would appear that they were less successful in actually talking with the foreigners and communicating to them their own conceptions of the world.

The symbolic power to define reality is always a stake in a political struggle that may intensify under conditions of intercultural contact and foreign domination.[7] Ritual authorities may represent the ideal wholeness of Mambai collective life, but that life is lived by individuals and groups who have different, socially patterned interests, and who may evaluate a collectively held premise in different ways. Significantly, the multiplicity of social discourses breaks out around what is perceived from one perspective as a failure of reciprocity. To Mambai, the abolition of the tribute system by the colonial government presupposes a collapse of exchange relations. And curiously, many Mambai do not hold their forgetful Malaia kin to blame for that act, but rather harbor dark suspicions about those of their own leaders most closely associated with the colonial state. The "walk of the flag" has its trunk in the Night of origins, but as the story comes down into the Day, it becomes a tale of growing tensions, antagonisms, and conflicts.

It was to this later, troubled part of the story that my presence was assimilated. My understanding of Mambai life arose in the context of a dialogical situation that I only intermittently controlled. Such control as I did exercise was ambiguous and had relatively little to do with my own training or personality. It derived primarily from the sociohistorical conditions in which Mambai had invested Malaia with a legitimate right to know. One result of the situation I inherited was that Mambai felt compelled to share their knowledge with me—not by virtue of my objective connection to colonial power, but by the way that connection was culturally constituted and lived. If I could be made into what they saw in me, a seeker of sacred knowledge, then they were who they imagined themselves to be, the guardians of the hidden trunk. On their part, the discourse that unfolded was a form of wish fulfillment, a performative enactment of hierarchical status. And

I, for my own reasons, some conscious, others not, became ever more compulsively complicit in their struggle to define reality.

In so singlemindedly using my book and pen to set down the story of rock and tree, I did little that actively encouraged Mambai to apperceive themselves as subjects of history. On the contrary, by acquiescing in their attempts to appropriate my presence into a mythological narrative, I may have held out to them a false promise of plenitude. So I am left now with this study, my substitute text of their discourses, and with the knowledge that what I have laid out here is still a tip, a partial understanding of a cultural order that has its trunk in history.

Notes

Introduction

1. In the editor's introduction to *The Flow of Life*, a collection of essays intended in part as a critical assessment of van Wouden's work, Fox asserts that van Wouden's emphasis on classification "testifies to the decisive influence of French sociology" (1980, 3).

2. Durkheim's fundamental claim in *The Elementary Forms* is that religion is a social phenomenon, but he presents the relation between religion and society in a number of different ways. Lukes (1972, 402–477) argues that there are three distinct hypotheses implicit in Durkheim's sociological explanation of religion. Lukes distinguishes these as the "functional hypothesis" (religion contributes to the maintenance of society), the "causal hypothesis" (religion has its origins in and is determined by society), and the "interpretive hypothesis" (religion represents social realities). The combination of these three hypotheses (which Durkheim himself did not differentiate) implies the precedence of the social over the symbolic order.

3. Lévi-Strauss set forth the idea of social life as communication in the essays on language and kinship which are collected in volume 1 of *Structural Anthropology* (1963, 31–97). The idea is central to his earlier study of alliance systems (1949; trans. 1969) and forms the connecting thread that binds his analyses of kinship and marriage to his later work on "savage thought" (1962a, 1962b), and to the four volumes of *Mythologiques* (1964, 1966, 1968, 1971).

4. See also Bourdieu's critique of the structuralist model of exchange (1977, 3–15). Bourdieu singles out the failure of the model to account for the political dimensions of exchange: "To reduce to the function of communication—albeit by the transfer of borrowed concepts—phenomena such as the dialectic of challenge and riposte and, more generally, the exchange of gifts, words, or women, is to ignore the structural ambivalence which predisposes them to fulfill a political function in and through performance of the communication function." A central element in Bourdieu's critique is his insistence that the temporal structure of exchange is what makes possible the misrecognition of political interests by the agents in a transaction. It should be emphasized that it is Lévi-Strauss's model, and not Mauss's, which obliterates the temporality of exchange relations.

5. Fox has claimed that there is a fundamental relationship between the

ubiquity of dual classification in eastern Indonesian cultures and the presence in these same cultures of special forms of speech characterized by strict semantic parallelism. These speech forms, or "ritual languages," are used on all formal occasions; they require the linking of lexical elements in pairs, determined by a variety of semantic criteria. The phenomenon of semantic parallelism is of widespread occurrence (Jakobson 1966) and provides a potentially productive way of approaching the internal structure of symbolic systems. Fox has pursued this direction in a series of articles on Rotinese ritual language (1971a, 1974, 1975). More generally, he has argued that a "linguistic view holds the key . . . to an understanding of the pervasive dualism that van Wouden noted" (1980, 16). In this study I provide numerous examples of the use of parallelism by the Mambai, and I often rely on ritual language pairs in determining culturally significant oppositions. However, I have not as yet conducted formal analyses of ritual language itself.

6. The inadequacy of van Wouden's model of dualism is a central theme in the essays collected in *The Flow of Life.*

Chapter One: Ritual and the Social Order

1. The Mambai phrase is *aim ten de seul*. Mambai conventionally adapt the Portuguese expression *ter que* to express necessity. *Seul*, which I have glossed as "to make restitution," conveys a notion of substitution, an exchange of dissimilar but equivalent items. Its range of meanings includes the exchange of money for goods, and of material gifts and services for life. In ritual contexts *seul* always implies a passage of time which separates an initial gift from a countergift. Thus ritual prestations are said to "pay for the fatigue and prostration" (*seul kolen nor lelan*) experienced over time by a donor of life. This exhaustion that demands recompense is represented as the inevitable outcome of the giving of life, and considerable emphasis is placed on the agonistic aspects of the process. In caring for others, a person expends his or her own physical vitality, becoming gradually drained and depleted. It is at the ritualized moment when life is totally "spent" that those who have benefited from it must provide recompense.

2. *Fu* and *lau* are symbolically associated with head (*ulu*) and feet (*oe*) respectively. In ritual, the base and tip of any significant object are equated with these body parts. Proper orientation entails that persons and things stand upright and erect, with their "heads toward heaven, their feet toward earth" (*ulun man leola, oen man raia*).

3. It is only in white ritual contexts that the right to play drum and gong is vested in designated social groups. The word *keo* is also used in reference to the final ritual stage in the "black" disposal of the dead. Anyone who so desires is theoretically free to hold a *maet-keon*, a mortuary ritual that involves percussive instruments.

4. I would like to thank Richard Huntington for bringing this passage to my attention.

5. Needham's conclusions regarding the prevalence of percussive noises in rites of passage are stated in the form of a proposition: "*There is a connection between percussion and transition*." Needham goes on to suggest that the connection, which appears to be universal, is grounded in the "general psychic character of mankind" (1967, 394). Huntington and Metcalf, who examine the pervasive use of percussion in mortuary rituals, focus on the diverse meanings attributed to percussion in particular cultures. They point out that different features of percussion may be emphasized in different cultures, and they underscore in particular the significance of loud noise, which links percussion to such natural phenomena as thunder and to cultural noise-makers such as guns, fireworks, horns, and sirens. In many cultures loud noises of various kinds are used to connote notions of divine power and are important in ritual contacts with the beings of the other world (1979, 48–52). The primary feature of drums and gongs in Mambai culture is the loud noise that they produce. Mambai seem to regard this noise, not as an evocation or representation of divine power, but rather as a mechanism for activating that power.

6. Young people are associated with the aesthetics of ritual in a double sense. Certain rites are intended to enhance the beauty of young people, whose conventional role in performance is also defined in aesthetic terms. Thus the young wear brightly colored clothes, and they perform songs and dances which are considered to be aesthetically pleasing. In contrast, old people are described as "ugly" (*soko*), and aesthetic criteria are not used in evaluating the acts they perform. These acts (which include invocations, immolations, and oblations), and not the singing and dancing of the young, compose the core of ritual performance.

In general, Mambai do not emphasize the aesthetic aspects of their rites. On the contrary, they will often stress the physical unpleasantness and non-aesthetic character of ritual occasions. Offerings of food, for instance, which are a central element in all performances, are never described as "beautiful," but are rather explicitly regarded as being of a distinctly grubby, unappetizing appearance, and as giving off an unpleasant odor.

7. The white ritual cycle in fact unfolds during the wet season, and for the groups that perform it, the periods of concentration and dispersion are seasonally distributed. But over the course of the dry season, different groups come together to perform the black mortuary rituals. Hence at the level of the total system, seasonal alternation corresponds to an opposition between two poles of ritual life.

8. In invoking this indigenous notion of hierarchy and inversion, Mauss implicitly departs from Durkheim's conception of a radical and absolute antinomy between the sacred and the profane.

9. *Leta* is used solely in reference, never in address. Mambai say that to address someone as a *leta* relative would be to emphasize the distance between addresser and addressee. Such verbal distancing of relatives is considered to be impolite.

Chapter Two: The Mambai and Their Land

1. Capell (1943) divides the Austronesian languages spoken on Timor into two subgroups, an eastern and a western one. In his classification, the western group has closest affinities with the languages of Roti and Solor. Fox, however, is of the opinion that Rotinese is more closely related to Tetum and Galoli than to the languages of the western group (1968, 17).

2. This population figure represents the situation prior to the Indonesian invasion of East Timor on December 7, 1975. Since then, war, famine, and disease have taken their tolls. Amid conflicting reports of the total number of the dead, I cannot estimate the present Mambai population.

3. For example, Tetum *asu*, "dog," becomes Mambai *ausa*; *manu*, "bird," becomes *mauna*; *mane*, "man," becomes *maena*, etc. In Mambai possessive constructions, nouns are demetathesized, as in *au asun*, "my dog."

4. Capell classifies all of these together with the Austronesian languages of Timor as a single subfamily. This subfamily is most closely related to the neighboring subfamily made up of the languages of Savu, East Sumba, West Sumba, Bima, and Endeh (Fox 1968, 17).

5. *Ai ura* and *ai foia*, the black and white eucalypti, are symbolically classified as a male/female pair on the basis of their habitats. The *ai ura* is said to be "like a man" because it grows on the wild, rough terrain of the mountain slopes, whereas the *ai foia* grows on the flatlands around the homesteads and is said to resemble a house-bound woman.

6. Swidden cultivation under conditions of irregular rainfall, a severe dry season, and impermeable soil can lead to ecological deterioration, and Ormeling (1956) has documented the disastrous results of Atoni swidden agriculture on West Timor. But the Atoni situation was complicated by the introduction of cattle by the Dutch after 1910, and subsequent overgrazing has contributed significantly to the erosion of the soil. On East Timor cattle were not a factor, and the overall ecological situation is superior to that of the western half of the island. Nevertheless, the area around Aileu showed signs of swidden deterioration (as do certain parts of eastern Timor), but I do not feel qualified to estimate how far the process may have progressed.

7. In Rotinese classification, for example, the four quadrants correspond to a congruent system of color categories, and each of these colors conveys a range of meanings (Fox 1973, 356). Needham notes similar structures in traditional Javanese symbolism (1979, 11).

8. I translate *teora* as "discourse," although the term could also be rendered as "language." But Mambai emphasis seems to fall on distinctive ways of speaking and on actual messages, rather than on the abstract linguistic code. The diverse languages and dialects spoken by the peoples of Timor are called *teora*. The totality of words (*teor-huan*, literally, "seeds of discourse") enunciated by the Mambai in the past and the present together make up *Mambai ni teran*, the "discourse of the Mambai." The expression

teora nirin sal means "a great deal of talk" or "too much talk," and in certain contexts it connotes idle chatter that promotes discord.

9. Mau Bere used to assimilate these names to riddles. He said that when he was first seeking knowledge, the elders would ask: "Who is it who rolls up? Who is it who opens wide?"

10. I am not certain of the translation. Neither Mau Balen nor Mau Bere could or would interpret the name. Their main concern was to identify it as a "trick" (*fiadas*, from Port.) of ritual speech, and to emphasize that there are no palm trees on top of Nama Rau.

11. In ritual speech there are references to "ten women/ten men" who seem from the contexts to represent the first ancestors of humanity. But when Mambai narrate the mythological origins of humanity, the total number of the ancestors born on the mountain varies from one account to another.

12. Mambai often allude to Father Heaven's partition of a patrimony when speaking outside of a storytelling context.

13. According to Mau Bere, the four guardians of Us Luli were formed out of hairs plucked from the navel of the First Being. Two of these figures have names that include the element *hul*, from *hulu*, "body hair, fur."

14. Us Luli is covered with strange shaped rocks. When I went on a trip that brought me within sight of the sacred mountain, Mau Bere identified these rocks as the debris from Heaven's labors.

15. Mau Balen and Mau Bere compared the mixture to cement.

16. The motif of a vine that once united the sky and the earth is widely distributed in eastern Indonesian myths. On Timor it has been recorded among the Atoni (Schulte Nordholt 1971, 148) and the Bunaq (Friedberg 1980, 280).

17. One day a very slight, barely perceptible tremor of the earth occurred. Mau Bere became very quiet. When it was over, he looked at me and smiled. "She has switched hands," he said softly. I did not understand him at the time, and he would not explain.

18. *Laif* means "to carry up, to bring up."

19. The word *leola* may refer to the firmament as a whole, or to the sun. Mambai also distinguish the sun as *leol-matan*. *Matan* means "eye" and also "cover" or "lid."

20. The pair *ina-salun/ama-kakun* refers to a female and a male water buffalo, but I am uncertain as to the correct translation for the terms *salun* and *kakun*.

21. In the period of organized nationalist activity that began in 1974, after the fall of the Caetano regime, these stereotypes of the Mambai took on political significance. "Mau Bere," a very common Mambai name which had been used as a derogatory reference to the hill peoples, was adopted by Fretilin, the nationalist party, as a symbol of Timorese unity. A central element in Fretilin political rhetoric was the slogan "Mau Bere, my brother." The intent behind the slogan, in my understanding, was to affirm Fretilin's solidarity with the mass of the population. To this end, they appropriated a name

that evoked the most "backward" of the indigenous peoples as a vehicle of a new national identity and pride.

Chapter Three: The Mythic Origins of Colonial Rule

1. The first permanent Portuguese settlement on Timor was established in the mid seventeenth century at Lifao on the northwest coast. After a century-long struggle with the Dutch, and with a Portuguese-speaking mestizo trading class, the Portuguese abandoned Lifao and moved their capital to Dili on the northeast coast. Sustained Mambai involvement with the Portuguese dates from this move. Mambai rulers are listed among the "loyal allies" who swore allegiance to the Portuguese crown at the time of the founding of the new capital, and they frequently appear in nineteenth-century colonial reports as defenders of the Portuguese against other rebellious native rulers. On this period see de Castro (1867). On the early Portuguese settlement of Timor, see Boxer 1947, 1969.

2. The term *malaia* is used throughout Timor to designate outsiders of various types. Within the category, Mambai distinguish *malai-butin*, Europeans; *malai-metan*, "black Malaia" or Africans; *malai-sina*, Chinese; and *malai-rai-klian*, "Malaia of the dry land." This last is sometimes opposed to *malai-taisa*, "Malaia of the sea," and it is used in reference to Timorese who are regarded as Westernized, typically, those who wear Western dress, speak Portuguese, and are educated in Portuguese-run schools. The category of Malaia thus includes all those who, by virtue of birth or upbringing, are conceptually located beyond the boundaries of the indigenous cultures.

3. The fundamental theoretical point here is that the members of a culture do not respond to objective conditions, but to meaningful situations. Confronted with changing experience, they put to new uses the interpretive means at hand, or conversely, they integrate new experience into a prior cultural system of meanings. I have discussed the hermeneutic claim at stake here in another work (Traube 1982; see also Sahlins 1981b, 5–8).

4. The Europeans whose names enter into Mambai ritual speech are those with whom the Timorese peoples have had direct or indirect contact, either through colonization (Dutch and Portuguese) or during World War II. Timor was occupied during the war by the Japanese, and it was liberated by Australian troops. Many Timorese cooperated with the Australians, and a tradition of friendship with Australia grew out of this experience. Australian tourists were common on Timor until 1975 and were regarded with respect by the local populations.

5. The number of brothers involved in the partition of the patrimony varied from one telling of the episode to another. When the explicit topic of the speech event was the relationship of Timorese and Malaia, narrators usually referred only to an elder and a younger brother. When the topic was "ancestors" (*tata*), the same narrators would describe a partition among three brothers, distinguished as "head man," "middle man," and "tail man."

6. In mythic accounts of the adventures of the ancestors, Au Sa is always identified as the blacksmith whom Father Heaven first instructs in metalwork. His primary role is to fashion the sacred ornaments and weapons that are displayed on ritual occasions.

7. Mau Balen and Mau Bere were explicitly regarded by others as representatives of Hohul and Raimaus. Their status was not without effects on speech situations. On a number of occasions it seemed to me that our hosts felt that they were being evaluated by the "masters of Hohul and Raimaus." If so, they were not far wrong. But the episode that I describe in the text was not typical. Usually, Mau Balen and Mau Bere listened respectfully to other speakers, and they only voiced any dissatisfaction they might feel with the account afterward, in private.

Chapter Four: The House as a Source of Life

1. On the importance of the house as a cultural category in eastern Indonesian societies, see the essays in Fox 1980 and the editor's introduction (10–12).

2. In Maori cosmogony, which bears many resemblances to Mambai traditions, the notion of human descent from the deities also implies participation in their nature (Sahlins 1981b, 14–15).

3. This type of double structure is prominent in Mambai symbolism and has affinities with the phenomenon known as "markedness" in linguistics. In cultural symbolism, however, the coexistence of inclusion with opposition characteristic of marking relations requires a manipulation of time. The encompassing, "unmarked" part is that which somehow resumes a temporal sequence. In Mambai symbolism, the encompassing part always stands for a totality before division and projects the idealized past onto the present. My understanding of how these temporalized structures operate in the articulation of hierarchy owes much to Valerio Valeri, especially a forthcoming article of his on dual organization in Seram. See also my study of Mambai dualism in the same volume (Maybury-Lewis & Almagor 1985).

4. Mambai occasionally refer to wife-givers and wife-takers as "people of one house," thereby emphasizing the interdependence of maritally allied groups.

5. The terms for "house" have a similar referential flexibility in other eastern Indonesian cultures. See, for instance, Barnes (1980).

6. In an earlier article (Traube 1980a, 295), I glossed the term *ria* as "homestead." I have come to prefer "origin village" or "village of origin," which suggests the distinction between place of origin and place of residence. What I call a "cult house" corresponds approximately to what Clamagirand describes as the Ema "core house" (1980, 136).

7. The same is true of many eastern Indonesian societies. See Valeri (1980, 182–185) for a lucid analysis of the situation on Seram with regard to descent.

8. Other eastern Indonesian peoples use relative age categories in similar ways, to assert hierarchical distinctions within groups or between groups of the same kind. See the essays in Fox 1980 for the range of variation in the actual groups designated by these categories.

9. In one myth, for example, an elder brother begins to perform a ritual during his younger brother's absence, and this act precipitates a split. It is not uncommon for brothers to quarrel over matters of ritual form. In one case that I witnessed, a younger brother was outraged when his elder brother allowed a water buffalo to be sacrificed at the wrong site (on the ground as opposed to on the altar), and he would not be mollified until a second water buffalo had been sacrificed in the proper way.

10. At the political level the shifting relations between centers and peripheries characterize what Tambiah calls the "galactic polities" of Southeast Asia (1976). A common feature in traditional models of the polity is the replication of the ruler's court by lesser order, formally dependent units. On the centrifugal tendencies inherent in such systems, see also Schulte-Nordholt (1971, 445–459) and Geertz (1980).

11. I discuss the word *luli* (glossed as "sacred") in chapter 7. *Kesa* comes from the verb *kes*, "to measure, to mark off," and pairs with *luli* in ritual speech. The association is based in a notion of the boundedness of sacred space, which is not adequately conveyed in my translation.

12. The origin village of Ol Fan is categorized as *kaka* to both Hohul and Raimaus. On a visit to Ol Fan I elicited two markedly different genealogical narratives of the relations among the ancestors. Neither account bore much resemblance to versions that I had heard in Raimaus, but the distribution of sacred objects in one of the Ol Fan versions was approximately the same as in the Raimus version. Mau Balen and Mau Bere expressed what was for them an exceptional degree of satisfaction with this Ol Fan account. They were not in the least troubled by the discrepancies between the two genealogies, which I called to their attention.

13. Many houses represent themselves and their sacra as *kaka nor ali*, but do not participate in one another's rituals. In some cases, there is an idea that houses related in this way should perform the yearly agricultural rites in a fixed sequential order, beginning with the eldest. There is also a convention that if members of one house should happen to attend the rites of any of their *kaka nor ali*, they ought to be treated as house members. Mau Balen and Mau Bere once accompanied me to the house-building ceremony held by their *kaka* Ol Fan. On that occasion they claimed to be affronted when the people of Ol Fan offered four covered baskets as our share in a ceremonial feast. Such baskets, they told the hosts indignantly, represented the portion reserved for strangers and were not appropriate for the "people of one house." Our hosts apologized profusely. The baskets were removed and replaced with plates containing the portion of "house masters."

14. *Lala*, "inside," is affixed to the names for types of vegetation and conveys the idea of a dense, thick cluster. Thus *ai-lalan* designates a cluster

of trees or forest; *kur-lalan* designates grasslands; *buk-lalan* designates a ring of *buka* plants.

15. *Um-boun* is a compound formed out of Tetum *uma*, "house," and Mambai *bou*, "shade." It pairs with *aif-mamun*, "warming fire," in ritual speech. The parallelism metonymically identifies the house by its twin protective functions. Foreign terms (notably Tetum, Ema, and Portuguese) are often used to construct pairs in ritual speech.

Chapter Five: The Renewal of Life through Marriage

1. Following Needham (1973a), I distinguish the relationship terminology from the rule of marriage and use the former as a criterion for determining the prescriptive or nonprescriptive character of the system. A prescriptive terminology, in Needham's sense, is one that is "constituted by the regularity of a constant relation that articulates lines and categories" (174). Classification of such a system as symmetric or asymmetric is also based on an examination of the relationship terminology. By Needham's criteria, the Mambai system is both prescriptive and asymmetric. Furthermore, the system meets Needham's requirements for "prescribed marriage," as distinguished from a "prescribed terminology" (177). Terminological relationships are socially realized through a positive asymmetric injunction. Where the situation becomes more complicated is in the determination of the actual social units of alliance.

2. Fox (1980, 7–14) provides a brief overview of eastern Indonesian alliance systems. Needham's essay in this volume analyzes the distribution of asymmetric prescriptive alliance in eastern Indonesia. From a comparative perspective, the Mambai alliance system most closely resembles that of the Ema, their neighbors to the south, as described by Clamagirand in the Fox volume. Both these societies exemplify what Needham calls the "standard systems of asymmetric prescriptive alliance" (1980b, 45). The Mambai and the Ema systems share a number of special features, including a tendency to mark and preserve alliances between primordial wife-givers and wife-takers. Both societies practice a form of adoption which extends alliance connections. Immediately prior to marriage, women may be formally transferred to groups that stand as wife-givers to the groups of the prospective husbands. These mediating groups then officially hand the women over to their own wife-takers. Among the Ema this is called a *bei bei* marriage, and alliance relations are so structured that it may result in closed three-partner alliance cycles, which the Ema value (Clamagirand 1980, 141–42). The corresponding practice in Mambai society is designated "to walk by the doorway" (*lolai damata*), where "doorway" refers to the mediating group. Giving women by a "doorway" is distinguished from cases where the woman "walks directly" (*lolai slol*) from a wife-giving to a wife-taking house. In some of the extended doorway arrangements, the woman's final destination is a group that stands as wife-giver to her own natal group, thereby creating the possibility of

closed alliance circuits. While the practice exists, Mambai do not present the potential for closed circuits as a salient feature of the doorway arrangements.

3. Barnes describes a situation similar in some respects for Kedang, on Lembata (1980). In Kedang, alliance "calls into play different types of collectivity, depending on context." Barnes argues that it is impossible to give a fixed definition to the notion of an alliance group in Kedang, since the particular collectivities that regard themselves as marital allies are of various structural levels. In practice, the Mambai system bears a greater resemblance to the Kedang system than may at first be apparent. There is an ideology of the house as the alliance unit, but the units designated as houses are variable and are constantly in flux. Moreover, what the ideology defines as ideal alliance marriages are only realized by certain individuals, who assert their status by claiming to represent their houses in their marital choices.

4. This type of situation is particularly likely to occur in the ceremony for the rebuilding of a group's cult house, an event which both agnates and affines are required to attend. When one group of participants stands in both a *kaka nor ali* and an *umaena nor maen-heua* relationship to the sponsoring group, Mambai distinguish between the different types of prestations incumbent on the visiting group.

5. Use of the cross-sex sibling tie to categorize alliances is another feature common to many eastern Indonesian societies (Fox 1980, 13). Even more prevalent is the use of the categories male and female to classify maritally allied groups, and much emphasis has been placed by analysts on the symbolic "maleness" of wife-givers. Schulte Nordholt identifies what he sees as a classificatory inconsistency in the multiple uses of gender categories by Atoni. He has in mind the apparent discrepancy between the superioriy of "female" ritual authorities and the superiority of "male" wife-givers in the alliance context. He goes on to argue that "a different set of principles must apply in each case" (1971, 205). My own view is that there is nothing "inconsistent" in the classifications, provided that analysis takes account of their diachronic dimensions. In Mambai classification, symbolically male wife-givers represent the original sibling pair, the totality before division. Their superiority is not a function of synchronic relations of opposition and correspondence, but rather reflects their status as the original sources of women and life. Among the Atoni, as Schulte Nordholt notes, wife-givers are classified both as *atoni amaf* (literally, "masculine father") and as *bab honit*, which he glosses as "life-giving, life-generating affine" (107).

6. This myth is discussed in Traube 1979.

7. As noted in chapter 3, there is a distinction between the "ban of the interior," the cosmic law imposed by Father Heaven, and the "ban of the sea," the jural power embodied in the Malaia flag. The Malaia also appear in a ritually recited variant of the myth of the origins of matrimonial regulations. In this variant, the sister goes "to wash and bathe in the water and sea" after having had sexual intercourse with her brother. She arrives at the coast, where she catches sight of the Malaia. She hastens to inform her kinsman Ki

Sa of what she has seen, and he sets out in search of "rule and ban." The implication is that the power to regulate marital relations is also obtained from the Malaia. In other contexts, however, Mambai distinguish marital status from political status within the larger community. The one, they say, "touches upon women and men," whereas the other "touches upon the ban." Yet marital proscriptions are also classified as a "ban," and it was only after I had pressed Mau Balen and Mau Bere on this point that they explicitly distinguished between a matrimonial "ban of women and men" and a political "ban of the sea." They went on to interpret this distinction, explaining that Ki Sa had in fact gone on two separate quests. On the first quest, they said, he obtained the flag pole (detached from Loer Sa's power tokens); on the second, he obtained the matrimonial ban. The product of their efforts was a coherent narrative account of the origins of regulations. The account was consistent with ritual discourse and with social classification, but I felt at the time that the consistency was a product of my questions. Had I not inquired into the chronology of mythical "bans," I doubt that the issue would have preoccupied my informants.

8. "Female blood and male blood" correspond to the categories of wife-taker/wife-giver and sister/brother. There is a reversal of categorical order in the stanzas quoted, since the term *umaena*, "wife-giver," precedes *maen-heua*, "wife-taker," whereas *lar-hinan*, "female blood," and *tbo*, "sister," are the first terms in their respective dyadic sets. Ritual speech is highly formulaic, and the sequential order of paired terms is fixed. Sequence expresses status in many contexts, according to the Mambai association of antecedence with precedence. The superiority of wife-givers is implicit in the formulaic sequencing of the categories, and to my knowledge, Mambai never depart from this order in ritual or ordinary speech. But while the term *hina* always precedes *maena*, as *tbo* does *nara*, it would be inaccurate to conclude that women are superior to men, or sisters to brothers. Mambai do assert that Mother Earth, the archetypal female and sister, "appears first" upon the scene, but they emphasize complementarity over asymmetry in their cosmological discourse, and I would argue that the deities are not absolutely ranked in relation to each other. Their temporal order of appearance is seen as the model for such fixed syntagmas as *hina nor maena*, *tbo nor nara*, and *ina nor ama* (but note also *leola nor raia*, "heaven and earth"). Overlapping formulaic constraints on lexical sequencing produce the slight skewing of dual categories in the passage cited in the text.

9. *Umaena* could as well be described as a metathesis of Tetum *umane*. The Mambai term for wife-taker, *maen-heua*, is a literal translation of Tetum *mane foun*, "new man."

10. Primordial affines are also marked among the Ema, who classify them as *ai mea*. Clamagirand defines this category as "wife-givers and wife-takers with whom the earliest marriage alliances were made" (1980, 141).

11. In ritual practice, however, any pair of marital allies may use this formula as a token of respect.

12. An in-married woman is more likely to attribute cursing power to people of her husband's house, and to women in particular. She may suspect her mother-in-law or her sister-in-law, especially if the mother-in-law (*kai*) is not originally of her own house. For a woman, then, marriage with a close patrilateral relative, ideally the father's sister's son, has distinct personal advantages. In such a marriage the wife may count on the support of her close female agnates in the new home. From a sociocentric perspective, however, it is wife-givers as a class who are deemed capable of causing mystical harm.

13. In theory, two groups that share a cult house should no longer intermarry, although their formal relationship is one of wife-giver and wife-taker. I also heard of arrangements of this kind in which the groups practiced direct exchange, despite official disapproval.

14. In this regard, Mambai death ceremonies contrast with those of other eastern Indonesian peoples who stress the ritual relationship between the mother's brother and the sister's child. See Fox (1971b) on Rotinese burial practices.

15. Mambai like to attribute improper unions to the *tea*, a circle dance accompanied by group singing. Young people are supposed to perform the *tea* at agricultural rituals and during the rites for the rebuilding of cult houses. *Tea* lyrics are often ribald, and the dance is conventionally regarded as an opportunity for lovers to arrange trysts. Mambai say that participants in the *tea* are easily overpowered by desire and thus form attachments that may be contrary to marital rules. From the one case of this kind that I actually witnessed, the general attitude toward these attachments is ironical. On the morning when the affair in question first received public attention, there were formal expressions of outrage on the part of the kin of the boy and of the girl. But when the young offenders appeared together at the *tea* that evening, they were greeted with laughter and cheerful sexual innuendoes. It should be noted, however, that the two were not closely connected by previous marriages. That is, while the girl's house was a wife-taker to the house of the boy, there had been no recent marriages between near kin of the individuals.

16. Clamagirand notes a similar representation among the Ema (1980, 142).

17. In an analysis of the theory of conception held by the Bara of Madagascar, Huntington warns against the tendency on the part of ethnographers to oversystematize symbolic categories and make more extensive use of them than do the people themselves (1978, 50). A full inquiry into such "theories" ought to compare and contrast formulations elicited from women and from men. Unfortunately, most of my materials on this topic come from Mau Balen and Mau Bere.

18. Struggling to elucidate the representation for a remarkably obtuse ethnographer, who was intent on getting the facts straight, Mau Balen once remarked: "After female blood has already gone out, then it counts as male blood." In other words, the "facts" are constituted by relations and depend on who is looking at them.

Chapter Six: The Ritual Community

1. In such cases Mambai say that a person or group "comes half from one side and half from the other side."

2. See van Wouden 1968 (48–58). But van Wouden himself was vague regarding the association between suku and clan. Later research indicates that the term *suku* or *fukun* refers in some societies to descent groups, and in others to territorial units. Among the eastern Tetum, suku are the immediate constituents of large political units. Hicks, who glosses the term as "prince-dom," says that such a unit consists of a number of villages, which are occupied by distinct aristocratic and commoner clans (1972, 99–100). Among the central Tetum, on the other hand, the term *fukun* designates a clan, and a number of these clans may occupy a single village (Francillon 1980, 248).

3. Prior to this date, Aileu was included within the administrative district of Ainaro.

4. In traditional eastern Tetum sociopolitical organization, the title of Liurai was applied to the head of the largest political unit, which Hicks calls the "kingdom" (1972, 101). Among the central Tetum in the Belu area of Timor, and specifically in Wehali, the office of Liurai was opposed to that of the Nai Bot, or Great Lord, the embodiment of supreme ritual authority. In theory, the Liurai was concerned with worldly affairs, and he symbolized masculinity and activity, but administrative affairs were regulated in practice by the Loro, the heads of peripheral princedoms (Francillon 1980, 262). In my understanding, the title Liurai itself evokes notions of masculinity and mobility. In Tetum *liu* means "to cross, to cross over, to traverse," and *rai* means "earth, land, realm." Thus the title could be translated as "he who traverses the realm," an appropriate designation for an active defender of order.

5. I have examined the historical context for this tension in another work (Traube 1982).

6. Hocart traced dual political structures back to an ancient, ritually en-acted dualism between a male sky and a female earth. Social divisions, Hocart argued, were modeled on this symbolic opposition, and had for their ritual purpose the promotion of life through the orderly interaction of male and female. From this dualism Hocart derives an opposition between a sky-king who regulates and an earth-king who executes, but it is not clear at this level whether the relationship should be understood in sexual terms (1972, 262–290). Van Wouden's analysis, on the other hand, implies that cosmo-logical and sexual symbolism are not coincident in eastern Indonesian diarchies. In his examination "Myth and Social Structure in the Timorese Ar-chipelago," he distinguished between "social dualism" and "local dualism." The former corresponded to the level of the kingdom as a whole and was based on a contrast between a female, elder, passive ritual authority and a male, younger, active executive figure. Within the kingdom, at the local level, van Wouden perceived a different system of classification, based on a cos-

mological contrast between a terrestrial internal power and a celestial external power. He concluded from these materials that eastern Indonesian peoples employed two different but overlapping systems of dual classification, which should be kept analytically separate. While this conclusion is unsatisfactory, van Wouden was accurate in his observation that the binary oppositions on which a classificatory system is based are not strictly coincident.

7. Needham places great emphasis on the distinction between relational similarities and affinities among the individual terms of different relations. Invoking Kant's definition of analogy as "a perfect similarity of relations between quite dissimilar things," Needham argues that "it is not the function of analogy to establish a kind or degree of direct resemblance" (1973b, xxxix). Homologies between terms may in fact be established, but Needham's point is that they are constituted by relationships, and not by the positing of direct equivalences. This implies that an analyst must determine through empirical investigation those terms that are most closely linked in indigenous conceptions, and also the semantic paths by which they are connected.

8. On the Indian separation of status and power see also Dumont 1970a (65–91).

9. I maintained my permanent residence in the household of the chief of Seloi.

10. This man, Alfonso, was the nephew of the Dom of Aileun, and I met with him on several different occasions. He was an interesting character, who had been enrolled for some time in the Segunda Linha, the Portuguese-run native militia. Consequently, he had spent many years outside of Aileu. He spoke fluent Portuguese and wore Western dress, but he also had a reputation as one who knew the "walk of the Koronels." He was a prodigious drinker and had a sense of humor that I alternately found ingratiating and maddening. I never felt even remotely in control during my conversations with him. The first of these took place in the company of the wife of the chief of Seloi, my Mambai "mother" and a relative of Alfonso's. It left us both amused, perplexed, and exhausted. I met with Alfonso again, over a year later, when I visited the origin village of Aileun, accompanied by Mau Balen and Mau Bere. It was on this latter occasion that Alfonso discussed the genealogy of his house, Bar Tai, and the atmosphere was notably tense. Mau Balen and Mau Bere said little in Alfonso's presence, but afterward and throughout our visit, they spoke bitterly of the "tricks" or *fiadas* (from Port. *piada*) perpetrated by Bar Tai people.

11. The tale of Bau Meta's misadventures with the ruler of Motain is frequently recounted by Mambai as a paradigmatic instance of their celebrated stupidity. According to prose tradition, Bau Meta received a book from the Malaia that made him the supreme ruler. But when he visited Motain, his rival learned of the book and instructed his wife to seduce their guest. While Bau Meta was thus occupied, the ruler of Motain crept into his room and stole the book, thereby usurping Bau Meta's status.

12. My impression was that the deference shown in Raimaus to Hohul priests reflected contingent circumstances rather than a formal tradition. The two leading priests in Raimaus were both relatively young men, and their father (the man who had taken over priestly responsibilities from the head of the Old House) had died when their training had barely begun. These two men always described themselves as "little children," who knew only the "tip of words." They deferred to the sons of the "old master" of Hohul, who deferred in turn to their own father.

13. The equivalent term in a western dialect of Mambai is *kaes-ubun*, "master of speech" (from *kase*, "to talk, to speak").

14. I had known Mau Balen for many months before I learned that he was the head of Nunu Fun, the Raimaus Old House. During a ritual meal held there, I observed that Mau Balen had received a special portion. When I inquired as to its significance, he and the priest who had served him explained that Mau Balen's was the portion of the special guardian of the house. It was Mau Balen's father who had relinquished public responsibilities many years ago. Mau Balen always insisted to me, with considerable vehemence, that he himself was not a priest. So too did Mau Bere, but this Mau Balen denied. And after I had known Mau Bere for some time, he told me that he could in fact be called a *kuka*. Like Mau Balen, however, he did not officiate at ritual performances, but rather played an active, off-stage role in managing such events. Mau Bere's father, on the other hand, was a "sitting priest," one who made offerings to a very special and sacred rock located underneath the Hohul Old House.

15. Men from lesser origin villages are also priests. Such persons officiate at local agricultural rites and at life-cycle rites.

16. On ritual occasions such persons are addressed as Dat Raia, not as wife-givers, and informants insisted that the two roles were distinct. On the other hand, the function of "showing the land" is often assigned in genealogical narratives to the trunk wife-givers of the group in question. The underlying idea seems to be that Dat Raia, like ordinary wife-givers, provide the two sources of life, women and land.

17. The disposal of fallen branches must be accompanied by *keo*. In Raimaus I was told that if a branch of Tai Talo should break, a water buffalo would have to be sacrificed in a special ceremony. When a branch did fall from a lesser banyan in Hohul, it was left untouched until the yearly agricultural rites had begun, thereby circumventing the requirement to hold a separate rite. After Dat Raia had ritually initiated the removal of the branch, they were assisted by other participants.

18. In this variant the ancestor Ki Sa begets a number of sons before he arrives at Raimaus. A group of these sons follow their father's path and converge at Raimaus, where they found Mau Nunun.

19. Exchange relations that link the peoples of the interior to the coastal peoples are common in the Indonesian archipelago and also on mainland Southeast Asia (Keyes 1977, 19–20). On Timor, the ruler of Wehali received

tribute from coastal chiefs who acknowledged his supreme ritual authority. The Wehali ruler also controlled the sandalwood-felling in the interior.

20. In ordinary speech the word *sau* is opposed to *luil*, a verbal form of *luli*, "sacred" or "prohibited." The meaning of *luil* is "to observe prohibitions, to avoid, to abstain from." *Sau* signifies the absence of prohibitions, that which is not under ritual restrictions. In translating it here as "release," I have in mind Steiner's interpretation (1967) of the similar Polynesian concepts *tapu* and *noa*, in terms of tying and untying.

21. I cannot say with certainty whether or not the rulers actually harbor such suspicions. My information was indirect, consisting largely of rumors that circulated within the ritual centers. My own position as a resident in the home of a suku chief added to the delicacy of the situation. I once discussed the rumors I had heard with the chief's wife, a person in whom I had complete trust. She dismissed them vigorously, although she admitted that there had been enmity in the past. I did not dare to pursue the matter with anyone else, for to do so might have worked against my friends in Hohul and Raimaus. But on the other hand, my very presence in those villages was cited by my friends as one cause of the displeasure of the rulers. Overall, I can only affirm that most members of Mambai ritual centers say that the rulers are hostile to them. My impression is that they are correct.

Chapter Seven: Divinity and the Social Order

1. For an extended critique of the functionalist reduction of meaning to social relations see Sahlins 1976 (55–125).

2. Bourdieu treats the relatively condensed character of certain symbolic objects as an effect of the application in practice of different schemes to the same objects (1977, 110–111). In these terms, the cosmological relationship of the deities is "subject to overdetermination through indetermination"; it is multiply defined by practically equivalent schemes, such as closing/opening, going in/going out, going down/going up, and also accumulating/dispersing, giving substance/giving form, perishing/enduring. Bourdieu points out that the multiple meanings of overdetermined symbols are not ordinarily totalized in practice, with its "poor," "fuzzy," "imprecise," or "economical" logic. On the other hand, there are cases where the agents, as well as the analyst, may have an interest in bringing together the plurality of meanings conveyed in their primary symbols, and myths are one means to that end. The polysemy of Mambai cosmology is more than a formal consequence of symbolic practices. It is also a hermeneutic tool that Mambai themselves use with varying degrees of competence.

3. I have borrowed this term from Todorov (1977, 132).

4. Following Peirce, I use the terms "icon" and "iconic" to differentiate a type or mode of sign relation. The class of icons is defined by the predominance of similarity or resemblance as the principle for linking sign and object. In Peirce's trichotomy icons contrast with indexes, in which the linkage is based on existential contiguity, and with symbols, which represent their

objects by virtue of a rule or convention. Peirce also distinguishes three subclasses of icons: images, where there is a similarity between a quality of the sign and a corresponding quality of the object; metaphors, based on a parallelism between sign and object; diagrams, in which the internal relations between parts of the sign exhibit the relations attributed to the object (1955, 104–15). Some of the general implications of iconicity are reviewed by Sebeok (1979, 107–127).

5. The use of the Portuguese term *estatua* suggests that the object in question is a Catholic icon of the Virgin Mary. Mambai have sacralized various classes of foreign objects and incorporated them into their ritual life. By and large, however, they have not appropriated European religious symbols, but have rather absorbed and reinterpreted objects symbolic of Portuguese political identity, such as the flag and the military drum. Unlike flags and drums, the Hohul "statue" is not regarded as representative of a larger class of objects. It is something unique to Hohul, where it is surrounded by restrictions. I never saw the statue, though it figured in many stories that I heard. For example, I was told of one occasion when a rumored visit from a group of Malaia necessitated special precautions. According to my informants, the statue was removed from its normal resting place in the White House and hidden in a lesser cult house, lest it be seen by the visitors. There it was said to remain at the time of my arrival in Hohul, and when a member of this cult house subsequently died, the funeral rites had to be adjusted to take account of the statue. Corpses are ordinarily laid out in the southern section of a cult house, but that was where the statue was supposedly lodged. I was told that this area had been "whitened" by the statue and hence could not receive the "black" corpse. In order to prevent "white from mixing with black," the corpse was displayed in the northern section of the house.

6. I saw nothing that resembled these carvings anywhere else, and I suspect that they are not of Mambai origin. Mambai say that they avoid looking directly at the carvings out of "shame" or "respect" (*etan sio*, literally, "hard body") for the nudity of the deities. This association of nudity with "shame" may reflect Christian influence, yet it recurs often in cosmological discourse. Mambai also say that Mother Earth's nudity is displeasing to Father Heaven, and they sometimes attribute her concealment beneath the ground to the shame that she feels over her naked body.

7. The species of bamboo that is used for the roof ornament is also classified as male.

8. Only in writing this passage did it occur to me that the triangular and quadilateral appearances of the two houses are probably associated with numerical symbolism, according to which three is for males and four is for females. These numerical values organize the placement of roof beams, which in turn gives rise to the distinctive appearances of the houses. Unthatched, the male house actually forms an extremely lopsided quadrilateral, with its two slanted sides converging on a short, horizontal roofbeam called "the one that remains and is separate" (*klik nor mdesa*). The thatch fills in this upper space of the house, creating a triangular appearance.

9. Peirce distinguished a subtype of icons "in which the likeness is aided by conventional rules" (1955, 105). On the other hand, it needs emphasis that there is a conventional element in all icons, inasmuch as perceived resemblances are culturally coded. Greenlee (1973, 72) suggests distinguishing "resemblance" from "similarity" as species and genus, reserving the former term for those similarities that are recognized by an interpretive community. By this argument, which seems consistent with the overall intent of Peirce's trichotomy, it is not similarity as such that underlies iconicity, but only similarity (collectively) determined as resemblance.

10. The term glossed as "god" is *maromak*, which Mambai regard as a Tetum word. Tetum serves as a lingua franca, and Catholic priests appropriated the term *maromak* to designate the Christian god. In Mambai ritual language, *maromak* pairs with Portuguese *deus* as a reference to Father Heaven, and I would argue that the foreignness of the vocabulary iconically evokes the stressed remoteness of the deity. *Nossa Senora*, "Our Lady," is occasionally used in ordinary speech to designate Mother Earth, but to my knowledge, this title never appears in ritual speech.

11. The word has a semantic complexity also characteristic of such religious concepts as Polynesian *tapu*, Hebrew *qadosh*, Latin *sacer*. Steiner argues convincingly for the nonuniversality of this "constellation of meaning" (1967, 35–36).

12. *Sau*, as I suggested in chapter 6 (n. 20), bears resemblances to the Polynesian concept of *noa*, which Steiner translates as "made common; not under *tapu* or under other restrictions" (1967, 36).

13. People who claim descent from Ki Sa trace their avoidance of water buffalo liver back to a mythological event. It is said that Ki Sa was once offered a human liver and was told that it was buffalo meat. Fortunately, his hunting dog discovered the ruse and warned him. Ki Sa refused the human flesh which, had he consumed it, would have marked him as a witch. His descendants say that they too would be regarded as witches if they were to eat buffalo liver. All food prohibitions may have similar mythological charters, but I could not always elicit them.

14. The Mambai concept of *lisa* bears resemblances to the Atoni *nono* concept. The Atoni word denotes a kind of liana, and it is also used of the prohibitions observed by descent groups. A group's cult practices encircle it like a vine (Schulte Nordholt 1971, 116).

15. *Maeta*, from the verb *maet*, "to die," refers to the dead themselves and to the final rites of passage. I think "mortuary house" is the appropriate gloss for *fad maeta*, since what is at issue is really the ritual treatment of death.

Chapter Eight: The Path of Rain

1. The rites for the rebuilding of a cult house are included in the category of white ritual, but Mambai distinguish them from the yearly rites.

Ideally, a house is rebuilt every seven years, but the actual occurrence of the rites is irregular. Moreover, the final stages of these rites activate marital alliance relations, which are not relevant in the rites of the agricultural cycle. Mau Balen once described the house rites as "just white enough," and another informant suggested that they might be called "red" (*mera*). She had in mind an important feature of the rites, which involves cooling the house to protect it against fire.

2. The exclusion of rice from the annual agricultural cycle corresponds to a mythological distinction between food crops. Unlike all other foods, which originate out of Mother Earth's body, the path of rice is traced back to the upperworld and Father Heaven. Rice is said to be of "recent" (*fnori*) origin in relation to other foods.

3. I never witnessed this opening rite. I attended only one Aif-Lulin, on my first visit to Raimaus. The opening rite was performed on the night of my arrival, while I was asleep, and I only learned of it on the following day. But I suspect that had I known of it and requested to attend, I would have been permitted to do so. For me, the Mambai often suspended ritual prohibitions that apply to young people and women, saying that what was *luli* to them was not necessarily *luli* to a Malaia.

4. It is said that if a young woman attends, she will become barren, and a young man's wife will desert him.

5. Nunu Fun, "Base of the Banyan," is said to be so named because it was formerly situated at the foot of Tai Talo.

6. If the woman is present, she receives the rear end, the traditional female portion. The two house masters receive the portion of the elders, the head and the neck, and the remainder is divided between their assistants.

7. Outside of a performance, people may go up to and down from the altar any way that they choose, but during performance all entries and exits are from the north.

8. In ritual speech the altar post is called *tar nifan/ai-otan*. *Ai-otan* means "tree branch," *nifa* means "tooth" or "prong," and *tar*, I believe, is the verb "to cut" or "to chop," ordinarily used in reference to trees.

9. In both Hohul and Raimaus the burial ground is located on the altar. In lesser origin villages corpses are buried outside of the village, and no part of the altar is used for black rites. Instead, black performances unfold on the ground below the altar.

10. The referent of the phrase "rock and tree" is ambiguous. When asked, informants identified either the altar post or the banyan as the tree. The rock could be either the altar or one or another of the sacred rocks in the village.

11. Raimaus itself is said to represent the navel of the earth, but Mambai are reluctant to discuss the significance of this representation. And when the referent of the term "earth navel" is narrowed to the hollow rock, then Mambai grow even more uneasy. They seem to avoid talking about the sacred rock, and I doubt that there is any strong consensus regarding its mythologi-

cal meaning. The atmosphere of fear and uneasiness that my questions provoked was sufficiently intense to discourage excessive probing on my part. Moreover, to search for some generalized mythological meaning would be fundamentally misleading, in my view. Ritual ministrations to the hollow rock are characterized by a high degree of privacy. Maun Koli, Ber Koli, and Tai Talo are approached in processions, but a lone and unattended priest makes the final offerings to the hollow rock. To most participants, the enclosed space around the rock is the province of the elders, the *mai mai*, who sit there at the opening and the closing of all performances. The generalized meaning of the rock is that it is the eldest, and that only the old ones understand its meaning.

12. This orientation varies according to the size and shape of the cairn. In Hohul, where the cairn is much smaller than in Raimaus, the entire space is reserved for men, and women perform their tasks upon the rim of the altar, beneath the cairn.

13. *Ferik* is a Tetum word that Mambai apply to any elderly or respected woman. The corresponding term for males is Tetum *katuas*, "old man."

14. Mambai told me that *suman* is a Kemak (Ema) word, equivalent to the Mambai term *mlala*, "cool." The number seven is odd, hot, and male in opposition to the number eight. But as the sum of four plus three, seven is also the Mambai number of totality, and certain offerings are computed solely in sevens. In these cases, "four touches the trunk, three touches the tip."

15. Within the house, east is considered hot and west is cool. The two cardinal points are respectively cooled and heated by means of offerings.

16. The altar post is one of several icons to which this function is attributed. The house post shrine and a pole that is erected during the rebuilding of a cult house are also identified as channels for contact with Father Heaven.

17. Mau Bere attributed another level of mythological significance to the collocation at the altar post. He said that Heaven had originally used his own bones to fashion the sacred swords and spears, and he explained that the weapons were placed upon the post to restore Heaven to wholeness: "It is as if his body were whole again."

18. As explained previously, Hohul priests often perform the orations in Raimaus ceremonies. Mau Saka, who is the head of Mau Nunun, orates in their absence.

19. I do not know why all speech at this performance was in *foder*. The Aif-Lulin was the first white ritual that I witnessed, and I was unaware at the time of the different ways of speaking used in most performances.

20. Mau Balen and Mau Bere received my report of Mau Lear's remarks with open derision. "Does he think it is like opening a water tap!" Mau Balen exclaimed.

21. The journey format is used in the exorcism of bush spirits, in the greeting and the dispatch of the dead, and in the consecration of a cult house.

22. *Mahu* is a verb used to describe the way that rain clouds come down and settle over the land. *Ma-mahun* relates to the stream of breath that is exhaled from the mouth, and the pair *er-inun/ma-mahun* is clearly based on a parallelism between exhalations from nose and mouth. Possibly, *ma* is from *lama*, "jaw."

23. *Doen nor salin/liman nor flan* designates the sacred spring, seen as the union of a pool of water and the underground canals that feed it.

24. Grass and bamboo are addressed with the suffix *sa*, which (as several people stressed) appears in the names of the original human ancestors. *Ora* is a species of bamboo, and the Mambai classify Betu Sa and Ora Sa as sister and brother.

25. These are the names of the eight sacred vessels kept in Us Luli.

26. These are the four guardians of the vessels, who are said to regulate the rains. The names are partially translatable: *us* (*usa*), "rain"; *keul*, "wind"; *kok*, "to show" or "to direct"; *toh*, "to pant" or "to exhale forcefully"; *rai*, "earth"; *hul*, "body hair."

27. *Koi*, the verb, is somewhat difficult to translate. It may be used in reference to the act of opening a door, but not a container. In ritual contexts *koi sisa* relates to the shredding of meat into tiny pieces which are placed upon offering stones. *Koi hauta*, literally "to shred (for) rocks," includes the act of shredding and placing offerings. Many offerings are said to serve the function of "opening a doorway," and shredding meat is in effect a ritual technique of opening passageways between separate realms.

28. Most of what I discuss in the text is drawn from a series of conversations with Mau Balen, Mau Bere, and with Mau Saka, who makes the offerings in Raimaus. Oblatory techniques are part of the knowledge that a priest acquires during his apprenticeship. The instructor teaches the novice how many bits must be shredded, at what place, and for what purpose. Younger priests, however, do not always possess a full understanding of the significance of their acts. Mau Saka plaintively insisted that old Leik Mau, the master of Hohul, had withheld critical knowledge. "He gave me only the tip," said Mau Saka. "He told me how many times to shred for each place, but he shut in the trunk. One remaining word, this he did not reveal." Leik Mau's own sons said similar things about their father.

Chapter Nine: The Meeting at the Spring

1. The term used in this context is *maen-ulun*, "head man." *Maen-ion*, "tail man," denotes the youngest.

2. As mentioned in chapter 8 (n. 1), the rites for the rebuilding of a cult house are a partial exception. Alliance relations become relevant in the final stage of such performances, which is called "to eat the water of the house" (*mu fad-eran*). Mambai speak of this stage as a juncture at which "we divide into wife-giver and wife-taker." When I attended the first stage of a performance, there were frequent allusions to the anticipated division.

3. Overall, the moon seems to play a muted role in Mambai myth and ritual. It does not figure centrally in narrative accounts of creation, and it is rarely addressed in ritual speech. If the Mambai connect the phases of the moon with the tides of the sea, I never learned of the connection. It should be remembered that the Mambai are a mountain people who have little or no direct contact with the sea. What they stress in their symbolic representations is the "otherness" of the sea. They regard the sea as a wild, mysterious, impenetrable realm, governed by laws of its own.

4. Each of the cult houses within a ritual center is associated with a unique spring, and each of these springs is visited in turn during the water-drawing ritual. Hence the events I describe in this chapter are repeated on separate days.

5. *Koli* and *talo* are common elements in personal names, but neither term, to my knowledge, has referential significance. The effect of the utterance *Maun Koli koli/Tai Talo talo* seems to be to call attention to the coming into being of the sacred rock and tree by using their names in a verbal construction.

6. Weeping is a culturally prescribed reaction to the ritual invocation of the dead, and one cannot necessarily read this cultural expression of emotion as an index of a particular inner state. On the other hand, I do not assume that the display of emotion is simply an external form, and that participants in fact feel no grief. By convention the return of the dead arouses sorrow in the living, yet the precise sources of feeling in individuals may vary. The rite may perhaps give rise to a sense of the inevitability of death, and it may also provoke remembrances of departed kin. On one occasion, shortly after we had returned from a spring, I was questioning Mau Balen very closely as to the identity of the returning shades. I wanted to determine if these included the recent dead as well as the long dead and, in a stunning display of insensitivity, I probed Mau Balen concerning his own father, who had been sent to the sea some ten years previously. Mau Balen, who had eagerly and cheerfully assisted me throughout the performance, suddenly burst into tears. He excused himself, saying that my questions had made him "remember the old man." Mau Bere, on the other hand, had a less personalized explanation for the grief conventionally evoked by thoughts of the dead. He claimed that in greeting the shades with tears, people expressed their blind dependence upon the ancestors who had passed down the forms of ritual action. "If we are doing right or wrong," Mau Bere said, "it is because of them, we tie everything to them. That is why they weep."

7. *An hoha/an taisa* signifies the peoples of Timor and the Malaia (see chapter 3).

Chapter Ten: The Journeys of the Dead

1. Funeral feasts held for leading members of a ritual center or for kingdom rulers are said to be extravagant affairs. I was told that the funeral gifts

for high status individuals are lavish and should include at least one water buffalo.

2. The funeral of an unmarried woman is a much simpler, private affair, conducted by the immediate family.

3. This rite is called *maeta ni hun*. *Hu* means "to lift, to raise, to carry." The expression *saun-hun*, literally, "lifted thing," is used of all individual rites in both white and black performances. I have never fully understood the significance of this expression.

4. In this they contrast with the southern Tetum, as described by Hicks (1976). Mau Balen used to profess considerable fear of the dead, and he cited his aversion as the reason for his decision to reside at a distance from Raimaus. However, he justified his reaction in terms of Raimaus's prominent place on the path of the dead. All departing spirits must visit Raimaus to request the "key" to the other world, and an individual might well find these continuous visitations disturbing.

5. Most misfortunes are not attributed to the dead, but to the "wild ears/wild eyes," the bush spirits or "masters of the outside," as they are also known. These spirits may maim or kill a careless traveler at any hour of the day or night. Their attacks are immediately recognizable by their violent character, for whereas the dead may inflict slow, wasting diseases, the bush spirits kill recklessly and swiftly, "like an arrow shot from a bow." Mambai bush spirits bear a resemblance to the Rotinese *nitu deak*, the spirits of the "bad dead" (Fox 1973). In contrast to the Rotinese, Mambai do not classify the bad dead as a separate category of spirits. When a bad death occurs a special, inverted funeral rite is performed outside in the bush to restore the deceased to a "normal" condition. Or so I was told, but I never saw such a rite performed.

6. This situation may be contrasted to certain Bornean practices of secondary burial analyzed by Hertz (1960, orig. 1907). The peoples examined in Hertz's essay also conceive of death as a protracted process. Prior to the final incorporation of the dead into the otherworld, they observe what Hertz called an "intermediary period" that lasts minimally until the flesh of the corpse has decomposed. Hertz argued that the soul's passage to the otherworld was metaphorically determined by the physical decay of the corpse.

7. I should make clear that I actively elicited Mau Bere's opinion on this matter. He himself had been planning a *maeta* for several years. Hohul death rituals are elaborate and can take even longer to organize than do those of lesser origin villages.

8. Postponing the journey to the sea gives individuals time to strengthen their ties with the personalized spirits who protect their own houses. It could be argued, moreover, that an individual who holds more than one *maeta* is also seeking to increase the reciprocal obligations of the dead, and so to secure a greater reward from the returning shades. I do not think, however, that Mambai reason in this way. The dead who pass overseas lose their individual identities and take on a collective personality. It would be unreasonable to expect such beings to calculate return gifts on the basis of the quantity of gifts dedicated to them before their apotheosis.

9. A man and his wife are usually dispatched together. Although Mau Rem did not mention this, I like to think that he had in mind a time when his own children would send their mother and father to the sea.

10. This pattern is in certain ways the inverse of the pattern of secondary burial rites discerned by Hertz.

11. One agnate of the sponsors is entrusted with keeping track of all the spirits implicated in the *maeta* and computing the gifts dedicated to them. Except for the priest, no one else claims to know the total composition of the spirit host.

12. I neglected to inquire into the significance of this designation. But the idea, which is implicit in the performance as a whole, seems to be that the kin of the dead, like the insects whose name they assume, are nourished on decay.

13. Representatives of the primordial marital allies of the sponsors must attend the *maeta*, whether or not there is a particular marital connection between the dead and their houses.

14. It should be stressed that wealth accumulated at one *maeta* is redistributed at another. Thus the "live water buffalo" that a sponsor may keep may well be sacrificed later on, when his own wife-givers summon him to their *maeta*. "Winning" in a mortuary ceremony is largely a matter of securing the wealth required to meet future ritual obligations.

15. This man was the youngest son of the old "master" of Hohul. I first met him officiating at a *maeta* held by a group that traced descent to his own house in Hohul. Later, we renewed our acquaintanceship at various Hohul rituals.

16. On hearing my account, Mau Balen remarked with obvious sarcasm: "It is the priest who knows."

17. Their credence or lack of credence in the Ki Sa myth became hard to determine. The question "Did Ki Sa really pretend to die?" simply made no sense, or at least, I could not hit upon a meaningful formulation.

18. Mau Bere used to relate every ritual detail to a corresponding narrative event, operating with the sacred myth much as others did with the Ki Sa myth. Yet I often sensed a forced element in his exegeses. Episodes that he had not previously narrated to me were rediscovered in ritual performance and reinserted into the myth.

19. I have borrowed the terms "oratorical" and "ostensive" from Fox (1979). The idea that either words or objects may predominate in a ritual system has a long history in anthropology. Tambiah (1981) reviews the whole issue of multiple media in his elegant argument for a "performative approach" to ritual.

20. Malinowski remarked that, despite the high "weirdness co-efficient" in the language of Trobriand magic, the words were not meaningless since the spirits themselves were said to understand them (1965, 213–223).

21. In order to tape a *toli*, I had to hush the crowd of onlookers repeatedly. The modicum of quiet that was eventually established was very clearly

in deference to me and my taperecorder, and not to the priest. The latter seemed imperturbed by the buzz of conversation, or by the even louder cries for silence taken up by those sitting near me.

22. Some people suggested that every cult house has a corresponding spirit house on the mountain. Others insisted that there is only one house on the mountain, which composes the "trunk" of all houses. Only one house is mentioned in the *toli*.

23. This rite is called *krau lulin*, "to gather up prohibitions."

24. Mambai tend to expect trouble on such occasions. Liquor flows freely and words follow suit. Moreover, "wild people" are often accompanied by the "wild ears/wild faces," the dangerous bush spirits. These creatures can possess human beings and cause them to become drunk and belligerent.

25. This rite is called by the same name as that of the previous day, *krau lulin*.

26. Candles are used in invocations of the deities.

27. Bees belong to the same class as decay-eating insects, the class of *saun-ubun*.

28. The buffalo sacrificed in the house ritual constitutes another type of "joining." Half of the buffalo is pronounced "white" and is consumed immediately, while the half that must rot upon the altar is "black."

29. Mambai have borrowed and make extensive use of the Portuguese word *dever*. To my knowledge, there is no single Mambai word that signifies owing and indebtedness.

30. MacAloon has built on Turner's notions of liminality, communitas, and antistructure to emphasize the "sociable" dimension of ritual performance. He differentiates types of performances, or aspects of a single performance, as rite, game, festival, and spectacle, which correspond to four "modes of human action," consecration, competition, enjoyment, and wonder (1981, 269). Sociability, the "play form of sociation" in Simmel's phrase (cited in MacAloon 1982, 263), is most pronounced in events framed as game, festival, or spectacle.

Valeri also calls attention to sociability in ritual, defined as "a bond that is immediately realized through the pleasure of play," and seen as dominant in the Hawaiian Makahiki Festival (1985, 219). In Valeri's model, which also has affinities with Turner's, pleasurable ritual play entails relative undifferentiation and hence would not encompass competitive performances constitutive of status distinctions. His notion of "play" corresponds approximately to "festival" in MacAloon's scheme.

In Valeri's terms, Mambai white rituals are more "playful" than are black rituals, inasmuch as the symbolism of white feasts entails a notion of undifferentiation. However, participants are only undifferentiated in relation to the affinal statuses enacted in black rituals. None of the rites that I observed among the Mambai are really analogous to the Hawaiian Makahiki Festival dedicated to Lonomakua, the playful god, opposite of Ku. But then in the Mambai pantheon there is no masculine counterpart to Father Heaven, the god of boundaries and structure, nor does he manifest himself in playful forms. When Mambai imagine a relationship of intimacy with a deity, it is in terms of their relative closeness to the female principle of the cosmos, and that intimacy has an agonistic content. I discuss the issue of pleasure in the conclusion to this book.

31. The lasting relevance of Hertz's essay on secondary burial lies in his implicit recognition of body and spirit as overdetermined ritual symbols. See Huntington and Metcalf (1979) for an assessment of Hertz's contribution to the anthropology of death ritual.

32. The role of metal sacra is more pronounced in white ritual than in black ritual.

Conclusion

1. Ricoeur acknowledges the philosopher Louis O. Mink as the source of the notion of a configurational act, which Mink interprets as "a grasping together" (cited in Ricoeur 1981, 174). Tambiah advances a similar claim in reference to ritual when he identifies meaning with "pattern recognition" or "configurational awareness" (1981, 134).

2. Readers familiar with the anthropology of ritual may recognize in these remarks an attempt to integrate a structural approach to ritual with some of Victor Turner's insights, in particular, his emphasis on the "multivocality" of ritual symbols. Although Turner developed his notion of liminality out of van Gennep's pioneering work on the tripartite structure of *rites de passage*, Turner himself pays more attention to the multiple meanings of individual symbols than to the systematic relations that constitute ritual sequences. This orientation was already apparent in *The Forest of Symbols* (1967).

3. The primary text is, of course, *Les formes élémentaires de la vie religieuse*, but the sui generis nature of collective thought is an implicit or explicit theme in all of Durkheim's work. The argument is forcefully laid out and defended in an 1898 article, published in *Sociology and Philosophy* as "Individual and Collective Representations" (1974). Although Durkheim's psychology is outmoded and his case overstated, his insistence on the relative autonomy of collective thought remains a critical component to any anthropology of the symbolic life.

4. Rieff (1959) calls attention to the utilitarian slant of Freud's thinking in the context of a critique of the psychoanalytic approach to art, dreams, and children's play. Play, for Rieff, is the modeling type in this paradigm, and Freud's reluctance or inability to foreground the play aspects of art and dreams is compared to the Aristotelian defense of poetry as catharsis. Rieff's rejoinder to Aristotle is eloquent: "But we do not drink for health or dance for exercise. Nor do we go to tragedies to get rid of emotions, but rather to feel them more abundantly: to banquet is not to be purged" (352). On the shortcomings of Freud's treatment of the dream-life, Rieff suggests: "What may be

liberating in the dream is not only the fact that certain suppressed contents are allowed expression but the very fact that the sleeper's emotion is dramatized, i.e., played out in a dream. . . . Dreams arise not only out of tension and distress and unfulfillment, but also out of a spontaneous pleasure in the mind's activity" (352–353). While this insight is implicit in certain passages in Freud, it is left undeveloped. On Durkheim's transfer of utilitarianism from individual to social "needs," see Sahlins 1976 (106–117).

5. To synthesize the Durkheimian sociology of ritual with psychoanalytic perspectives was one of Turner's objectives in *The Forest of Symbols*, and Beidelman has also urged anthropologists to take account of the unconscious meanings of ritual symbolism (1966). I single out these two authors, not because they are unique in turning to psychoanalysis, but because they carefully avoid any simple reduction of ritual symbolism to psychological processes.

6. Freud introduced the new dualism of the instincts in *Beyond the Pleasure Principle* (1955; orig. 1920). It came increasingly to dominate his thought in his last works.

7. Sahlins (1981b) provides a close interpretation of the differential, culturally conditioned responses of Hawaiian nobles and commoners to colonial contact.

References

Augé, M. 1982. *The anthropological circle: Symbol, function, history*, trans. M. Thom. Cambridge: Cambridge University Press.

Barnes, R. H. 1974. *Kédang: A study of the collective thought of an Eastern Indonesian people*. Oxford: Clarendon Press.

———1980. Concordance, structure, and variation. In *The flow of life: Essays on Eastern Indonesia*, ed. J. J. Fox. Cambridge, Mass.: Harvard University Press.

Beidelman, T. O. 1966. Swazi royal ritual. *Africa* 36: 373–405.

Bourdieu, P. 1977. *Outline of a theory of practice*. Cambridge: Cambridge University Press.

Boxer, C. R. 1947. The topasses of Timor. *Koninklije Vereeniging Indisch Instituut* 73 (24):1–22.

———1969. *The Portuguese seaborne empire, 1415–1825*. New York: Alfred A. Knopf.

Capell, A. 1943–1945. Peoples and languages of Timor. *Oceania* 14:191–219; 311–337; 15:19–48.

Clamagirand, B. 1980. Social organization of the Ema of Timor. In *The flow of life: Essays on Eastern Indonesia*, ed. J. J. Fox. Cambridge, Mass.: Harvard University Press.

De Castro, A. 1867. *As possessões Portuguesas na Oceania*. Lisbon: Imprensa Nacional.

Dumézil, G. 1948. *Mitra-Varuna*. Paris: Gallimard.

———1970. *The destiny of the warrior*, trans. A Hiltebeitel. Chicago: University of Chicago Press.

Dumont, L. 1968. The marriage alliance. In *Marriage, family, and residence*, ed. P. Bohannan and J. Middleton. New York: Natural History Press.

———1970a. *Homo hierarchicus: The caste system and its implications*. Chicago: University of Chicago Press.

———1970b. *Religion, politics, and history in India*. The Hague: Mouton.

Durkheim, E. 1965. *The elementary forms of the religious life* (translation of *Les formes élémentaires de la vie religieuse*, 1912). New York: Free Press.

———1974. *Sociology and philosophy*, trans. D. F. Pocock. New York: Free Press.

Durkheim, E., and Mauss, M. 1963. *Primitive classification* (translation of *De quelques formes primitives de classification*, 1903). London: Cohen & West.

Fox, J. J. 1968. The Rotinese: A study of the social organization of an Eastern Indonesian people. D. Phil. thesis, Oxford University.

———1971a. Semantic parallelism in Rotinese ritual language. *Bijdragen tot de Taal-, Land-, en Volkenkunde* 127: 215–255.

———1971b. Sister's child as plant: Metaphors in an idiom of consanguinity. In *Rethinking kinship and marriage*, ed. R. Needham. Association of Social Anthropologists Monograph 11. London: Tavistock Press.

———1973. On bad death and the left hand. In *Right and left: Essays on dual symbolic classification*, ed. R. Needham. Chicago: University of Chicago Press.

———1974. Our ancestors spoke in pairs: Rotinese views of language, dialect, and code. In *Explorations in the ethnography of speaking*, ed. R. Bauman and J. Sherzer. London: Cambridge University Press.

———1975. On binary categories and primary symbols: Some Rotinese perspectives. In *The interpretation of symbolism*, ed. R. Willis. Association of Social Anthropologists Studies 3. London: Malaby Press.

———1979. The ceremonial system of Savu. In *The imagination of reality: Essays in Southeast Asian coherence systems*, ed. A. L. Becker and A. A. Yengoyan. Norwood, N.J.: Ablex Publishing Corporation.

———ed. 1980. *The flow of life: Essays on Eastern Indonesia*. Cambridge, Mass.: Harvard University Press.

Francillon, G. 1980. Incursions upon Wehali: A modern history of an ancient empire. In *The flow of life: Essays on Eastern Indonesia*, ed. J. J. Fox. Cambridge, Mass.: Harvard University Press.

Freud, S. 1953 [1900]. *The interpretation of dreams*, Standard Edition vols. 4–5. London: Hogarth Press.

———1955 [1920]. *Beyond the pleasure principle*, Standard Edition vol. 18, 3–64. London: Hogarth Press.

Friedberg, C. 1980. Boiled woman and broiled man: Myths and agricultural rituals of the Bunaq of central Timor. In *The flow of life: Essays on Eastern Indonesia*, ed. J. J. Fox. Cambridge, Mass.: Harvard University Press.

Geertz, C. 1980. *Negara: The theatre state in nineteenth-century Bali*. Princeton, N.J.: Princeton University Press.

Greenlee, D. 1973. *Peirce's concept of sign*. The Hague: Mouton.

Hertz, R. 1907. Contribution à une étude sur la représentation collective de la mort. *Année Sociologique* 10:48–137.

———1960. *Death and the right hand*, trans. R. and C. Needham. New York: Free Press.

Hicks, D. 1972. Eastern Tetum. In *Ethnic groups in insular Southeast Asia*, vol. 1, ed. F. LeBar. New Haven: Human Relations Area File Press.

———1976. *Tetum ghosts and kin*. Palo Alto: Mayfield Publishing Co.

Hocart, A. M. 1970 [1936]. *Kings and councillors: An essay in the comparative anatomy of human society*. Chicago: University of Chicago Press.

References

Hubert, H., and Mauss, M. 1964. *Sacrifice: Its nature and function* (translation of *Essai sur la nature et la fonction du sacrifice*, 1899). Chicago: University of Chicago Press.

Huntington, R. 1978. Bara endogamy and incest prohibitions. *Bijdragen tot de Taal-, Land-, en Volkenkunde* 134:30–62.

Huntington, R., and Metcalf, P. 1979. *Celebrations of death: The anthropology of mortuary ritual*. Cambridge: Cambridge University Press.

Jakobson, R. 1966. Grammatical parallelism and its Russian facet. *Language* 42:399–429.

Jakobson, R., and Halle, M. 1956. *Fundamentals of language*. The Hague: Mouton.

Keyes, C. F. 1977. *The golden peninsula: Culture and adaptation in mainland Southeast Asia*. New York: Macmillan Publishing Co.

Leach, E. 1961. *Rethinking anthropology*. London School of Economics Monographs on Social Anthropology 22. London: Athlone Press.

Lévi-Strauss, C. 1949. *Les structures élémentaires de la parenté*. Paris: Presses Universitaires de France.

———1950. Introduction a l'oeuvre de Marcel Mauss. In *Sociologie et anthropologie*, Marcel Mauss. Paris: Presses Universitaires de France.

———1962a. *Le totémisme aujourd'hui*. Paris: Presses Universitaires de France.

———1962b. *La pensée sauvage*. Paris: Plon.

———1963. *Structural anthropology*, vol. 1. New York: Basic Books.

———1964. *Le cru et le cuit*. Paris: Plon.

———1966. *Du miel aux cendres*. Paris: Plon.

———1968. *L'origine des manières de table*. Paris: Plon.

———1969. *The elementary structures of kinship*. Boston: Beacon Press.

———1971. *L'homme nu*. Paris: Plon.

———1976. *Structural anthropology*, vol. 2. New York: Basic Books.

Lukes, S. 1972. *Emile Durkheim: His life and work*. New York: Harper & Row.

MacAloon, J. 1981. *This great symbol: Pierre de Coubertin and the origins of the modern Olympic games*. Chicago: University of Chicago Press.

———1982. Sociation and sociability in political celebrations. In *Celebrations*, ed. V. Turner. Washington, D.C.: Smithsonian Institute Press.

Malinowski, B. 1965. *Coral gardens and their magic*, vol 2. Bloomington: Indiana University Press.

Mauss, M. 1967 [1954]. *The gift: Forms and functions of exchange in archaic societies* (translation of *Essai sur le don*, 1923–1924). New York: W. W. Norton.

———1979. *Sociology and psychology*, trans. B. Brewster. London: Routledge & Kegan Paul.

Mauss, M., and Beuchat, H. 1979. *Seasonal variations of the Eskimo: A study in social morphology*, trans. J. J. Fox. London: Routledge & Kegan Paul.

Maybury-Lewis, D., and Almagor, U., eds. 1985. *Dual organization: A study of social and symbolic dualism*. Manuscript.

References

Needham, R. 1963. Introduction to *Primitive classification* by E. Durkheim and M. Mauss. London: Cohen & West.

———1967. Percussion and Transition. *Man* n.s. 2: 606–614.

———1973a. Prescription. *Oceania* 43:166–181.

———ed. 1973b. *Right and left: Essays on dual symbolic classification.*

———1979. *Symbolic classification.* Santa Monica: Goodyear Publishing Co.

———1980a. *Reconnaissances.* Toronto: University of Toronto Press.

———1980b. Principles and variations in the structure of Sumbanese society. In *The flow of life: Essays on Eastern Indonesia*, ed. J. J. Fox. Cambridge, Mass.: Harvard University Press.

Ormeling, F. J. 1956. *The Timor problem: A geographical interpretation of an underdeveloped island.* Jakarta and Groningen: J. B. Wolters.

Peirce, C. S. 1955. *Philosophical writings*, ed. J. Buchler. New York: Dover Publications.

Ricoeur, P. 1974. *The conflict of interpretations.* Evanston: Northwestern University Press.

———1976. *Interpretation theory: Discourse and the surplus of meaning.* Forth Worth: Texas Christian University Press.

———1981. Narrative time. In *On narrative*, ed. W. J. T. Mitchell. Chicago: University of Chicago Press.

Rieff, P. 1959. *Freud: The mind of the moralist.* Chicago: University of Chicago Press.

Sahlins, M. 1972. *Stone age economics.* Chicago: Aldine Press.

———1976. *Culture and practical reason.* Chicago: University of Chicago Press.

———1981a. The stranger king. *Journal of Pacific History*, vol. 16 (3): 107–132.

———1981b. *Historical metaphors and mythical realities.* Ann Arbor: University of Michigan Press.

Saussure, F. 1969 [1916]. *Cours de linguistique générale.* Paris: Plon.

Schulte Nordholt, H. G. 1971. *The political system of the Atoni of Timor.* The Hague: Martinus Nijhoff.

Sebeok, T. 1979. *The sign and its masters.* Austin: University of Texas Press.

Steiner, F. 1967. *Taboo.* Baltimore: Penguin Books.

Tambiah, S. J. 1976. *World conqueror and world renouncer: A study of Buddhism and polity in Thailand against a historical background.* Cambridge: Cambridge University Press.

———1981. A performative approach to ritual. *Proceedings of the British Academy* 65:113–169.

Todorov, T. 1977. *The poetics of prose.* Ithaca: Cornell University Press.

Traube, E. G. 1979. Incest and mythology. *Berkshire Review* 14:37–53.

———1980a. Mambai rituals of black and white. In *The flow of life: Essays on Eastern Indonesia*, ed. J. J. Fox. Cambridge, Mass.: Harvard University Press.

———1980b. Affines and the dead: Mambai rituals of alliance. *Bijdragen tot de Taal-, Land-, en Volkenkunde* 136: 90–115.

References

————1982. Order and events: Responses to colonialism in Eastern Indonesia. Manuscript.

Turner, V. 1967. *The forest of symbols*. Ithaca: Cornell University Press.

Valeri, V. 1980. Notes on the meaning of marriage prestations among the Huaululu of Seram. In *The flow of life: Essays on Eastern Indonesia*, ed. J. J. Fox. Cambridge, Mass.: Harvard University Press.

————1985. *Kingship and Sacrifice*. Chicago: University of Chicago Pres.

Van Wouden, F. A. E. 1968. *Types of social structure in Eastern Indonesia* (translation of *Sociale structuurtypen in de Groote Oost*, 1935). Koninklijk Instituut voor Taal-, Land-, en Volkenkunde Translation Series, vol. 11. The Hague: Martinus Nijhoff.

Waismann, F. 1965. Language strata. In *Logic and language*, ed. A. Flew. New York: Doubleday.

Yalman, N. 1967. *Under the Bo tree: Studies in caste, kinship, and marriage in the interior of Ceylon*. Los Angeles: University of California Press.

Index

Index

Book and pen, xviii–xix, 55, 245.
See also Malaia
Botanic metaphor: for alliance,
92–93; for house formation,
68–69; for time, 14–16. *See
also* Trunk/tip opposition
Bourdieu, Pierre: on practical
logic, 6, 138, 198, 262n 2
Breath: and death, 221, 231; in
poetic speech, 267n 22; of
shades, 194
Buffalo, water: as gift from shades,
185, 193; marital allies as, 86;
as sacrifice to spirits of dead,
218, 219, 221, 225, 226; as sacrifice to steady house, 206,
207; as tribute item, 47
Burial: and decay, 200–201; of
Mother Earth, 38–40; re-
enacted, 220, 221–24. *See
also* Corpse; Funeral

Center: of altar, 161; opposites
united at, 37, 46; vs. periphery,
28, 29–30, 69; as trunk, 74
Coastal peoples, xii, 49
Colonialism: and culture, 52, 244;
Mambai responses to, 53–58,
61–65. *See also* Diarchy; Malaia; Portuguese
Communal meal, 44, 47, 168, 183,
191–92
Community: at Er-Soia ritual,
179–84; structure of, 98–100
Complementarity: and asymmetry,
4, 15, 74; and antagonism, 97,
144; of deities, 37–38,
147–49; of male and female,
80, 94, 242; and ritual system,
11–12
Conception, theory of, 93–94, 96,
173. *See also* Rain
Cooking fire: origins of, 43, 44, 46;
in ritual, 158
Corpse: and alliance, 97; attitudes
toward, 206–7; disposal of,

200–201; substitutes for, at
maeta, 214, 220, 221–22. *See
also* Body; Burial; Funeral;
Mother Earth
Correspondences, 5, 102–3, 108–9
Cosmogony: and Mambai collective identity, 45–46, 243; communication of, 31–34, 178–
79, 237; narrative account of,
36–115; and ritual, 15–16,
187–88; as trunk, x. *See also*
Knowledge; Trunk/tip opposition
Cosmos: and alliance, 97; silence
of, 18; and society, 5–6,
13–14, 134–36, 184, 198–99
Creation myth. *See* Cosmogony
Cross-cousin marriage, 5, 81–82,
85
Cult: and house, 70; vs. *luli*, 141,
143–44; mythic origins of, 84;
and wives, 72, 88
Cult house. *See* House

Dat Raia: in altar rite, 166, 167–68;
in Er-Soia, 182, 183, 191; status
of, 114; as wife-givers, 261 n. 16
Dead, spirits of: ascend to mountain, 217–21; attitudes toward,
202–5, 268n. 6; vs. body, 230–
32; descend to sea, 224–28;
and Father Heaven, 232–34; as
life-givers, 211–12, 216, 220.
See also Body; Corpse; *Maeta*
ritual; Shades
Death, chapter 10 passim; and human condition, 242; ritual, origins of, 212–13, 214; ritual,
stages in, 200–202. *See also*
Burial; Dead, spirits of; Decay;
Funeral; *Maeta* ritual; Mother
Earth
Decay: and fertility, 40, 144, 197–
98, 222–24; vs. Father Heaven,
136, 144–45; potency of, 206–
8; and Ritual Lord, 103–4. *See*

282